Hugh Mackay is a social researcher and the author of sixteen books – ten in the field of social analysis and ethics, and six novels. He is a Fellow of the Australian Psychological Society and has been awarded honorary doctorates by Charles Sturt, Macquarie, New South Wales and Western Sydney universities. In 2015, Mackay was appointed an Officer of the Order of Australia. He lives in the Southern Highlands of New South Wales.

www.hughmackay.net.au

Other books by Hugh Mackay

Non-fiction

Reinventing Australia

Why Don't People Listen?

Generations

Turning Point

Media Mania

Right & Wrong

Advance Australia . . . Where?

What Makes Us Tick?

The Good Life

The Art of Belonging

Fiction

Little Lies

House Guest

The Spin

Winter Close

Ways of Escape

Infidelity

The Good Life

Hugh Mackay

First published 2013 in Macmillan by Pan Macmillan Australia Pty Limited
This Pan edition published 2016 by Pan Macmillan Australia Pty Limited
1 Market Street, Sydney, New South Wales, Australia, 2000

Cataloguing-in-Publication entry is available from the National Library of Australia:
http://catalogue.nla.gov.au

Typeset in Bembo by Midland Typesetters, Australia
Printed by McPherson's Printing Group

To Sheila

Contents

Preface		1
1	The Utopia complex	3
2	How the pursuit of happiness can make you miserable	41
3	Seven false leads	69
4	A good life or a good time?	125
5	Do unto others . . .	157
6	Living the good life	193
7	A good death	235
Postscript		255
Further reading		258
Acknowledgements		259
Index		260

Preface

If you've picked up a book called *The Good Life*, chances are you've already given some serious thought to what goodness is and what kind of life might be called 'good'. It's easy to get lost in the language, so I'd better spell out exactly what I mean when I say 'the good life'. I'm referring to a life that is characterised by goodness, a morally praiseworthy life, a life valuable in its impact on others, a life devoted to the common good. This type of life is marked by a courteous respect for others' rights, a responsiveness to others' needs (including, most particularly, their need to be taken seriously) and a concern for others' wellbeing. A person living this life will be motivated by kindness and compassion.

If you were hoping for a book about how to *feel* good, how to find happiness or how to reap some reward for your goodness, I'm sorry to disappoint you: this is not that book. All those things might happen when you're living the good life, but if you set out to be good or to do good because of what's in it for you, then you'll have missed the whole point of the journey.

Virtually every philosophical and religious tradition (to say nothing of our common sense) tells us, with the clarity and urgency of a ringing bell, that there's only one good way for humans to live. If we want to contribute to a civil society by promoting the peaceful, harmonious and mutually supportive communities which are our natural habitat, we must learn to treat other people in the way we ourselves would wish to be treated – the so-called Golden Rule. That sounds straightforward enough, but our experience of life soon teaches us that the Golden Rule is easier to admire as an ideal than to put into practice. We may aspire to lead a life animated by kindness and based on respect for others, but, for all kinds of reasons to do with our personalities, our temperaments and our circumstances, our life often falls short of that gold standard.

In the following pages, we're going to explore that dilemma together and see how, in spite of all the temptations and pressures to do otherwise, we may be able to make the dream of the good life come true. Along the way, I hope to convince you that these three rather overworked words – the good life – can point to an inspiring truth about what it means to be human; an encouraging, uplifting truth about us that is easily overlooked in the rush of a busy life.

As a social researcher, I've spent my working life listening to many thousands of people tell their personal stories. *The Good Life* draws heavily on those stories, interpreting them in the light of musings on the subject of goodness by philosophers, poets, scientists, theologians and psychologists. At various points through the text, you'll come across vignettes, slices of life, designed to illuminate some of the themes of the book through glimpses into the experiences of several different people – some real, some imaginary. There is also a sprinkling of verbatim quotes from people I've listened to over the years – participants in my research projects, colleagues, friends, family members, people I've heard on radio, strangers on a bus – whose stories or comments illustrate points in the text. The quotes have been edited, where necessary, to disguise the speaker's identity.

I offer *The Good Life* to you in the hope that you may recognise yourself somewhere in these pages. I also hope you will be encouraged to think that if your life sometimes seems a bit too demanding, if there isn't quite enough Me time or if people have been slow to tell you how much they appreciate you, it might still be a very good life indeed.

Hugh Mackay

1

The Utopia complex

To many people in the West, this feels like a Golden Age. And why not? Extraordinary advances in medical science; the explosion of information and communication technology that stimulates, informs and entertains us like never before; swift and cheap international travel; efficient, reliable, affordable cars; promising talk of a clean-energy revolution; online shopping; a plentiful year-round fresh food supply that defies the four seasons; ever-smarter manufacturing and distribution processes that whisk tulips from Amsterdam to florists in Melbourne, and European fashion labels from their Chinese factories to warehouses all over the world; to say nothing of the sophistication of modern marketing techniques that stroke our egos with seductive skill. If ever we were going to be able to live the good life, surely this would be the time.

That impression of a Golden Age might not be so easy to sustain if you were to peep beyond the borders of affluent, peaceful Western societies into the teeming squalor of the world's refugee camps, the ravages of continuing wars (driven, as usual, by religious rivalries or territorial greed, or both), the eternal tensions of the Middle East, the nuclear stand-off between India and Pakistan, or the looming problem of global food security. In fact, even in the West's comfortable and relatively secure cities and suburbs, our dreamy blue skies are sometimes clouded by the frightening possibility of global warming wreaking ecological and geopolitical havoc on our planet. But in the busy round of daily life, most of us manage to put such thoughts out of our minds. We have a more appealing, more immediate agenda: the pursuit of perfection – *woo-hoo*! Being twenty-first-century Westerners living with unprecedented material prosperity, mobility, convenience and comfort, who would dare say we're not entitled to the best of everything? Far from fearing that a deep malaise may have us in its grip, we are inclined to feel lucky to be alive in such a place and at such a time in history.

And yet, the more you examine our Utopian fantasies and our energetic attempts to turn them into reality, the more you wonder if the very things we're so desperate to acquire as symbols of this imagined good life may be insulating us from deeper and more enduring satisfactions, fuelling our dreams while limiting our vision, encouraging us to settle for the most trivial and fleeting meanings of 'good'. Our teeth should remain perfectly bright, white and, of course, straight, regardless of their age. If we are female, we ought to have perfectly formed or re-formed breasts that resist the sagging once thought to be a natural consequence of breastfeeding and the passage of time. We should be able to track down the perfect latte, the perfect investment vehicle (perfectly safe but astonishingly lucrative) and the perfect movie (uplifting, funny, sexy *and* memorable). Even a storm can now qualify as a perfect storm.

It's no longer enough to have a couple of days off at the weekend to sleep in, catch up on chores, do a bit of reading or internetworking, and perhaps take the kids to a park or catch a movie. No, *Have a great weekend!* has become the standard Friday-evening send-off, and *How was your weekend?* the standard Monday-morning greeting. (You'd better have your awesome weekend story ready.)

Holidays should be havens of happiness: islands of perfection in a choppy sea of imperfection. We should plan them carefully and execute them in ways that allow us to come as close as possible to our ideal selves. (Slight problem here: in 2012, *The Psychologist* quoted UK research suggesting that the inevitable post-vacation let-down is greater and more rapid for perfectionists than for those with more modest expectations.)

Work should be fun, or, if not fun, then at least stimulating and satisfying. So should marriage, and if it isn't, then we should strive for a perfect divorce in which we and our former partner will behave in the civilised and responsible way we couldn't quite manage during the marriage. And *our* divorce should have zero impact on the kids.

The kids themselves should be gifted in ways that make them worthy of special attention by perfect teachers who are perfectly attuned to the peculiar talents and circumstances of each child (especially ours) and to the expectations of its parents (especially us).

> I went to the school and I said, 'Look, if I have a rattle in my Mercedes, I expect the service people to fix it. I paid a lot of money for that car. Well, I'm paying thirty thousand dollars a year to this place, and there's a serious rattle in my son's maths. So you'd better fix it'. They seemed offended. What planet are they living on? I'm the fee-paying parent, for God's sake.

In the future, such rattles might be bred out of our children as biotechnology edges us ever closer to perfect embryos. (Here's a recent innovation from the frontier of biotechnology likely to set a true Utopian's heart racing: the three-parent baby, conceived in vitro after defects in a cell taken from the mother's egg have been corrected and purified through the use of a cell from another woman's egg.) In the meantime, we must deal with our children's messy imperfections, and our own, as best we can.

Our counsellors, it goes without saying, should be gurus: people of infinite wisdom capable of coming up with perfect strategies for dealing with the problems we bring them. We should be able to visit only the very best doctor, and our uniquely wonderful doctor should prescribe the proven-perfect treatment for our condition, based on the perfect drug – highly efficacious, with no side effects except perhaps the prolonging of life into a richly rewarding old age.

Sex should be blissful and deeply satisfying, every time. Orgasms should be unfailingly spectacular and available to both sexes on demand.

Sport? It's all about winning, of course: losing has no place in Utopia. Whatever it takes, from cutting-edge equipment for the Under 10s to performance-enhancing drugs for the professionals. Gamesmanship, sometimes disguised as the pursuit of excellence, replaces sportsmanship in the drive for victory. Sports psychologists abound, not just to motivate us but to help us deal with the shock of — (don't mention the word).

Our cars should be perfectly safe, and the roads we drive them on should be so brilliantly engineered that the possibility of road trauma is virtually eliminated. We should have access to automotive technology that will protect us from lapses in our concentration, deficiencies in our driving technique or our sheer incompetence. (Surely the perfect car is already on some German designer's drawing board?)

The state should leave us alone to get on with our lives in peace but should exert tight control over the behaviour of other people who mightn't be as responsible or competent as we are. And it should of course be ready to support us whenever we think we're entitled to help.

In our perfect world, blame is easy to affix, revenge is sweet, and outcomes are always positive (for us). Life should proceed from one thrilling gratification to the next, banners triumphantly aflutter, joy unbounded.

All we want is heaven on earth. Is that too much to ask?

I exaggerate, but not by much. Here is an actual statement from Neale Donald Walsch's *The Storm before the Calm* (2011): 'The function of life is to recreate yourself anew in each golden moment of Now, in the next grandest version of the greatest vision you ever held about who you are'. Our language has become inflated by Utopian hyperbole. *Fantastic!* says the waiter, when I've successfully negotiated the challenging task of signing my name on a credit card voucher. 'Fabulous' has replaced 'good', and 'great' now means 'okay'. We're busily establishing centres of excellence everywhere, from primary schools to car showrooms. We're hooked on the idea of happiness as a natural entitlement, a bit like universal healthcare. We have enshrined towering self-esteem as a cardinal virtue and the greatest gift we can pass on to the rising generation. Utopians are conditioned (and are busily conditioning their children) to assume that perfection in anything should be within their grasp.

Teaching our children to expect too much

The real victims of the Utopia complex are our children. We can learn to swallow our own disappointment; we can cope with the realisation that we've made fools of ourselves by our pursuit of an unreachable goal; we can slink off to a therapist in search of a reality check. But the children of parents in the grip of the Utopia complex might not get off so lightly. They might have been so deeply and consistently conditioned to expect the best to be provided for them – admiration and rewards for everything they do and constant support and guidance from parents anxious to remove every obstacle from their path – that their arrival on the threshold of adulthood will actually come as a shock. Children are likely to struggle when confronted by the demands of independence if they have been cosseted in a state of prolonged dependency and fed a rich diet of self-esteem-boosting praise. (*Good try!* is the response to failure currently favoured by parents, even if the failure was actually the result of zero effort.)

In a 2011 article in *The Atlantic* provocatively titled 'How to Land Your Kid in Therapy', US psychotherapist Lori Gottlieb reported on the growing number of young adults arriving in her consulting room with symptoms suggesting they are anxious and confused about how to handle the independence expected of them. Typically, these are people who report a happy, secure childhood, loving parents, a good education and a highly supportive environment in their formative years. They have often had a good academic record and may be in a loving relationship and holding down a well-paid job. So where did this emerging sense of emptiness and confusion come from? Though she is working with purely anecdotal evidence based on the cases she sees personally, and though a person's emotional state is bound to be the result of many interacting factors, Gottlieb thinks she may have an answer to that question. Her view, supported by some other therapists, educators and social theorists, is that this is the first crop of adults to have emerged from the self-esteem movement: the first crop of over-parented, over-protected kids to have reached adulthood under the influence of so-called positive psychology. Gottlieb notes that rates of depression among college students have risen along with rates of self-esteem, and she is inclined to see some causal links there.

The people Gottlieb is encountering may be victims of their parents' Utopia complex. After all, if everything is supposed to be perfect, and your children are lavishly praised and rewarded for doing *anything*, what is likely to be the long-term effect on them? Gottlieb consulted Jean Twenge, a professor of psychology at San Diego State University and a co-author of *The Narcissism Epidemic* (2009), and explained her concern about this new breed of clients who should have been well prepared for adulthood by such happy childhoods but who now seem dissatisfied and bewildered. Twenge was not surprised. In her view, what begins as a healthy self-esteem can quickly morph into an inflated view of oneself, 'a self-absorption and sense of entitlement that looks a lot like narcissism'. According to Twenge, 'Narcissists are happy when they're younger, because they're the centre of the universe. Their parents act like their servants, shuttling them to any activity they choose and catering to their every desire . . . constantly telling their children how talented and special they are'.

This sounds to me exactly like parents who are in the grip of the Utopia complex, trying to create a perfect childhood for their children by being perfect parents, possibly imagining that, since they tried so hard, the result will be perfect children. (Perhaps they haven't heard of British psychoanalyst Donald Winnicott's theories about the *good enough* parent.) The inevitable implication is that, as they grow older, these over-praised and over-indulged children will discover they are not the centre of the universe. That discovery can be both shocking and painful.

Carla's separation meltdown

Carla has been raised by loving parents in a comfortable middle-class home in a thriving regional community. All through school she was something of a star, both academically and musically. Her parents praised and encouraged her lavishly, provided extra coaching to address a couple of weak spots in maths and took a keen interest in everything she did. She was the apple of her father's eye and, according to her mother, 'more like a friend than a daughter'.

Friends of the family sometimes worried that Carla was being cast as the symbol of her parents' success, as though her parents were determined Carla should conform to the ideal of a child they could be proud of, a child worthy of all the love and attention they were giving her. From outside the family, it sometimes looked as if the parents were confusing love with praise, support with control.

Though she was clearly destined for university, Carla took a gap year after high school so she could spend one more year at home with her parents before moving to the city. During that year, she fell in love with Hank, a local boy who was studying at TAFE while apprenticed to his father as a plumber. Carla's mother loved Hank and prided herself on the fact that Carla told her everything about the blossoming relationship. When it became clear that Carla wanted to start a sexual relationship with Hank, her mother organised an appointment with the family doctor to give Carla a prescription for the contraceptive pill. And then, rather to Carla's surprise (and even more to Hank's), she booked and paid for a luxurious room in a resort in a nearby town for Carla and Hank to spend their first weekend away together.

A year later, it was time for Carla to enrol at university. By then, she had tired of Hank (her mother, in any case, had decided he wasn't good enough for Carla), and Hank had found someone new – someone, he confided to his best mate, whose mother wasn't under the bed. Carla's parents had found her a place in a university college where the principal seemed to warm to her in the admissions interview. She had assured Carla's parents, in a separate, private interview they had requested, that she was sympathetic to Carla's situation, having herself come to a city university from a country background, twenty-five years ago.

At first, Carla phoned her mother every day, often sending chatty text messages as well. She was finding the lectures challenging but engrossing, and she had teamed up with another girl from the country, also living in her college.

Barely a month into the first semester, Carla had what her mother later described as a 'meltdown' (a word she preferred to 'breakdown'). Carla became depressed, anxious and unable to concentrate. She couldn't sleep. Her parents went to the city for a week, taking a room in a motel near the campus so they could spend time with her. They found her sullen and unresponsive, prone to occasional outbursts of guilty crying over the fact that she had let them down. She simply could not cope, she told them.

Her parents tried to reassure her. She had not let *them* down, they said (though she didn't believe them), but they were anxious that she shouldn't let *herself* down. They reminded her how precious she was to them and what a special person she was. They quoted from her school reports (having memorised the best bits) and pointed to the music awards they had insisted she bring with her to sit on the desk in her college room.

After a week they returned home, Carla having assured them she'd give it another try. She didn't call them. She didn't respond to their calls. Her mother interpreted this as a good sign, hoping it meant that Carla was knuckling down to the work.

Carla had agreed to see a counsellor on the campus, who urged her to rethink the course she was enrolled in. She fell out with her friend, who accused her of being arrogant and self-absorbed. She found herself constantly bursting into tears. Finally, she phoned her mother and asked to be picked up and taken home. Her parents found her standing outside the front door of the college, bags packed and tears streaming down her face. She had withdrawn from her course, having been assured she could re-enrol the following semester if she wanted to.

Back home, Carla felt wretched and confused. She couldn't decide what to do next. She was offered her gap year job back and took it without enthusiasm. Her parents offered to buy her a return ticket to Europe, to clear the cobwebs, they said. She declined, knowing the problem wasn't cobwebs and recognising another of her parents' attempts to smooth things over with euphemisms. They, too, were confused. Until now, everything had seemed so perfect, so full of promise. They had been so proud of Carla. She was their princess.

Jean Twenge believes that receiving the constant message that you're special is counterproductive, not only because it creates an unhealthy inflation of self-esteem but also because it tends to alienate those around you. These are kids, she says, who 'grew up in a bubble, so they get into the real world and start to feel lost and helpless. Kids who always have problems solved for them believe that they don't know how to solve problems. And they're right – they don't'.

'You Are Not Special!' was the title of the 2012 commencement address at Wellesley High School in Massachusetts, delivered by David McCullough, a teacher of English at the school. He clearly believed the graduates needed a reality check, and his rather bracing message was that, if you're so special, then what about the other 3.2 million seniors graduating from more than thirty-seven thousand high schools across the United States? Even if you are one in a million, he told the students, that means there are seven thousand other people exactly like you on the planet. Noting how values have changed, McCullough complained that 'no longer is it how you play the game, no longer is it even whether you win or lose or learn to grow or enjoy yourself. Now it's "So what does this get me?"' In a direct swipe at the entitlement–dependency mentality, McCullough said, 'The fulfilling life, the distinctive life, the relevant life, is an achievement, not something that will fall into your lap because you're a nice person or Mommy ordered it from the caterer'.

Lori Gottlieb describes one client who is typical of this new breed of young adult as 'bright, attractive, with strong friendships, a close family and a deep sense of emptiness'. This young woman, like Carla, was troubled by the feeling that she was less amazing than her parents had always told her she was. Though she regarded her parents as her 'best friends in all the world', it hadn't occurred to her (and why would it?) that they had actually set her up for disappointment, disorientation and anxiety by transmitting to her the values and expectations of their own unrealistic vision of Utopia. 'Could it be', asks Gottlieb, 'that by protecting our kids from unhappiness as children, we're depriving them of happiness as adults?'

School teacher Jessica Lahey worries about the kind of parents who won't let their children learn; whose over-parenting has the potential to 'ruin a child's confidence and undermine an education in independence'. Writing in *The Atlantic* ('Why Parents Need to Let Their Children Fail', 2013), Lahey describes an incident where she called a student's mother to inform her that her daughter was to be disciplined for plagiarism.

'You can't do that. She didn't do anything wrong,' said the enraged mother.

'But she did. I was able to find entire paragraphs lifted off web sites,' Lahey replied.

'No, I mean *she* didn't do it. I did. *I* wrote her paper.'

We have a long history of believing that damaged adults are likely to be the products of a lack of adequate parenting, and that continues to be true in many cases. As the Utopia complex tightens its grip on our culture, we may also have to start looking out for adults who were damaged in childhood by the very opposite: over-parenting. It's a disturbing thought, but it may turn out that recruiting our kids in our own mad quest for Utopia is actually a form of child abuse.

In a seminal 2011 article published in the *Journal of Youth Studies*, 'A New Narrative of Young People's Health and Well-being', the Australian social analyst Richard Eckersley challenges the widely accepted view that young people's health is steadily improving. He notes that while death rates (including deaths from road accidents and suicide) are falling and young people's own reported levels of personal happiness remain high, the incidence of mental illness and obesity-related health problems and risks among the young has increased markedly since 1990. He also points out that these health problems are no longer to be found primarily among the marginalised and disadvantaged, but in society's mainstream.

Eckersley acknowledges that such deterioration in the health and wellbeing of the youngest members of a society must be the result of many interacting factors. He identifies a wide range of problematic health behaviours, including inadequate sleep (the internet never sleeps, and many of its heavy users are trying to get by on less sleep than they need), poor diet, drug and alcohol use, and insufficient physical activity. He also describes such societal factors as social inequality, family upheavals, educational pressures, the growth of mass and social media, the decline of religion, changes in youth culture including the growth of the so-called night-time economy, with pubs and clubs open all hours and people not only drinking more but becoming both sleep-deprived and more disposed to violence as a result. In Eckersley's view, 'Fundamental features of modern Western societies, including those that have contributed to past progress, are now working against mental health'. Along with many other social analysts, he links the increase in mental and obesity-related health problems to the big shift in Western culture towards greater materialism and individualism. Eckersley is in no doubt about the consequences of such a shift:

> A cultural focus on the external trappings of 'the good life' increases the pressures to meet high, even unrealistic, expectations and so heightens the risks of failure and disappointment. It leads to an unrelenting need to make the most of one's life, to fashion identity and meaning increasingly from personal achievements and possessions and less from shared cultural traditions and beliefs. It distracts people from what is most important to wellbeing: the quality of their relationships . . . which, ideally, contribute to a deep and enduring sense of intrinsic worth and existential certainty. As Goethe warned, things that matter most must never be at the mercy of things that matter least.

Marketing Brand Me

The Utopia complex fills a vacuum where political passion, religious faith or social idealism once inspired dreams of a better world rather than a perfect life. Having fallen for the blandishments of the consumer society, many of us have adopted materialism as our driving philosophy, sometimes managing to marry it with religious or political faith. In the West, the capitalist model of materialism has captured our hearts and minds, and mass marketing is its most obvious face.

Consider the role of advertising in our lives. Most advertisements, taken singly, strike us as being somewhat outrageous, occasionally silly (*An insult to our intelligence!*), but essentially harmless. They are outrageous in the sense that they typically offer emotionally charged benefits from using a product or service that we know, when we bother to reflect on it, can't possibly be realised. Coca-Cola, believe it or not, won't guarantee your popularity or enhance your social skills; it might not even quench your thirst as successfully as water. A new car might well be better than the old one, but it will still crumple when someone runs into it and will soon be outmoded by an even more desirable, newer model. Today's state-of-the-art smartphone is tomorrow's yawn.

> I was being driven somewhere by the son of one of my friends. As we were driving, I felt my mobile vibrate and took it out of my handbag to check the message. My friend's son was staring at the phone with a look of incredulity. At first I thought he was disapproving of me for checking my phone when I should have been talking to him. As if! No, it turned out he was genuinely amazed at how antiquated my phone was. I said to him, 'Are you laughing at my phone?' and he said, 'Well, it would look good in a museum'. They really do think your mobile phone says something about you, don't they?

Most advertisements are judged by most people to be harmless. That's either because we know that, in the scheme of things, purchase decisions are generally pretty trivial, or because we take advertisements with a grain of salt anyway. We understand their mission is to sell us things, and, while we may tolerate or even appreciate them for their entertainment value, we know that, in the end, we have the power to ignore or reject them – though, rather oddly, many people believe that while they themselves are largely immune to the effects of advertising, others are more easily sucked in.

> I wouldn't say I was particularly vulnerable to advertising – not the way some people seem to be brainwashed by it – but I do get cranky when the supermarket hasn't got my favourite brand of something, even though my brain tells me that, for most products on the shelf, one brand is just as good as another.

Many attacks on advertising are uninformed and misguided. They usually presume that advertisements have far more persuasive power (even hidden power) than they actually do. In fact, advertising works best when it is designed to reinforce what we already think rather than to attempt to change our minds. It is actually one of the weakest of all the marketing factors when compared with more direct influences on consumer behaviour like price, packaging, promotion, distribution and display, to say nothing of the quality of the product itself or the personal recommendation of a friend.

But the fact that individual advertisements might seem harmless enough can blind us to a deeper and more insidious cultural effect of the whole caravan of modern mass marketing. All those TV and radio commercials, posters, pop-ups, glossy ads in magazines, price promotions, glitzy displays and product demonstrations add up to something greater than the sum of their parts. It's not just that they encourage greed; it's not just that they reinforce our reliance on material values by encouraging us to define ourselves in terms of what we have rather than who we are. No, the deeper problem for us, as a society and as individuals, is that they join together in a loud and seductive chorus of entitlement and invite us to sing along. While each marketing campaign is going about its legitimate business of reinforcing consumers' beliefs about Brand X and its superiority over Brand Y, another reinforcement is also taking place: our Utopia complex is being stoked. Instead of recognising it as a complex – a syndrome, a neurosis, a disorder – we begin to believe the idea brand marketeers are consistently presenting to us, day after day, year after year: that the good life is about getting what we want. (*We can have all this stuff! We can be as glamorous as that! We can have a better time than we've been having! Life will be richer and more satisfying, and we will become happier, better people if we jump on the bandwagon!*)

In response to the relentlessness of all this conditioning, something else happens as well: we start to think of promotion as a way of life. We may even adopt the idea that we ourselves are rather like brands – Brand Me and Brand You – jostling for attention and recognition in a crowded marketplace called 'society' or in that other, intangible marketplace called 'cyberspace', where social media like Facebook and Twitter provide a ready-made platform for self-promotion. Facebook profiles are roughly equivalent to the brand personalities constructed by marketing strategists to position their products in the consumer marketplace.

In the age of promotion, everything's a brand. Cities are promoted like brands. Political parties and politicians themselves are brands, increasingly marketed in the same sloganistic way as commercial products and services, with the predictable outcome: a loss of voters' esteem. In thrall to the marketing-minded strategists who advise them, politicians are stuck with being seen as brands rather than law-makers, which almost inevitably means they will be accorded less respect, less loyalty and less attention. They will be expected to be attractive and entertaining rather than visionary and thoughtful. The twenty-four-hour news cycle has become a drain on the imagination and intellectual capacity of politicians and those who feed them their lines. Media personalities have always been brands, scarcely distinguishable from the commercial brands that sponsor and sustain them. Celebrities are brands. Perhaps it was inevitable that some families would start promoting themselves like brands, by posting *My Family* pictures on the rear window of their car.

There's nothing new in the preoccupation with self or the wish to lead a life based on economic security and material comfort. As a species, we've been focused on these ever since our forebears started storing food for the winter and lining their caves with animal skins. Looking after our own interests is natural; it's even necessary, up to a point, for our physical and emotional survival. In a modern capitalist society pursuing the goal of endless economic growth, the health of the economy depends on every consumer being driven by self-interest. (In fact, the relentlessness of mass marketing tends to reinforce our self-interest, risking some stifling of more noble tendencies, such as altruism.) What's changed is that the self we are increasingly being encouraged to indulge is a buffed-up, idealised self that doesn't always correspond to the person we know ourselves to be, or to the life we know we are really living.

The truth about us all is that we are frail, flawed, fragile and feeble, as well as many more flattering things. Yes, we are sometimes bold, funny, thoughtful and even wise. Yes, we can succeed in all kinds of endeavours; we can prosper. Yes, we can be wonderfully compassionate and caring; we can fight for justice and win; we can create beautiful objects, words and pictures; we can offer unstinting service to others and expect no reward for it; we can give and receive love and be enriched by it. We are all that and more, and the 'more' contains as much darkness as light. We are bound to fail sometimes. Life will frustrate us. Friends and family will disappoint us. Some of the lessons we will learn about ourselves will be hard to take. We won't always want the truth to be told about who we really are and what really drives us.

When we surrender ourselves to the Utopia complex, we can too easily forget who we really are. We can fall for the idea that frailty is not our nature but a weakness to be overcome or perhaps to be masked by the thrill of a new outfit. If we're not careful, we can start to 'believe our own bullshit' – an inelegant but accurate description of what happens when we buy the idea that perfection is possible; that we can have it all, have the best, be the best. Our folklore reminds us that no one is easier to con than a con man: if we're intent on the marketing of Brand Me, we may find that we have become the foolish victims of our own hype.

A tale of two leaders, part 1

Kieran O'Toole sweeps into the small conference room attached to his office and takes his place at the head of the table. He looks around him, checking that all the people he has summoned to this meeting are present: the head of his new sub-department (Recreation for the Ageing), his chief of staff, his political advisor, his media advisor, three people from the PR company he has put on retainer (at his own expense

– Kieran is independently wealthy) and his personal assistant. No one present is over the age of thirty, except Kieran himself, who is thirty-eight, and the department head, who is in her early forties.

Kieran has just been appointed a junior minister in the state government, one of three juniors reporting to the same Cabinet minister, a party heavyweight with years of experience in government who is deeply suspicious of Kieran for his flashy wealth and naked ambition. Kieran has been told that his style is a bit brash and he needs to listen more, to consult. He is trying.

'Welcome. Thank you for coming. I want to explain to you why we're here and what I expect of you. But perhaps some of you would first like to tell me what *you* think our priorities are.'

There's some shuffling of papers and clearing of throats.

The department head, unused to silences, jumps in. 'We want to revolutionise the leisure and recreation sector to take more account of the needs of an ageing population. Our most urgent priority has been clearly established and agreed by all our stakeholders – that is, the development of more age-friendly infrastructure, through the construction of new facilities and the modification of existing assets held by both the public and private sectors. Access. Adaptation. Accountability. These are our watchwords, Minister.'

'Really?' Kieran is new to this. He is unprepared for such fluency. 'Those are our watchwords? So, anyone else?'

The head of the PR firm, Jon, quickly sides with the department head. A private contract with an ambitious junior minister is one thing, but there are many lucrative possibilities lurking within the department itself, to say nothing of the wider public service. 'Took the words right out of my mouth, Polly', he says, smiling warmly at the department head, who stiffens at the familiarity: she's used to being addressed as 'Secretary', especially by people she's never met before. Jon goes on, 'Our job, as I see it, is to raise the profile of the ageing and to highlight the virtues of recreation, physical and mental, right through the, er, final, er . . . '

The PA is scribbling furiously. The political and media advisors are looking expectantly at their new minister, hoping for something a little more piquant than this. Their wishes will shortly come true.

'All good, all good', says Kieran. 'That's probably all we need from you this morning, Polly. We'll get on and discuss the political side of things – no need to concern you in any of that.'

'Quite so', says Polly tartly, rising to leave. 'Just one other thing, Minister, if I may?'

'Of course.'

'As the PR people are employed in a personal capacity by you, they should not properly be meeting on departmental premises.'

Kieran tries to smile but ends up smirking. Polly leaves. Jon wriggles awkwardly in his seat.

Once the door is securely shut behind Polly's departing back, Kieran turns to Jon. 'Don't worry about that. We'll have you sorted with a departmental brief a.s.a.p. – nothing too grand to begin with. But perfectly legit.' Kieran sits back in his chair. 'Anyone want to say anything else before I begin?'

No one does.

'Well, then,' says Kieran, 'pieties aside, I want to leave you in no doubt of our priorities here. I want to be minister for Planning and in the inner Cabinet within two years. Treasurer within five. Premier? We'll see. If I want it, I'll go for it, but I might not want it. I want to see the job up close before I decide. And if anyone quotes me outside this room, I will deny this conversation ever took place and terminate your contract forthwith. Understood?'

Everyone appears to understand. The PA's pen is frozen.

Kieran relaxes. 'So you lot are the team to get me there. Team O'Toole. You were right about profile, Jon, only it's mine you have to be worrying about. You did it for that bishop; you did it for that judge; you did it for that miner; and now I want you to do it for me.' As he says this, Kieran taps himself on the chest with the index finger of each hand. 'This job may have been given to me as a sop to the faction,' he says, 'but we're going to treat it as a launch pad, pure and simple. I want profile like you've never seen profile before. I want to be borne aloft on an ever-rising thermal of good news'. (Someone once told Kieran to harness the power of metaphor.) 'I want no embarrassments. No gaffes. No fuck-ups. Image. Profile. Exposure. Got it? I want Brand O'Toole to shine as brightly as possible, all the time. I want to be the punters' perfect politician.'

He turns to the media and political advisors, one at each elbow. 'You boys do what Jon tells you, okay? I want you to keep me informed at every turn – that's your job – but I want Jon to call the shots.'

*

Just a block away from the Department of Recreation for the Ageing, another leader is taking up her new job. Kate Sherman has been appointed CEO of an aged-care agency that is funded partly by government, partly by a religious charity with a long history of welfare work and partly by private donations. Kate has been in the job for just one week and has spent that time sitting with staff members of all levels, trying to understand the workings of the place as well as catching the mood. This is her first meeting with her senior executive group, and it's taking the form of a light lunch in the conference room.

After some animated chatter, Kate taps her water glass for silence. 'It's such a privilege to be here, and I know some of you must be wondering why an outsider got the job. I don't know, either, but here I am, and I'm going to have to rely on all of you to give me as much support as you can. I'll be listening very hard and learning as quickly as possible. And I'm sure I'll make mistakes. But there's one thing I guarantee: I'll listen to anything you want to say to me and I'll treat each of you the way I'd expect to be treated myself. No exceptions to that.'

Kate looks around the room at her six new colleagues. Two, she knows, applied for her job and might now be thinking of looking elsewhere. The other four seem genuinely welcoming and pleased to have her onboard. Everyone is smiling.

'I'm no autocrat, but there are just two things I'd like to insist on, right from the start. One is that you, too, treat each other and everyone in the organisation the way you yourself would like to be treated. No exceptions to that, either.' Kate notices a couple of pairs of downcast eyes, but the others are still shining at her. 'The other thing is, I would really like to get rid of that silly sign in the foyer that says, "Excellence in Aged Care". Of course we want to do our best, and occasionally we may even do something excellent, but we'll all stumble sometimes. Mistakes will be made. Clients will be disappointed in us. I don't want that sign hanging over our heads like a hollow promise or a vague threat, as if to say, "Excellence in aged care, or else!" And I don't want it intimidating our clients and their families, either. I don't think they'd ever say they want excellence from us. They might say they want us to be nice to them. Supportive. Efficient, certainly. But warm and human, mainly. Fully present for them. Attentive. Patient, even when things get a bit tense and chaotic. Treating them the way we'd like to be treated, in other words. I'm not sure "excellence" really captures all that. Any dissenters?'

Far from dissent, there is actually a ripple of applause from the group of six.

'Oh, one other thing, if I may. We're not competing with each other. Everyone in the organisation has a specific job to do, and we are all on the same side, all in the same team. I understand there used to be weekly awards for staff members. That has to stop. No awards from now on. No more Service Provider of the Week, or anything like that. Okay? We're in this thing together, and everyone is to be valued for what they contribute.'

Amid all this striving for excellence, perfection and self-esteem, it's easy to overlook a fundamental fact about our species. We humans are, by nature, social creatures – herd animals – and the process of socialisation, learning how to live harmoniously in social groups, is actually designed to restrain our self-interest and curb excessive competitiveness. To hear the merchants of self-esteem, though, you wouldn't think so. *Winners are grinners!* they tell us, and so, from an early age, our children are being trained to expect recognition and rewards for everything they do, so they'll feel like winners. A gold star for breathing. A certificate for turning up. Lavish praise for functioning like a reasonable kid. This is dangerous stuff, because it creates an impression that life is about recognition and rewards, that Utopia consists of winning glittery prizes, that if you keep winning you will be taken more seriously than the losers. This is the inevitable product of our neurotic embrace of materialistic Utopianism. (The ironic truth, of course, is that if there were ever a real Utopia, it would be a haven of harmony, cooperation and egalitarianism.)

It takes some of us a long time to realise that we can be diminished by rewards. They can too easily become ends in themselves, distracting us from the intrinsic value of worthwhile activity. Rewards can actually limit the satisfaction we obtain from a job well done or from the performance of a virtuous act, by putting the focus on Me – on the actor rather than the action. The worst effect of the reward mentality is that we may eventually lose interest in doing things for which there is no reward-based incentive, no recognition, and thus further reinforce our sense of entitlement.

I used to despair of getting the kids to clean their rooms. One of my friends wised me up. 'Give up the struggle', she said. 'You have to resort to simple bribery – just pay them money. Works every time.' Well, it did work, I suppose. There was some hard bargaining about what a clean room is worth (I'm sure Darren will be a trade union official when he grows up), but they stuck to the deal. Next thing, there was a price on everything I expected them to do. Putting out the garbage. Emptying the dishwasher. Eventually, I jacked up. I realised I'd backed myself into a corner, so I told them I just wanted them to do all these things because they are members of the household too. Complete failure. Not a flicker. I'm still trying to work out what to do next. Maybe I need a Kid of the Week award, like Man of the Match.

Man of the Match is a particularly unfortunate sign of the times, already, inevitably, winding its way into children's games. The whole idea of a team, like the idea of a community or an organisation, is that we pool our various talents in order to promote the common good. How can anyone be Man of the Match when the very essence of teams is that they are about Us, not Me? The answer is clear: the Utopia complex creates an insatiable appetite for heroes and celebrities whom we are supposed both to adulate and to emulate. Courtesy of Twitter, we can even feel connected to our heroes in ways previously unimaginable: as we narrow the gap between celebs and us common folk, we can all share the limelight; we can all indulge in the pleasing illusion that celebrity is within our grasp and we are part of the magic circle.

The Brand Me mentality has entered the world of writers, many of whom are rather introverted, reclusive types who recoil from the idea of celebrity and wish their work could speak for itself. (*But, no, you'll have to promote it, and if you can't be a celebrity then at least try to be a personality.*) Celebrity chefs, celebrity bishops, celebrity doctors, even celebrity intellectuals. You might think intellectuals would be free from this sort of nonsense, given that we once demanded that they should be dispassionate, sceptical, rigorous and, above all, uninterested in personal popularity. But there are now polls to choose Australia's most popular public intellectuals: this has become just another product category ripe for branding in the media marketplace. Far from being intellectuals in the classical sense, people so branded are likely to be passionate advocates or shameless entertainers.

How did Brand Me become such a phenomenon? It might be an expression of the desire to find something to control in a world that seems increasingly beyond our, or anyone's, control. We may not be able to control the climate, the exchange rate, the European debt crisis, the worrying rate of US unemployment or the mad ambition of politicians, but we can control Me, or, at least, the public persona we choose to project as Me. Some of us compensate for our apparent powerlessness by becoming obsessed with our personal appearance – witness the rash of breast implants, facelifts, Botox injections and tattoos – or with our house and garden, our food or the number of Facebook 'friends' we've accumulated, all designed to project an image of someone who's well on their way to a personal Utopia.

Facebook may have created the perfect vehicle for personal brand marketing, but this isn't just about the influence of Facebook, Twitter or reality TV shows, the cult of celebrity or the insidious effects of marketing and PR machines that promote hollow values and promise more glitz and joy than they can ever deliver. This is about an entire culture that runs on the promotion of self-esteem and feeling good about yourself, regardless of whether you've done anything to warrant such feelings.

In the jangle of tawdry awards, prizes and promotions designed to pump up our self-esteem, an important idea is in danger of being overlooked. According to Roy Baumeister, professor of psychology at Florida State University, the key to a satisfying life is not self-esteem but self-control – a far cry from the blazing guns of self-promotion on the glory road to some imaginary Utopia. Like many psychologists, Baumeister once believed that self-esteem held the promise of being 'a powerful key to mental health and successful behaviour'. But his research over two decades led him to the conclusion that the beneficial effects of self-esteem are actually quite limited and that, in fact, self-control is one of the most important traits found in people who lead a satisfying life. Writing about his research in *The Psychologist* in 2012, Baumeister describes self-control as our 'moral muscle' and points to its centrality in sound decision making and in the restraint of our impulses towards self-indulgence in ways necessary for the effective management of our lives.

This meshes with common sense. Doesn't our own experience teach us that moderation is generally preferable to excess; that self-discipline is more likely than self-indulgence to preserve our self-respect; that self-aggrandisement is usually a symptom of self-delusion, or, at least, emotional insecurity? Martin Seligman, widely regarded as the high priest of positive psychology, has reached the same conclusion as Baumeister. Research published by Seligman and Angela Duckworth in 2005 rather controversially found that self-discipline, not self-esteem, is actually more useful than IQ as a predictor of all-round high-school performance.

In the noisy contest to construct and promote a Utopian image for Brand Me, particularly via our status symbols and online bragging, it's easy to forget that we may be sacrificing the very thing that will lead to the deepest sense of satisfaction: self-respect based on self-control. There is no shortcut to that, and no amount of self-promotion will get us there.

The rise of infantilism

China's one-child policy is famous, but, without government coercion, birthrates in most Western countries have fallen to record lows, commonly around 1.5 babies per woman, though hovering around 1.8 in Australia and dipping as low as 1.3 in Italy and Spain. These rates are way below the population replacement level of 2.1 babies per woman, which is why immigration, often involving the resettlement of refugees, is seen as a way to sustain economic growth.

The obvious implication of more adults choosing to remain childless is that children now represent a smaller proportion of the total population of many societies than ever before in our history. A sustained low birthrate tends to make societies less child-centred and potentially less child-friendly with our child-free resorts, apartment blocks and restaurants, and our greater willingness to criticise other people's children. Yet, at the same time, we are in danger of slipping into mass infantilism, as if one facet of our Utopia complex is to retain our childishness. Is this an unconscious compensation for the diminished presence of children in our midst?

Is it because innocence is part of the Utopian dream? Perhaps. Whatever its origin, we do seem to be developing a growing sense of infantile dependency, on governments to fix everything, on banks to lend us enough money to buy whatever we want, on the latest techno-toy to give us a thrill, on drugs to relieve us of the challenges, or even the tedium, of reality.

From the craze for cosmetic surgery to reduce the signs of ageing to the Brazilian wax treatment that transforms the appearance of the genital area of a fully mature woman into that of a prepubescent girl, from the increasingly hysterical cult of celebrity that's reminiscent of childish jostling for playground popularity to burgeoning information technology corporations with childish names like Google ('Barney Google, with the goo-goo-googly eyes'), Yahoo, Facebook, Crikey, Twitter and Apple, we seem to be on a cultural spiral that is drawing us back towards childhood. 'Kidults' is the label created for young adults who resist the idea that adulthood starts anywhere before thirty, and 'adultescence' the word used to describe the stretching of adolescent attitudes and behaviour well into early adulthood.

For all the attempts to persuade fashion designers and women's magazines to use models that look like real women, the trend towards childishness in the body shape of models continues, with breasts and hips de-emphasised, the childish pout often deployed on the catwalk and models as young as fifteen recruited into the industry. We may tut-tut as much as we like, but the fashion industry well knows that part of the Utopian fantasy is that we might retard the process of ageing.

When mothers report that they and their daughters are able to share some wardrobe items, this is sometimes said with irritation at daughters who simply help themselves to their mother's clothes. More often, the remark is tinged with pride in the discovery that a mother's clothes actually suit a woman as young as her daughter. The increasing casualisation of dress, language and manners looks like an attempt to stay young, and nowhere is the trend more apparent than in the persistent wearing of blue denim jeans well beyond middle age.

The dumbing down of newspapers, the rise of reality TV and the steady degeneration of talkback radio all point to a more infantilised culture fed on a diet of homogenised and predigested information. There are still broadsheet fundamentalists, who think traditional-format newspapers are the cornerstone of a civilised society, but their numbers are shrinking along with newspaper readership. The infamous ten-second grab on radio and TV news is a distant memory: two or three seconds is all you'll get now, and sometimes no more than a few words. The advent of dedicated news channels appears to have softened the core of news and current affairs programs on traditional free-to-air entertainment channels, allowing them to relax into the populism that favours human interest over public interest. (Generalisations about TV are increasingly difficult to make, however. Replaced by the internet as the love-to-hate medium we consume voraciously and attack mercilessly, TV has been freed to fragment, as radio did before it. While reality TV thrives at one end of the spectrum, high-end TV drama is challenging movies as the medium where the best writing, acting and production take place.)

Politics has become infantilised, too. Leaders who tailor their remarks to the media's relentless demand for sound bites, who are trained to stay on message and to recite today's slogan like a mantra (rather like a child who has mastered a new multiplication table), should not be surprised when the electorate's esteem for the political process sinks to new levels of cynicism. As suggested earlier in this chapter, if political parties adopt the simplistic tone and techniques of commercial mass marketing, they should expect voters to respond by taking them no more seriously than brands. The yearning for visionary statesmanship may not have entirely evaporated, but it is hardly encouraged by the perception that politics is a game being played by people who, in the parliamentary chamber – the forum in which we dare to expect the best of them – often resort to behaviour that strikes us as childish.

Even tertiary education is not immune from infantilisation, with lecturers being expected to entertain as well as inform, in anticipation of being assessed by their students. In some universities, the staff refer to these assessments as the 'happy scale', since their real purpose is to ensure that the students are happy with the institution, just like satisfied customers or contented, well-fed babies. On our largest university campuses, the sheer number of students means that they must often be treated more like high-school pupils than budding scholars. And fee-paying students typically believe that, having paid the price of their chosen degree, they are entitled to receive it, with some institutions allegedly being complicit in this by discouraging academic staff from declaring that any fee-paying student has actually failed.

The tendency for young adults to stay in the family home for longer than any previous generation certainly reflects both an unaffordable housing market and a generational shift towards postponing commitment to home ownership (or anything else). But it is also partly explained by the culture of childish dependency and entitlement. Of course, some parents drive this trend by encouraging their children to stay in the family home well into adulthood, as a way of continuing the practice of removing obstacles from their children's pathway (in this case, the financial hurdle of housing costs), as well as reassuring themselves that they are 'close to the kids' and even that they are 'staying young' by remaining members of their young-adult offspring's social circle.

We may deplore the growing sense of dependency, yet we lap it up. We bemoan the nanny state and nod sagely in response to talk of smaller government or of getting the government out of our lives, yet we appeal with childish eagerness for help, or for someone to blame, as soon as something goes wrong, or whenever we catch a whiff of some government concession that seems to disadvantage Me. *Why can't we get the tax cuts too?* say the rich, stamping their metaphorical feet.

My country, right or wrong

The Utopia complex afflicts governments, too. Politicians consistently make outrageous claims for the likely effects of their policies (every initiative is a 'reform') and try to convince us that we are blessed with leaders who are uniquely bold, competent, honest, trustworthy and selflessly committed to public service and the wellbeing of the citizenry, with not a hint of self-interest to be found in their ranks and nothing ever done for reasons of political expediency, blah, blah, blah. Most people are sceptical in the face of politicians' claims about their own virtue. We don't automatically think of politicians as being a force for good; we don't necessarily associate politics with goodness (though, at its shining best, it can be). We demand a higher standard of personal behaviour from politicians than from each other while not seriously expecting it, and yet our cynicism never quite gets the better of us: we seem endlessly prepared to back up for another try, always ready to invest fresh faith in a new leader.

In the Australian context, an interesting proposition has been advanced by Laura Tingle, political editor of *The Australian Financial Review*, to explain why we so constantly feel let down by leaders in whom we have placed such faith. In her 2012 *Quarterly Essay*, 'Great Expectations', Tingle argues that in spite of radical reductions in the power of the government to influence either the economy or the lives of ordinary citizens, politicians continue to employ rhetoric that might once have been appropriate but no longer reflects the actual situation. 'Our post-deregulation politics has been dominated by politicians reluctant to admit that one implication of opening up the economy is that they don't have quite as much control as they once did', she writes. As examples, Tingle cites the government's loss of direct control over wages and work conditions, the value of the dollar and the setting of interest rates. The steady removal of tariffs and subsidies that protected industries has left the government less able to resist the economic pressures of global markets. Yet our faith in the system tends to be undiminished by economic upheavals, cultural revolutions, political mayhem, disappointment after disappointment or disenchantment upon disenchantment. It would, though, wouldn't it? Patriotic pride is a crucial component in the Utopia complex.

The German-born US senator Carl Schurz gave us the phrase 'my country, right or wrong', but we have conveniently forgotten the rest of what he said: 'My country, right or wrong: if right, to be kept right; and if wrong, to be set right'. (Utopia-hungry patriots don't like that last bit. *Wrong? Us?*) Revolutionaries and cynics aside, most people seem content with the idea that, whatever the flaws of their politicians, their country's system of government is about as good as it can be, though this belief may turn out to be less robust among members of the increasingly globalised younger generation. Being more globally connected, they are likely to be less constrained by nationalism, more aware of a global consciousness and more prepared to live and work – and fall in love – anywhere in the world. As a result, we should expect them to have a less rose-tinted view of their domestic political system than their parents might have. This certainly seems to be the case in Australia, where a 2012 Lowy Institute poll found that only 39 per cent of Australians aged from eighteen to twenty-nine years believed democracy was better than other forms of government. Commenting on that poll in *The Weekend Australian*, sociologist Frank Furedi suggested that this indicates the socialisation of young people in Australia is seriously flawed; but there are alternative interpretations of the Lowy Institute finding, including the possibility that young people may be looking around the world and deciding democracy is not all it's cracked up to be.

Politics aside, we all need to believe we're best at something, even something buried in our glorious past. The Greeks cling to the idea that their country was the cradle of Western civilisation, the British sing 'Rule Britannia' with a gusto undimmed by the harsh geopolitical and economic facts, New Zealanders believe they have 'God's own country', Americans pride themselves on living in 'the land of the free and the home of the brave', and Australians like to think 'we punch above our weight' in everything from international sport to the winning of Nobel prizes (though the Australian national anthem makes the breathtakingly modest claim that 'our home is girt by sea'). If, in spite of all this patriotic zeal, we fail to convince ourselves that our birthplace is the best on earth, we may decide to live away from our homeland for a while to see what else is going on, or, more radically, to emigrate to somewhere that promises to come closer to our ideal. Having moved there, we'll probably then regale the residents of our new Utopia with romanticised tales of the one we left behind.

When perfection is the dream, recurring disappointment is the inevitable consequence. But, since the Utopia complex is a neurosis, perhaps even an addiction, we don't learn from our disappointments, whether in politics, in the consumer marketplace or in our quest for sexual perfection. Each disappointment only spurs us on.

Inevitably, inexorably, sex

For millions of people around the world, the miracle of internet-based information technology has come down to this: unlimited access to pornography and erotica. Who's surprised? When we abandon ourselves to the idea of a materialistic Utopia, pleasure and gratification are likely to overtake self-control and self-sacrifice as personal ideals, so it's not hard to imagine how sex soon becomes central to our yearning.

Any culture in the grip of the Utopia complex is ultimately going to commodify its dreams. The short step from a preoccupation with the pleasure and gratification of retail therapy to the pleasure and gratification of sex is easily taken: notice how often 'Ten Steps to Great Sex' (or minor variations on the theme) appears as a teaser on the front cover of glossy magazines. The use of implicit or explicit sexual imagery to promote products and services, and the surrender to erotica and internet porn, are part of the same pattern. The commodification of sex is entirely consistent with the values of mass-market materialism: compulsive acquisition, self-indulgence, exploitation and constant replacement.

For a growing number of Westerners, the sexual has become the spiritual, the logical end point of our dreams of perfection. Hence the cultural obsession with perfect sex, reliable orgasms, sexual adventuring fuelled by performance- and pleasure-enhancing drugs, with sexual possession as the ultimate possession, and porn the symbol of ultimate sexual liberation: no holds barred, no consequences, no regrets.

When a culture becomes saturated in sex, obsessions that were once marginal or hidden become part of the mainstream. Both the pornographers and the anti-pornographers are reinforcing these obsessions. Those who encourage the sexualisation of pre-pubescent girls for commercial gain or as a source of misplaced parental pride and pleasure, as well as those who constantly rail against the sexualisation of girls as though that's the only thing, or the main thing, to be said about youth culture, are all complicit in this increasingly obsessive drive to keep sex on the agenda, to keep us thinking about sex, noticing sex and ultimately, perhaps, inadvertently training our children to accept that sex *is* a commodity that occupies just another place in the market. (As we know only too well, nothing reinforces a fashion, a prejudice, a belief or a practice like constant attacks on it.)

The Utopia complex traps us in a neurotic obsession with a life lived for Me and my pleasure. If the conditions are right and the partner sufficiently skilful, it's no secret that I can get the most intense pleasure of all out of sex. Where else can I find a constantly renewable source of stimulation and gratification to keep me happy all the way into a Viagra-fuelled old age? And if the drive to make my sex life more interesting and rewarding demands a constant parade of new sexual partners, then that's consistent with the Utopia complex, too: there's a good reason why 'new' has always been a magic word in the commercial marketplace.

If that sounds like a corruption of the best that sex can be – a vehicle for expressing love, commitment, devotion, mutual support and comfort, while also having fun with your partner – then so be it. After all, that's only an extension of the corruption of moral values inherent in any pursuit of a material Utopia. Sex for the sake of sex, or sex solely as an expression of lust, is equivalent, in every way, to acquiring stuff for the sake of having it.

Hey, what about *fun*?

It goes without saying that we all need a good laugh to bring us back to earth. There is such a thing as the joy of sex. It's true that vigorous physical exercise can induce feelings of euphoria. Aesthetic pleasure – visual, musical, tactile – can be therapeutic. Communing with nature is relaxing; so is curling up with a good book (or even, occasionally, a bad one). Buying a new car is a thrill for many people. Regular holidays are essential for our health and sanity. There's nothing wrong with throwing a self-indulgent treat into your supermarket trolley, reading a trashy magazine over a restorative cup of coffee or reviving your flagging spirits with a new hairstyle. Apart from the fun involved in some of these purchases, we need to buy things to keep the engine of commerce ticking over and to keep each other in jobs. In fact, if you can afford it, there's economic virtue in paying someone else to clean your house or mow your lawn, just as you pay someone else to educate your children, build your house, grow your food and make your clothes.

There's a big difference, though, between occasional harmless fun and the neurosis that traps us on a treadmill of wanting everything to be fun. There's a big difference between enjoying the thrill of an occasional self-indulgent purchase and getting hooked on shopping as a primary source of stimulation, pleasure and gratification in your life. When that happens, you're at risk of developing the Utopia complex (*This is good, so more must be better!*). But we were not born to shop. We will not find much sense of meaning and purpose in a retail mall. Stuff won't save us.

Obviously, not everyone suffers from a full-blown case of Utopianism, but, one way or another, few are immune to its effects. The Utopia complex fuels the notion that the good life is about how much money you've got, the amount of power you wield, the size of house you live in, the make of car you drive, your personal appearance, the school attended by your kids, the places where you eat, the sophistication of your information technology kit, your favourite holiday destinations and the kick you get out of sex. In other words, Me, Me, Me.

No one truly believes that the acquisition of more and more material possessions, a succession of ever more exciting sexual partners, a younger-looking face, smarter clothes, straighter teeth or brilliant bathroom fittings are likely to add to the sum of goodness in a life. Yet, once we have thrown ourselves willingly into the swiftly flowing Utopian stream, it's hard to find a reason to swim for the bank and clamber back onto dry land. We might be left behind; we might miss something; the next thrill might be just around that next bend.

The good life is not a contest. There are no winners or losers. You can't be left behind; you can't miss out. The good life, as we shall see, is lived with a quite different Utopia in mind.

Jack and Jill went up the hill . . . *then* what?

Jack and Jill Thurkettle have been married for thirty-eight years, have raised three children, who have all left home (though their youngest keeps popping back in the breaks between relationships), and feel, like many others before them, that having climbed the hill *there's nothing there*. They don't want to take a tumble like their nursery-rhyme namesakes, but they are conscious of a nagging anxiety, or perhaps it's a vague sense of unfulfilment. Life has come to feel not empty, exactly, but somehow incomplete; unsatisfying.

They discuss it often. Interminably, in fact. Their recurring theme is that something is missing from their lives and that, after all their material and even their parental success, they should be feeling a deeper sense of contentment. When they look back, in search of what's missing, they remember a constant sense of anticipation, always looking forward to the next stage, the tingling feeling that something was constantly happening, or about to happen, in their lives. Falling in love, getting married, furnishing their first flat, having children, buying a house, raising the family, establishing their careers, planning family holidays, kids' birthday parties and Christmas, surviving the chaos of home renovations: it was like a rushing tide that swept them along without leaving much time for making sense of it all. Now, at a stage in their lives when they had assumed there'd be so much to look forward to, they seem to be floundering, struggling to find a focus, unable even to relate to each other as they once did, though their sex life continues much as before, a pleasant habit.

In moments of quiet reflection, Jill asks herself, *Is this all there is?* and can't bear to face the possibility that, yes, perhaps it is. *What's it all about?* occasionally floats into her mind, and she has no idea of the answer. Such questions are a bit too confronting for Jack, though Jill knows he must be sharing her sense of quiet despair.

Sometimes they speculate about the possible advantages, emotional and social, of returning to the church where they met as young people, but their forays in that direction have been discouraging. To be frank, they felt . . . what? Superior to the rest of the people they met? They don't like to use that kind of language, but, yes, that's how they felt. Jill still wonders whether they should seek out a more fashionable church, or a bigger church, where there would be a greater chance of finding 'people like us', but Jack favours the idea of taking up golf, or perhaps bridge, something they could do together to help fill the time that used to be swallowed up by the children's activities. Even as the children left school and entered young adulthood, their lives were a source of endless fascination to Jack and Jill, along with the normal amount of angst and irritation. But even the angst, in retrospect, was engaging; at least something was happening.

They often find themselves commenting on how much they miss the children. They are wistfully noticing how far apart from each other they seem to have drifted. They had not expected this to happen, hadn't noticed it happening, and are saddened by it, but determined to recapture some of the magic that brought them together and sustained their relationship for so many years. Meanwhile, movies are their favourite distraction.

They are well off. Comfortable. Jack is a middle-ranking manager in a large insurance company, and Jill is working for an information technology consultancy, having given up teaching when she had three children in rapid succession and never felt like returning to the classroom. Financially, their combined income puts them within the top 20 per cent of Australian households. Everything says they have reached the top of the hill, or, at least, *their* hill, the hill they chose as their personal summit. They know they are the envy of many of their friends who have suffered disappointing setbacks to their careers, children who have gone off the rails, separations, divorces, affairs or bereavements. The Thurkettles have had none of that to contend with. Yet here they are, up the hill, the hard climbing all done, and it suddenly seems rather pointless and meaningless.

'I'm just not *happy*', Jill has said to Jack, several times. 'Do you think it's us? Have we run out of steam, you and I?' Jack has always been uneasy about getting into these emotionally intense encounters with Jill. Though he knows they are important to her, he often feels out of his depth, unsure where the conversation might go or what Jill's hidden agenda might be. There's a particular reason for his reluctance in this case: a woman in his office has been making it clear she's available for a no-strings-attached dalliance. Jack enjoys the flirting but has resisted the temptation to take it any further. He hopes Jill would do the same if confronted by a similar offer at her own work. He knows the marriage is not all they had both hoped it would be, but it's still profoundly important to him, partly because his pride won't let him become another statistical cliché.

As time passes, they each begin to wonder if the problem is, indeed, with them and the quality of their relationship. Is the empty feeling the result of hearts that have been hollowed out by the relentless process of living a busy family life? It's true that the kids got most of the attention and energy, and Jack and Jill often felt more like parents than partners.

'Isn't life supposed to be better than this at our age? At this stage?' Jill wants to know. 'Aren't we supposed to be living the good life? We're both well educated; we're healthy; we've got good jobs; we've plenty of time on our hands; the kids are fine . . . Come on, Jack, what is it with us? Why aren't we having more fun? We always used to have so much fun!'

It's easy to mock Jack and Jill; easy to believe we know what's wrong with them. They've had it too easy, we may say. The hill they climbed wasn't steep or rocky enough. They haven't lived through a war or a plague or experienced the kind of tragedy or trauma that sharpens people's values and clarifies their priorities. When they go casting around for something, apart from their children, to give their lives a sense of meaning and purpose, we may shake our heads at how pathetic that seems. We may criticise their exploitative approach to religion, though many people go to church for social and emotional reasons – tribal reasons – that have little to do with specific religious beliefs. We may wonder why their work doesn't fulfil them more than it appears to, or why it hasn't occurred to them to do something useful in the community with some of their spare time. (If they did, they would undoubtedly encounter like-minded people doing the same.)

In some ways, the Thurkettles are typical of the postwar baby boomers, born between 1946 and 1961, who, at least on the surface, seemed to have an easier passage through life than their parents: no world war and no Great Depression, for a start. Yet, like every generation, theirs had its challenges: the boomers were buffeted by a series of cultural, technological and economic upheavals that forced them to confront their parents' conceptions about the nature of society and, in many cases, to chart a quite different course from the one their parents had mapped out for them. As they moved into early adulthood, fired by a spirit of protest and by signs of revolutionary change around the world (the new wave of feminism that sparked a gender revolution, student and worker protests across Europe, anti–Vietnam War demonstrations, political assassinations, nuclear disarmament rallies, the Age of Aquarius with its messages of peace and love), many boomers became social pioneers, cultural warriors and iconoclasts. They deserted institutional religion in large numbers, and their quest for non-religious meaning led many to experiment with Eastern mysticism, especially via yoga and meditation, and with quasi-mystical personal development programs. Others, like the Thurkettles, maintained a vague connection with religion but seemed more focused on climbing their own little hill, cashing in on the pervading sense of prosperity, setting goals that were largely material and then wondering why there wasn't more of a thrill attached to achieving them.

For those who used their children as a primary source of meaning and purpose in their life, there was always going to be a difficult period of adjustment when the nest finally emptied. Adapting to the sexual and gender revolutions, they sent the divorce rate through the roof and, aided by the contraceptive pill, started the birthrate on its long descent. They revolutionised family life, redefining the very word 'family' to include ever more diverse groupings, and they institutionalised the two-income household.

Their parents dubbed them the Me Generation, because they seemed, from the beginning, to be so intent on going their own way, whether pleasing themselves or imposing their will on the world. The boomers coined the term 'retail therapy', which was taken up with glee by their children. They racked up record personal debt but preferred to think of it as credit. They were famously reluctant to save, partly because, being the children of the Cold War with its ever-present threat of a nuclear holocaust, they felt their future was uncertain and their lives might be cut short at any time. That sense of living on borrowed time was deeply implanted in the boomers' psyche by the experience of growing up in the Fifties and Sixties, and it affected more than their saving and spending patterns; it made them reluctant long-term planners, as well. For many, like the Thurkettles, reaching their sixties came as something of a shock: either they hadn't expected to live this long, or, if they had, they hadn't given much thought to what they would do when they got here.

It's taking Jack and Jill a long time to discover that the secret of the good life has very little to do with having fun. When they finally work that out, their priorities will shift, their sense of purpose will acquire a new clarity and their offspring will be relieved to find they are no longer expected to engage so closely with the lives of their middle-aged parents. Whether the Thurkettles will also have more fun remains to be seen.

2

How the pursuit of happiness can make you miserable

One of the craziest manifestations of the Utopia complex can be found in the popular idea that happiness is our default position, our natural state, and that everything we do is – perhaps even should be – calculated to maintain a chirpy disposition and a state of perpetual wellbeing. The more you think about that idea, the weirder it seems, yet it continues to be asserted as an axiom: however much we may cloak it in worthy-sounding rhetoric, we're told, all we're ever really doing is trying to maximise our own happiness. To present this as if it's a deep insight into human behaviour is to ignore some well-established truths about us, such as our capacity to behave in utterly selfless and even heroic ways that bring us no obvious pleasure; our willingness sometimes to act solely out of duty; the fact that we learn most of our most important and character-forming lessons from so-called dark experiences, like sadness, failure, disappointment or loss; and the inconvenient reality that the goodness of a life actually has very little to do with fluctuations in our emotional state. But the view persists as one of our favourite modern myths, its advocates often touting happiness as one of the brightest, shiniest symptoms of the good life.

If this were true, it would make sense to pursue happiness. Just go for the attractive stuff, the positive stuff, the pleasurable stuff. Calculate the satisfaction you'll get out of something before agreeing to do it. Avoid the tough challenges unless you can be sure of getting a high from meeting them. Don't, whatever you do, get caught up in other people's problems: they might drag you down and diminish your prospects of happiness. (*A problem shared is a problem doubled . . . Hey, there's a good reason to keep clear of people in need.*)

If you were to espouse happiness as the appropriate goal of your existence, you'd be perfectly entitled to use 'feeling good' as the benchmark for assessing whether you were having a good life. You'd equate success with happiness and, presumably, failure with unhappiness; you'd think only happy people could be living well; you might even think of happiness as a sign that someone has their life under control. That last one is a killer: imagine falling for the idea that getting your life under control is a pathway to happiness. A life under control? Would that be at the very end, perhaps, when you've paid all your debts, fulfilled all your obligations and taken your place in a rocker on the verandah of the Eventide Home, with a rigid daily routine, bowel motions monitored and everything right where it's supposed to be? Or would it be when you've finally got all your books arranged in order (or thrown them out in favour of a Kindle), your sock drawer organised, the crossword completed and in bed by nine? Or would it be when your children turn out as you'd expected and none of them ever calls with a problem?

And what about the fashionable belief that we are in control of our own happiness; that we can make it happen? How should we put that into practice? Are we supposed to keep an eye on whatever is happening to us to make sure we're getting enough happiness out of it, and find ways of escape if we're not? This would be a total surrender to the ego. If you fall for the proposition that happiness is within your control, you'll feel as if black days, or even blue days, are a signal that your life is out of control. And that's nonsense. Trying too hard to achieve happiness or to hang on to it when it pays you one of its fleeting visits will only increase your feelings of frustration and disappointment. Barry Schwartz, a professor of social theory at Swarthmore College in the United States, puts it like this: 'Happiness as a by-product of living your life is a great thing. But happiness as a goal is a recipe for disaster'.

A devout Christian of my acquaintance, long ago deceased, was fond of drawing a distinction between happiness and joy. He liked to play the phonetic game of equating happiness with happenings – things that happen to us that have an emotionally positive impact on us – whereas joy, to his mind, was about an enduring state of inner serenity and contentment. The distinction was religiously motivated in his case: he believed it was only religious faith that could produce such serenity and contentment. Even if you are not animated by any particularly religious impulse, there is some wisdom in the distinction. It's true that for many of us the idea of happiness depends on events and experiences that give us pleasure, encouragement or positive stimulation of some other kind. 'Joy' might not be the word you'd choose to describe something more enduring, something that doesn't rely on external stimuli, but many people, with or without religious faith, describe a grounding, a calm confidence that keeps them balanced even in the face of turbulent or challenging events – and phases of unhappiness.

What such people are describing is a clear sense of purpose which is neither generated nor influenced by our ever-changing emotional state. If you're clear about how you mean to live your life, the day-to-day (or hour-to-hour, or moment-to-moment) question of whether you happen to be feeling happy or sad hardly seems to matter; those emotions are no more than interesting signals about your response to the passing parade.

A day at the beach

Jason and Peter, not yet twenty, are friends and rivals, each thinking himself an emerging poet, and each eager to be first in the affections of their creative-writing tutor, Tabitha Trent. Spending Saturday together at the beach has become a pleasant habit for them, emphasising their freedom from the years of compulsory sport at the school they had both attended.

They sit, perched on a rocky headland overlooking the bay where they've spent most of the day swimming and sunbathing. The silence between them is a much-practised art. Jason once read a story about two famous poets who met only once and were unable to find anything to say to each other. He and Peter are training themselves to be comfortable with silence.

Below them, a small yacht is skimming across the blue water of the bay, leaning over in a stiff breeze, its sails straining to contain the rush of air. It's enough to move any young poet to words.

'Look at those sails', says Jason, immediately wishing he'd waited for Peter to speak first. 'Don't you love the way they swell and lift with the wind? That's a perfect picture of optimism, don't you think?'

'Go on', says Peter, bracing himself for another of Jason's excursions into positive psychology, his current obsession.

'I hear the cynicism in your voice. But look: it's only with that fullness in its sails, that lift, that the yacht can get up such impressive speed. It's a metaphor for optimism.'

'No it's not. It's simple physics. That's how yachts work.'

'Don't be such a literalist. We all need to be like those sails – open to the wind and the sky, swept along by the force of nature. Sheer joy. If I had to draw happiness, I'd draw that yacht with its big, ballooning sails.'

Peter gazes out to sea, both wanting and not wanting to prick his friend's bubble. He clears his throat and Jason looks at him doubtfully. 'All right, Pete, say what's on your mind. You can't see the inner beauty of it, the poetry of it – that's your problem. I know perfectly well how yachts work. I'm just saying that picture, right there, is a metaphor. Why can't you let your poet's heart be filled like that sail, uplifted, swept along wherever the wind takes you?' Jason is rather pleased with that and plans to do some more work on the idea when he gets home.

'I wonder', Peter says, taking pleasure in the gravity of what's coming, 'if I might say a word on behalf of the keel? Your blissfully ballooning sails would capsize that boat in an instant if it were not for the heavy keel keeping the boat upright and driving it forward. No keel, it would just go sideways and – plop!'

'Very amusing. You're actually a keel kind of person, aren't you, Pete? It comes out in your poetry. All dark and deep. Leaden. Didn't I hear Tabby Trent suggest you might lighten up a bit? Are you actually against happiness?'

'Are you against keels and counterweights? If you're going to talk in metaphors, may I point out that life, even in a case as blameless as yours, is not all bright and breezy? I will say just one word: Eloise.'

Knowing where this might take them, Jason desists.

'Can we agree, then', says Peter, 'that yachts need wind, sails *and* a keel?'

'Of course', says Jason, wishing he'd kept his metaphor to himself, but determined to knock the tutor sideways, keel or no keel, with next week's poem. 'And water, obviously', he adds, keeping intact his reputation for having the last word.

The popular idea of happiness is focused on a pleasant sense of uplift, maximising the possibility of positive emotional experiences, such as pleasure, gratification or fulfilment; nurturing a generally positive attitude. It goes without saying that we enjoy that uplift and sometimes seek out experiences that will create it. But if we go further and yield to the temptation to confuse or conflate such happiness with the good life, we create some emotional and cultural hazards for ourselves – even some moral hazards. The most obvious one is that all the talk about happiness puts the emphasis on Me and how I'm feeling, whereas the goodness of a life, as we shall see in chapter 5, is about moral sensitivity and integrity rather than emotional wellbeing. If you accept that (and I hope you will at least have given it some serious thought by the time you reach the end of this book), it follows that the measure of a good life could hardly be based on some assessment of how happy we are;

it will depend primarily upon how well we treat others, regardless of how that makes us feel.

Another hazard is that we will find ourselves privileging happiness above all the other colours in the spectrum of emotions that make us who we are, as if Jason's yacht doesn't need both sail and keel to make progress. Out of all the emotions available to us, why pick on one for favourable attention, especially if, on reflection, it turns out to be the one that has least to teach us about what it means to be fully human, fully engaged with the life of the world we live in? In particular, an obsession with happiness can make us scared of sadness and rather unhealthily relentless in our pursuit of the positive.

I once attended a conference where a speaker urged us all to 'write down, every night, three good things that happened to you today'. I was dying to ask, *Why? Why single out good things?* Her purpose, presumably, was to encourage us to inculcate feelings of happiness at the end of each day and put us to sleep with a smile on our face. Yet happiness is just one among the many emotional states – some pleasant, some unpleasant – that we must learn to recognise and embrace as signs of our humanity. If I were to urge you to write down three reflections on your day (and I never would), I'd be suggesting you look for the contrasts: What range of emotions did you experience today? Where did they spring from? What did each of them teach you about your journey through this day's events?

Without sadness, we would never know what happiness is. Yet sadness, however justified it might be by circumstances or natural mood swings, is too often and too quickly put under the microscope in case it turns out to be an early sign of the disease we have learnt to call 'clinical depression'. (This is a bit like our penchant for describing a light head cold as the 'flu.) Some forms of depression are indeed 'clinical' – serious illnesses requiring specialised medical treatment – but the boundaries of its diagnosis seem to have become so elastic that we are a bit inclined to lump together all our emotional troughs, from the blues to a perfectly normal melancholia, and call them 'depression'.

Writing in *The Psychopath Test* (2012) about the United States' notorious *Diagnostic and Statistical Manual of Mental Disorders*, published by the American Psychiatric Association, Jon Ronson notes that there has been such an explosion in the number of conditions now chronicled in the manual as treatable mental disorders that surveys designed to test the prevalence of symptoms concluded that 50 per cent of the US population was suffering from a mental disorder of some kind (which would, presumably, imply that 'disordered' is the new meaning of 'normal'). 'It was truly a revolution in psychiatry', Ronson writes, 'and a gold rush for drug companies who suddenly had hundreds of new disorders they could invent medications for, millions of new patients they could treat'.

We're living at a time in medical history when labels for mental and emotional disorders are proliferating at such a rate that many people may yet find themselves diagnosed with a condition or syndrome not previously heard of. Perhaps having a label pinned on your condition could be a source of comfort if you're feeling a bit troubled, a bit neglected or a bit less focused than usual. (According to Ronson, the architects of the mental disorders manual rejected the apparently serious suggestion that Atypical Child Syndrome be included in the list of new disorders.)

Clinical depression, unlike sadness, is never going to visit most of us, and for that we can be grateful. Most people are not going to be savaged by the black dog or shrouded in the rough blanket of despair that smothers its victim with feelings of hopelessness and helplessness and, in the extreme case, with an urge to end it all. Most won't be crushed by the sense of futility, relentless anxiety or terminal bleakness that depression can visit on those who suffer from it, and who clearly need professional support and careful treatment. Perhaps our current obsession with happiness is partly a result of our heightened awareness of the Western epidemic of depression. We want to avoid becoming depressed, just as we want to avoid heart disease, cancer or diabetes, and perhaps we think being happy is a preventive strategy, a bit like keeping fit or watching your diet. Yet the truth is that to be fully human – to be normal, to be healthy – is to be occasionally engulfed by waves of grief or sadness, stymied by feelings of despair, paralysed by doubt or crushed by disappointment.

We grow through pain

We should be wary of pursuing happiness as the main goal of our life, not only because happiness is one of the most elusive and unpredictable of emotions, but also because so many people report that their most valuable experiences of emotional growth and personal development have come from pain, not pleasure. And, to further complicate the picture, isn't there a kind of sweetness about some forms of pain and sadness?

Of course, we enjoy moments of feeling happy and positive. When we're miserable, as we inevitably and appropriately are, from time to time, it's tempting to feel that life is being unkind or unfair to us. So it's easy to see why we might think of happiness as the natural state to be in – our default position. But that overlooks an important truth about the experience of being human: sadness is not only as authentic an emotion as happiness, it's also far more instructive. The fleeting moments of bliss and joy, and even the deeper sense of contentment that occasionally envelops us, make sense only because they represent such a contrast with the experience of pain, trauma, disappointment or sadness, or even with those times when we feel ourselves trapped in the drudgery of a tedious, dreary routine.

Dreary routine? In fact, the emotional flatline we associate with the routines of daily life is not as flat as we sometimes imagine it to be. We might scarcely notice the momentary ups and downs, but they punctuate every day, prompted by events, encounters and memories: pinpricks of sadness; bursts of bliss; little flashes of panic or angst; surging waves of joy that recede, like any waves, as quickly as they build; and all those other patches of sunlight and shade, those moments of pleasure and irritation, that pop in and out of our psyche. They are all reminders that the emotional spectrum is broad, and that to miss any of it – yes, even the disappointments, the failures and the tedium – would be to diminish the spectacular experience of wholeness.

Be happy! strikes me as an odd thing to say to anyone, in every way as odd as *Be sad!* I'd never want to wish a positive emotional state on anyone, particularly if they were wrestling with some difficulty, dealing with a tragedy or simply experiencing a rather bleak patch. I'm with Benjamin Disraeli on this: 'There's no education like adversity'.

> You wouldn't want to wish misery on anyone. I wouldn't wish my husband's illness on my worst enemy. But dealing with it has been the best thing for our marriage. It sounds trite, I know, but it really is the tough times that make you realise what matters.

'Happiness is not a horse; you cannot harness it', says an old Russian proverb, capturing an idea that permeates much religious and moral teaching on the subject: the more you seek happiness, the less likely you are to find it. 'Happiness is not found in self-contemplation', wrote Samuel Johnson; 'it is perceived only when it is reflected from another'. Self-absorption, like puffed-up self-esteem, is never the pathway to fulfilment, let alone enlightenment. *How can I become happier?* is a classic sign that we've missed the point.

It goes without saying that some emotions are harder to deal with than others. Most of us have no trouble handling happiness, satisfaction, pleasure, euphoria, contentment or triumph. Even a little bliss is quite nice, occasionally. But the fact that such emotions are so easy to manage is precisely the reason they don't have much to teach us. In fact, too much euphoria can blind us to the truth of our situation.

Take falling in love. Most people experience that heady state as a sublime form of happiness, and yet from the outside it looks more like a mild neurosis. When we're head-over-heels in love, we're typically quite dysfunctional, distracted, disorganised and inclined to make absurdly optimistic assessments of the state of the world, along with hopelessly unrealistic judgements about all the wonderful qualities miraculously combined in the person who has become the object of our affection. To a lesser extent, we do the same when we 'fall in love' with political leaders, investing unrealistic measures of hope and optimism in them and their ability to change society for the better.

I once heard a positive psychologist encouraging people to give their doctor a piece of chocolate before he or she made a diagnosis, on the grounds that the sugar hit would produce an emotional high that would enhance the doctor's ability to make an accurate diagnosis. *Really?* I thought. Then I reflected on something we all know to be true, from our own experience: when we're well fed, we tend to make more charitable judgements about what's going on and, in particular, about other people. In fact, some disturbing UK research reported in *The Psychologist* in 2012 has shown that prisoners coming before a parole board have a much better chance of obtaining favourable treatment if they are seen after lunch. So I wondered if there might be something in the chocolate idea . . .

Then I came across the results of research conducted by Joe Forgas at the University of New South Wales that would certainly discourage us from offering our doctor chocolate. Forgas's work suggests that, in some circumstances, there are actually advantages in being blue. Unhappy people – not depressed, just not happy – are apparently less gullible, more attentive, more easily able to communicate, more sceptical and actually likely to make better decisions. Other studies have likewise suggested that people feeling overly positive can tend towards recklessness and less responsible judgements: not the characteristics you'd be looking for in a doctor's diagnosis. On the other hand, being cheerful and positive can apparently be good for our cooperativeness and creativity (but not always: look at the infamously cranky Beethoven, evicted, for various offences, from dozens of apartments).

In fact, research on the effects of happiness and unhappiness is telling us what we know, intuitively, to be true: all our fluctuating moods have something useful to offer us, and if we try to limit their range by controlling them (with drugs, for instance), we will diminish our capacity to learn from the emotional richness on offer. Happiness is far from the ideal state we sometimes imagine it to be; it would certainly not be healthy as a permanent condition.

We might do well to resist drawing too many neat conclusions about any of this, or making too many sweeping generalisations, except this one: we need to experience all the emotions available to us if we are to be 'whole' human beings. Indeed, the cluster of emotions we sometimes think of as dark, demanding or tough should not be considered negative at all. The difficult emotions are actually our greatest teachers. That's why our folklore insists that we grow through pain and learn more from failure than success.

> Retrenchment? Tell me about it. Three times it's happened to me. I'll tell you what it meant – the last time, anyway. It meant I reassessed everything. I got my work in perspective; I got my marriage in perspective; I got my kids in perspective. I'd previously been married to the job, no question. I'll never fall for that again. I know I'm the driven type – I get passionate about what I'm doing and then I get trapped in it. Well, you have to decide what really matters, don't you? In my case, it took losing my job three times. Three times! Slow learner, see? The point is, I never learnt anything much from all the previous success I'd had. It was the retrenchments that taught me what I needed to learn.

The champion Australian swimmer James Magnussen attracted worldwide attention when he swam well below expectations in a men's relay event at the 2012 London Olympics. He was said to be 'gutted' after the race. Following widespread speculation that he would be unable to recover his morale and his form for other races, Magnussen declared he had learnt more about himself in the twenty-four hours following the relay than in the previous twenty years of his life. He subsequently won a silver medal in the one hundred metres freestyle, one-hundredth of a second behind the United States' Nathan Adrian – an experience which no doubt held still more lessons.

The propositions that we grow through pain and learn more from failure than success are both so obviously and inarguably true that you have to wonder why, when emotions like disappointment and sadness visit us, we want to banish them as quickly as possible. *Give me a pill! A drink! Music! Sex! Distract me; protect me; cheer me up! Give me a shortcut back to the easy, pleasant stuff!* Euphoria has always appealed to us as the Great Escape. The truth is that we will learn nothing from our sadness, our suffering, our disappointments or our failures unless we give ourselves time to experience them to the full, reflect on them, learn from them or, in modern parlance, process them. Another bit of our folklore reminds us that time is the great healer, and we can look at that truth in another way: healing takes time.

Why then are so many parents prepared to declare that their greatest wish for their children is that they should be happy? Is this just another symptom of a Utopia complex that ranks our emotions according to how desirable they are? If happiness is at the top of your list, you'd naturally want it for yourself and your children in doses as large as possible.

No one would wish sadness upon their children, but the simplistic wish for happy children is such an unrealistic goal, to say nothing of vacuous and misguided, it's tempting to ask: Is that *all* you want for them? Do you really want them to be as emotionally deprived as that? Don't you want them to learn how to cope with failure, frustration, disappointment and even unfairness:

a friend who's disloyal, a teacher who plays favourites, a sporting contest they were a certainty to win but lost? Don't you want them to know there are cheats who get away with it, referees who make wrong calls, teachers (and parents) who aren't always sweet tempered and even-handed, cats and dogs that look cute but snarl at you if you try to pat them? And don't you want to help them recognise the blues as part of life, something to be accepted, dealt with and learnt from? None of that means we should seek sadness, for ourselves or our children, any more than we should seek any other emotional state. It would be strange to welcome disappointment or trauma into our lives, but we might do well to accept that a noble, courageous, well-lived life is one in which we are equipped to experience and negotiate the full range of emotions: neither seduced by the lure of happiness nor obsessed by the grim and gritty aspects of life, but open to whatever comes and ready to learn from it all. Bereavement happens. Relationships break down. Illness takes its toll. Children (and parents) disappoint us. Friends let us down. We fail. What should we do? Pretend we're not upset? Take a happy pill? Deny ourselves the chance of experiencing the full richness of human existence?

A very short lesson in Greek

The question underlying this whole discussion is, of course, this one: what do we mean by 'happiness'? As is often the case, it's helpful to start with the ancient Greeks. When, during the fifth century BCE, the playwright Sophocles declared that wisdom is the chief element of happiness, what do you think he meant by 'happiness'? Not pleasure, if wisdom is its 'chief element' – except perhaps that fleeting pleasure we take in acquiring insights, learning something, *getting* it. Not contentment, either, since wisdom and understanding may sometimes fuel a restlessness in us: an urge to make the world a better place, a desire to advocate on behalf of the poor, the marginalised or the underprivileged, or to spread the word on behalf of a worthy cause. No: the ancient Greeks had a more nuanced idea of 'happiness' than we have today, and the claim that wisdom is its main ingredient gives us a clue as to what that idea might have been.

In the following century, the philosopher Aristotle taught that the ideal life was the life of *eudaimonia*, a word that has been popularly – but rather simplistically – translated as 'happiness'. When we examine what Aristotle actually said, we can begin to see why that ancient idea occupied such an important place in Greek thought and perhaps we can also see why the pursuit of happiness – in that original sense – was indeed a worthwhile goal. Aristotle was certainly not talking about sensory pleasure, cheerfulness, euphoria or a life so dreamily disengaged from the real world as to create the illusion that things are better than they really are. This was not a life of 'positive outcomes'. Aristotle's brand of happiness involved living in accordance with reason, fulfilling one's sense of purpose, doing one's civic duty, living virtuously, being fully engaged with the world and, in particular, experiencing the richness of human love and friendship – in other words, something that sounds remarkably like the contemporary concept of 'wholeness' (a word which shares its origins with the religious word 'holiness').

When contemporary Westerners speak of happiness, we don't usually mean anything as noble or virtuous – or complex – as those ancient Greeks had in mind. In our culture, we typically mean something more emotionally restricted, and relentlessly positive, than the state implied by Aristotle: 'happiness' and 'wholeness' are by no means interchangeable terms in the modern world. I might believe that we'd all be better off if we were to focus on wholeness rather than happiness, but I admit this is not a popular position. Happiness, in the increasingly narrow modern sense, has our culture by the throat. From nursery tales to Hollywood's romantic comedies, 'happily ever after' is presented to us as the gold standard.

> I went to one of those happiness conferences. Some of it was quite helpful: I got some good tips on how to minimise stress, and how to live in the moment. But some of it was beyond weird – people telling us we were responsible for our own happiness, and if we weren't happy, that meant we didn't really want to be – all that stuff about how you can get what you want just by wanting it badly enough. Reach out to the universe. All pretty old-hat, actually. The woman sitting beside me had a son who was dying of cancer, and she eventually left in tears.

Fortunately, there are signs that the happiness industry is losing some of its momentum: books and conferences are beginning to pay attention to the idea that this may have been a lopsided and potentially dangerous period in our cultural history; a period when we held out false hope to too many people. If you encourage people to pursue happiness single-mindedly as their primary goal, either they are going to risk surrendering to the delusion that it's possible – desirable, even – to float through life in a bubble of joy, seeing the world through a happy haze, or they're going to be frequently disappointed and frustrated. Neither is a healthy outcome. We need to change the agenda. Let's not crown happiness as the sovereign emotion. Let's leave it where it belongs, as one among the many emotions that, taken together, make us who we are.

In *Reason in Art* (1905), the Spanish philosopher and novelist George Santayana wrote that 'to be interested in the changing seasons is . . . a happier state of mind than to be hopelessly in love with spring'. Most of us prefer one season to the others, but the sane and balanced person learns to appreciate the seasonal changes of light, tempo and weather, and the resulting differences in the food we eat, the clothes we wear, the places we go and the things we do. And so it is with our emotional state: most of us prefer one mood to the others, but the sane and balanced person learns to accept and appreciate the changing emotional seasons. To focus on any one emotion (but especially happiness) to the point of pursuing it is, after all, to risk becoming self-absorbed and even narcissistic. *Am I happy? Why am I sad? Am I fulfilled? Why am I feeling like this? Am I content? Why am I stressed?* We will ask some or all of those questions occasionally, but to become obsessive about any of them, to turn them into our quest in life, is to miss out on the thrill of wholeness.

Composers know that a rich musical experience includes harmony and counterpoint, discords and resolutions, themes and variations. They know we need major *and* minor keys. We need uplifting melodies to whistle, and dark, complex material to stir us more deeply, even to disturb us. We need the good ol' blues. We need slow, reflective movements embedded in symphonies, along with all their other musical hues and tempi. If music is indeed the 'food of love', then it must, like food, offer us the rich variety of a balanced diet; it must also, like love itself, illuminate all the emotional possibilities of the human heart. Novelists, playwrights and poets, similarly, understand that the arts are not (or not *only*) about happiness; they're about the representation and interpretation of life as it really is, in all its complexity, ambiguity and mystery. (Who doesn't enjoy a good cry at a sad film?) A happy ending only makes sense through its contrast with what has gone on before.

Positive thinking is all very well – better than thinking negatively, no doubt, and shown to be therapeutic for some people burdened by depression. But we don't recommend a daily dose of antibiotics for people who are not fighting a bacterial infection, and, for people not wrestling with mental illness, thinking positively may actually interfere with the ability to think realistically.

The glass is half full, says the optimist.

The glass is half empty, says the pessimist.

That glass is twice as big as it needs to be, says the engineer, and realists are a bit like the engineer. We don't need to put a positive spin on everything: if the water reaches halfway up the glass, that's the reality we're presented with; that's the reality we need to deal with.

Jill goes to LOL Club

Jill Thurkettle has lost patience with her husband, Jack, and their recurring conversations about the lack of direction in their lives. She thinks she may go mad if Jack utters the phrase 'spinning our wheels' one more time. Their quest to find a church that suits them has been fruitless. Jill has been discouraging Jack from rushing out to buy a dog: she recognises his sudden yearning for a pet as a symptom of a man in need of more love, and is uneasy about its implications. Their growing suspicion is that this (whatever 'this' means) may be all there is, yet neither is prepared to settle for that.

Jill has accepted an invitation to join a local book club – seven or eight women in their fifties and sixties. The club has been running for years, but they recently adopted the name 'LOL' after one of their members came to a meeting breathless with the news that a colleague in her office had joined a group called the Happiness Club and had taken to quoting the club's slogans at every opportunity. 'Happiness is a decision', she would tell anyone who happened to be having a rough day. 'You can be happy right now and for every moment to come for the rest of your life', she would announce over morning coffee, causing some consternation among her colleagues, who would respond with such comments as 'Do we have to?' or 'What, *every* moment? No time off for bad behaviour?'

Amused by their friend's account of all this, the members decided that their humble book club should also be given a name. Misery Club was the first suggestion, rapidly followed by Whingeing Women, Mad Cows Society and The Avengers. They finally hit on 'LOL', delighted by its multiple ambiguities (including, said one, 'luscious older ladies'). To their husbands or other outsiders, though, it remains a mere book club.

The invitation to join has come from Franny, a friend from a mixed tennis group that Jack and Jill have belonged to for years. When Franny raised it, it felt more like a firm request than an invitation.

The night of the meeting is cold and wet, and Jill is grateful to Franny for having offered her a lift. On the way, Franny gives her quick biographical sketches of the other six women who will be there. Jill is daunted by the intellectual credentials of two of them, both academics, but they all sound interesting, mostly working women in similar situations to hers.

They are met at the door by Liz, the hostess, and Jill is warmly welcomed, a glass of red wine is put in her hand and introductions swiftly made. It all feels unexpectedly intimate and wonderfully alive with . . . what? Energy? Goodwill? Jill has a momentary pang of guilt, thinking of Jack slumped in front of the TV, but quickly banishes it.

A woman called Prue, somewhat older than the others, is in the midst of an account of her recent separation – 'trial separation', her husband has told her, but everyone except Prue seems to have known he had his eye on someone else.

'Not all men are treacherous, faithless bastards, Prue', the woman beside her remarks. 'They are just hooked on their own testosterone. Follow their dicks to the ends of the earth. Shoot first; ask questions later.'

It emerges that another of the women has recently moved in with Prue, to help her through the transition to solo living. Jill is impressed by the matter-of-fact way this is all being discussed, and by the unconditional support flowing between these women.

The discussion broadens into some frank exchanges about the state of some of the other women's relationships, all delivered with a candour that Jill finds slightly unnerving. She remains silent, struggling to connect the strands of the stories, scarcely able to believe some of them, smiling sympathetically whenever anyone looks at her. She is privately coming to the conclusion that Jack is the salt of the earth, though one of these women appears to have left a previous partner on the grounds of nothing more heinous than that he was boring. (Jill wonders, *Is Jack boring? Am I? Is that our problem?*)

More wine is poured, and the decibel level rises as strategies are discussed for ridding life of tiresome or wayward – or controlling and possessive – husbands or partners. Jill can't put Jack into any of those categories. A bit dull, perhaps? But Jill is herself feeling a bit dull in the face of all this intensity.

'Book time, girls!' says Liz, suddenly.

Jill glances at her watch. Nine-thirty already. She told Jack she'd be home by ten.

More wine is poured, and the women briefly share their reactions to the book. Jill would have loved more discussion, but it's as if the book part of the evening is a ritual they go through on the way to something else. Clearly, there are more layers to be peeled away. The book's plot and characters provide the catalyst for a rolling series of deeper conversations about love, deception, families, faith, money, the varieties of liberation and enslavement, difficult mothers, headstrong daughters, health, men. There's no laughter now.

Jill can feel her own world tilting as she catches glimpses of the lives of these women. She has never known such caring, healing love outside a parent–child relationship, or such willingness to accept and deal with sadness and loss. (No one is saying *Cheer up!* to anyone.)

The mood changes, the tone lightens, as if the group is returning to the surface from a deep dive. There is some salacious gossip from a couple of the women's workplaces and then they are all on their feet. Tight, bonding hugs and kissing of cheeks.

Jill and Franny drive home in silence.

As they pull up in front of Jill's house, Franny says, 'I hope you'll come again next month. They need you'.

'*Need* me? Are you serious?'

'Dead serious. Why on earth did you think I invited you?'

Jill is silent, wondering what she has to offer such interesting women.

Inside, Jack is waiting like the father of a teenager out on her first date. Jill, unsure of how to describe her first encounter with this stimulating group, refuses to say anything until they are in bed with the light out.

'No, this is *not* all there is, Jack', she murmurs into his shoulder.

The *feel-good* life?

If the good life were a life of self-indulgence, feeling good would be the goal of everything we did. Fun and laughter would be our highest priorities. But there's more to life than pleasant stimulation, and no one is likely to be satisfied with a life lived in the single-minded pursuit of one emotion – happiness or any other.

Our emotions are the body's reactions to things that happen to us day by day: the people we meet, the experiences we have, the challenges we face. They are like the soundtrack to our lives, signalling to us the character and intensity of our responses to what's going on around us. They sometimes act as alarm bells, warning us we're in danger of being harmed (or of harming ourselves). They sometimes reward us with lovely little moments of euphoria. They often send us darker signals as well, like sadness, disappointment or anger, alerting us to some lesson that needs to be learnt. They leave us in no doubt when we've done something embarrassing, shameful or stupid. And sometimes they are simply telling us about the state of our digestion, our hormone levels or the condition of our liver.

Our moods fluctuate naturally. It is only when the highs are uncontrollably euphoric or the lows uncontrollably depressed, or when we become stuck at one point in the natural cycle of waxing and waning emotional states, that we need professional help. But most of us don't experience those extreme mood swings: we learn to recognise and accept changing moods for what they are, sometimes triggered by events, sometimes by thoughts and sometimes by body chemistry.

I remember when my youngest was about seven, he used to get really, really worried when he felt a bit sad. I tried to explain to him that our emotions go up and down, and it's nothing to worry about. I compared it with the weather: we wouldn't want sunshine and blue skies every day; grey days are good, too. Eventually he got it. Then he started giving us regular bulletins on how he was feeling – I must say that got a bit tedious. But when he hit puberty, he became quite good at recognising when his mood was down and he'd just take himself off to his room for a while and tell us he didn't want to talk about it. By then, he'd learnt how to cope with it and he wasn't spooked by a bit of sadness or emptiness. He could usually work out where it had come from, and even if he couldn't, he'd just accept that this was a mood that would pass. Considering how he used to be – almost panicking about it – I was very proud of how he came to deal with it.

Emotions feel powerful in their effects on us, yet they are remarkably easy to manipulate. Advertisers do it all the time. So do composers, film-makers and chefs. So do politicians with a gift for the rhetorical flourish, or preachers with a passion for souls. Parents try to do it to their children and lovers to each other. And, of course, we regularly try to manipulate our own feelings through the use of all kinds of drugs – legal and illegal – that have been smoked, drunk, chewed or otherwise absorbed into the body since the dawn of humanity. The goal of all this manipulation of emotion is clear: to replace an authentic emotion with an artificially induced one; perhaps to prolong or intensify a natural high. That can be a harmless enough practice when so-called soft drugs are used as an occasional stress-buster or social lubricant. The danger, of course, is addiction: getting hooked on euphoria to an extent that limits our capacity to function within the normal range of emotional responses.

When I get home, I need to have a glass of wine straightaway. I can't face the kids or the cooking until I get that first one under my belt. I know all about alcohol-free days, but you try living my life without it.

Some of us also try to control our emotional state through the use of meditative disciplines that aim to break the nexus between events and feelings, often with brilliantly therapeutic effects in the reduction of stress and the bolstering of our ability to resist distractions.

In fact, it seems to be an almost universal human tendency to seek ways of relieving ourselves from the relentlessness of our emotions so we can feel relaxed, elevated, excited or calm on demand. It's no accident that the happiness movement has coincided with an explosive increase in the use of recreational drugs in the general population and mood-altering drugs in psychiatry. The same culture shift may well have contributed to the West's high levels of obesity caused by the overuse of comfort foods and drinks (whether sugar saturated or alcoholic) designed to make us feel better, at least in the short term. Indeed, the proposition that we can control our own happiness could easily sound like an invitation to *induce* feelings of happiness. And, if there were no other considerations, who wouldn't prefer to feel euphoric rather than troubled or confused, high rather than low, happy rather than sad, proud rather than ashamed, triumphant rather than disappointed?

But for most people, free-flowing emotions are as important to our ability to monitor and cope with life as any of the body's other warning systems and response mechanisms. An emotion that can be summoned at will is not an authentic emotion. Yes, we can get into bad habits, slipping too easily into anxiety, relying on stress to motivate us or always expecting the worst in any situation, and we may need therapeutic assistance to break those patterns if they are disturbing or disabling us. And, as noted earlier, there does seem to be evidence to support the idea that people struggling with mental illness may benefit from a disciplined attempt to think positively. Outside clinical practice, though, there's an inherent danger in chasing inauthentic emotions. It's important to be able to recognise the state we're in and to explore the factors that led us to this point. If we allow ourselves to become preoccupied with the manipulation of our emotions, we risk becoming emotionally disabled, unable to function without artificial support.

An important step towards understanding and embracing the good life is to acknowledge that it has nothing to do with how you happen to be feeling from moment to moment. Living the good life isn't always going to make you feel terrific; it isn't necessarily going to make you rich (or poor); it won't necessarily lead to worldly success (or failure). It is not about any of that. Depending on your particular circumstances, a life animated by kindness and compassion, a virtuous and even noble life, *may* produce inner calm, moral confidence and a deep sense of wellbeing. That's a formidable combination, and you might even want to label it 'happiness'. But there's a very fine line here: if we are acting compassionately, virtuously or ethically in order to feel good about ourselves, we've missed the whole point. A kind or virtuous act performed for our own emotional benefit amounts to exploitation of the person towards whom we've acted charitably. We need to delete our own happiness from the list of motives for any act that is going to count as noble or virtuous: such acts are exclusively about the benefit to others, without counting the cost, let alone the benefit, to ourselves. To claim them as pathways to our own happiness is to misread the whole idea of morality.

The pursuit of happiness? Sounds like a wild-goose chase to me. To seek it, to desire it, to yearn for it is to miss it. It's not like money, food, power or status: you don't get it by going after it. When it comes to you, that's a bonus all the more welcome for being unexpected. But unremitting happiness is not the mark of a life well lived – a good life – any more than unremitting sadness is. *Wholeness* is the thing to aim for.

What is this thing called 'wholeness'?

One of my psychological heroes, the non-directive, client-centred psychotherapist Carl Rogers (1902–1987), wrote passionately about wholeness, though he never used that word. He referred instead to 'the fully functioning person'. (I say Rogers was a *psychological* hero: that's a willing admission of intellectual and professional admiration.

Up close, according to his biographer David Cohen, Rogers was as emotionally frail and psychologically flawed as anyone, and rather hard to admire.) In an influential paper titled 'A Therapist's View of the Good Life', published in *On Becoming a Person* (1961), Rogers described three characteristics of a fully functioning person. The first is an ever-increasing openness: 'the polar opposite of defensiveness' was how Rogers put it. He spoke of the need to be open to the full range of emotions that flow from our experience, in particular to the experience of fear, discouragement and pain. (Interesting, isn't it, how often those powerful teachers, the so-called negative emotions, crop up in discussions of wholeness and goodness?) For Rogers, the fully functioning person is not only able to experience all his feelings, but is unafraid of them.

Second, Rogers believed a fully functioning person develops the ability to live completely in the moment – to experience each moment as new. He wrote that such a person would realise that 'what I will be in the next moment, and what I will do, grows out of that moment, and cannot be predicted in advance either by me or by others'. Living in the moment involves an absence of rigidity and a maximum of adaptability: 'To open one's spirit to what is going on *now*, and to discover in that present process whatever structure it appears to have . . . is one of the qualities of the good life, the mature life'. This comes very close to the Buddhist emphasis on an attitude of 'mindfulness'.

The third characteristic of Rogers's fully functioning person is a willingness to trust their own 'gut instincts' (Rogers called them 'total organismic reactions') rather than trying to adhere rigidly to a set of pre-coded rules laid down by some institution, and a refusal to be unduly influenced by the opinions and judgements of others or constrained by previous experience.

Rogers summed all that up in the term 'psychologically free'. By that he meant being able to acknowledge, openly and fully, all our feelings and respond to them as they come to us via each new experience.

The emphasis here is on the idea of being open to all our feelings and reactions – not trying to filter out the hard stuff or the dark stuff, as if we should selectively seek out only those experiences that will bring us the emotion we prize. What a bizarre way of living that would be! Imagine, in your pursuit of happiness, trying to avoid any experiences that might call on you to deal with disappointment or loss. (For a start, you'd need to insulate yourself from most of the human race, in all its chaos, confusion and despair.)

Rogers also emphasised the importance of creativity in the good life. He regarded individuals who are psychologically free, unshackled from excessive conformity, as being able to express their emotions freely. Like so many other psychologists, teachers and philosophers, he recognised creative self-expression as a healthy pathway to wholeness. In fact, Rogers thought the psychologically free person would be most readily able to adapt and survive under changing environmental conditions. He regarded the whole person – the free person, the creative person – as 'a fit vanguard of human evolution'.

Nowhere in his work did Rogers refer to happiness as one of the distinguishing marks of a fully functioning person, let alone as one of the prerequisites of the good life. Indeed, he included 'happy' in a list of adjectives (along with 'contented', 'blissful' and 'enjoyable') he regarded as quite inappropriate to any general description of the good life, though he conceded that any fully functioning person would inevitably experience those emotions at appropriate times. Like anyone who's serious about the good life – anyone who's interested in living a whole life rather than a merely happy life – Rogers considered words like 'exciting', 'rewarding', 'challenging' and 'meaningful' to be more suitable descriptions of the life you might expect.

Wholeness is not for the faint-hearted. It involves a special courage, which Rogers called 'the courage to be' – in other words, a willingness to plunge into the stream of life, open to whatever it may bring, fully focused on the moment. This is an echo of Aristotle's idea that the good life involves full engagement with the world, including engagement with our civic duty and all the richness and complexity of personal relationships.

Rogers acknowledged what we all know to be true: a person who is liberated from the bounds of conformity and is prepared to embrace wholeness may sometimes be unhappy. Such unhappiness could occur partly because reality does indeed 'bite'; partly because there is no escape from disappointment and sadness if you enter fully into your encounters with other people in a spirit of openness; partly because the person who is psychologically free and fully functioning may have to face the tricky realisation that they are out of harmony with some rather constrained or conformist aspects of the prevailing culture.

That reference to becoming who one truly is needs to be interpreted in the light of Rogers's broader view of life. He wasn't talking about a narcissistic form of authenticity or some self-indulgent expression of the ego; he believed in the fundamental goodness of humans and assumed that if people are encouraged to discover and become who they really are, this will lead them to embrace and express goodness in their lives.

The achievement of wholeness is probably the goal of everyone who reads a book with a title like *The Good Life*. If you aspire to live that kind of life, you will almost certainly receive wonderful little flashes of happiness and even bursts of joy along the way. There will be rewarding moments of triumph, gratification and contentment. You'll also experience sadness, frustration, grief, failure, disappointment and loss, and you'll be called upon to endure tedium and an occasional sense of helplessness and weariness. 'Wholeness' means what it says: brace yourself for the full spectrum, the works, the whole enchilada.

The experience of happiness, pleasant though it is, requires no courage, no nobility of purpose and no commitment to serve the common good – indeed, no particular commitment to goodness at all, except in the sense of feeling good. I repeat: there's nothing wrong with feeling good – enjoy it while you can – but the feeling will evaporate as soon as you pursue it. The experience of wholeness, by contrast, equips us to enter into the distress, the disappointment, the suffering of others, to bask with those who want us to share their fleeting moments of triumph, and to be reliably present for those grappling with life's uncertainties. Pollyanna is not our best role model.

Rogers wasn't keen on the idea of rewards for living the good life. But he did refer to the possibility of 'maximum satisfaction of our deepest needs' when we become fully functioning people. What might those 'deepest needs' be? In the context of our examination of the good life, I would say they include the need to know we have lived a useful life and that we have responded as well as possible to the needs of others, contributing to their wellbeing in whatever ways we can. Those are the great satisfactions of a life well lived. Beside them, what is the point of asking, *Am I happy?*

Perhaps you feel I've sold happiness a bit short, that I've oversimplified the idea of 'the pursuit of happiness' or that I've overestimated the popular emphasis on the quest for positive outcomes, the fostering of a spirit of optimism and the yearning for pleasure. I admit it's possible that some people really do mean something like *eudaimonia* (implying wholeness, or even wisdom) when they say 'happiness'. They may be using it as a code word for the satisfaction that comes from a life well and nobly lived – duty done, sacrifices made in the service of others, suffering endured courageously, virtue nurtured, compassion selflessly offered. I hope so. I'd like to believe that's what we mean when we talk about the idea of a good life, rather than feeling the need to resort to descriptions of an emotional state, especially one as ephemeral and accidental as happiness.

The crucial test of a life well lived is the quality of our responses to the needs of others. Everything else is peripheral and mostly trivial. From our chance encounters with total strangers to our long-term associations with family, friends, neighbours and colleagues, our connections with other people form the testbed of our sensitivity, our moral courage and our capacity for love. After all, our relationships, whether fleeting or enduring, are the source of life's richest meanings, but, as we struggle to establish them, nurture them and sometimes forsake them, they teach us that happiness and sadness are mere accidents of our fluctuating emotional state, incidental to the great realisation that it is in loving we are made whole. And yet love's work is the hardest work of all, which is why this book is about the good life, not the easy life.

Helen Keller, the remarkable American who, despite deafness and blindness, became one of the twentieth century's most outspoken humanitarians, asserted that 'happiness is not attained through self-gratification, but through fidelity to a worthy purpose'. On the same theme, the German philosopher Immanuel Kant wrote, 'Morality is not the doctrine of how we make ourselves happy, but how we make ourselves worthy of happiness'. At the core of both those statements, and of so much of the world's wisdom, is the belief that happiness is at best a by-product, not the goal, of a well-lived life.

To live as fully engaged members of the society that sustains us, we must learn to be sensitive to each other's needs, kind in our disposition towards other people (including strangers) and willing to accept some responsibility for the wellbeing of those around us. It goes without saying that if we live like that, we will experience some disappointment and pain. Given the right circumstances and a dollop of luck, we will also experience moments of towering satisfaction and occasional sparks of happiness.

3

Seven false leads

If we pursue happiness as though that is the most important thing in life, we're bound to be frustrated and disappointed, for all the reasons set out in chapter 2. That's why I would describe happiness as a false lead: it seems like a reasonable goal until you pursue it, and then you may find your focus has become so narrow and so selective (*Always be positive!*) that you actually begin to resist the idea of wholeness. When that happens, you run the risk of diminishing yourself as a person and your value to others.

There are many other false leads on the pathway towards a good life, including the yearning for certainty, an unhealthy curiosity about what the future might hold, a preoccupation with 'finding yourself', and the search for the meaning of Life. There is nothing inherently wrong with any of those pursuits or with any of the other false leads discussed in this chapter, but they, like the search for happiness, can easily distract us from the goals of the good life. Each has the potential to become an obsession, almost like an idol we worship, because each has undeniable appeal, and some (like the quest for the simple life) may well have a worthy purpose. The best way to keep them in perspective is simply to remind ourselves that none is necessarily about goodness.

Certainty

The most interesting questions we ask about ourselves defy precise answers, because most of the things we want to know are unknowable:

Is there a reason why we're here, or are we a cosmic and evolutionary accident?

What will become of us, as a species?

What happens when we die?

How big is the universe, and how many other planets out there support species like ours? Billions? One? None? Does it matter?

How can there be an edge of space?

Before the Big Bang, there was . . . what? And what before that?

Does it make more sense to believe in a god or not to believe in a god? And even if it makes no sense, what do we lose by believing?

Can all religions be right, or all wrong, or only one right, or is believing not about being right or wrong?

Are religion and science incompatible or simply two different ways of looking at the world?

Is one system of governing ourselves better than all others?

Are the rise and fall of civilisations inevitable?

Must so many people suffer?

Will science one day have all the answers, sweeping aside the theories of theology, philosophy and psychology and even determining our moral code?

It is part of human nature to ask such questions, and when we can't find answers that offer us the certainty we crave, we are quite capable of making up our own. That doesn't mean we're gullible, stupid or blind in our beliefs; it just means that, faced with so much mystery, most of us find it hard to settle for simple awe. We want answers, and so, drawing on our intuition and imagination, we create our own belief systems, fed sometimes by experience and sometimes by hope.

And then we place our faith in them.

And then we start believing that what we have chosen to place our faith in is true; that the things we have come to *believe* are just like the things we *know*.

And then someone gently points out that many of the things we think we know as objective truths in the scientific realm are themselves based on assumptions that are subject to uncertainty. This doesn't please us: we would prefer certainty. Yet Albert Einstein wrote that 'the most beautiful experience we can have is the mysterious. It is the fundamental emotion that stands at the cradle of true art and true science. Whoever does not know it and can no longer wonder, no longer marvel, is as good as dead, and his eyes are dimmed'. Einstein was no religious believer, yet he was certainly prepared to marvel at life's mysteries and not look for answers to everything. He was interested in far more than the scientific, material, quantifiable world: 'Not everything that matters can be measured, and not everything that can be measured matters'. (As a qualitative researcher for most of my working life, I've always warmed to old Albert for saying that.)

Faith is the work of the imagination; a creative act; a leap; a tentative, hopeful encounter with the numinous; a reaching-out for certainties that keep eluding us. Faith is also about trust, about deciding to settle for answers to questions we scarcely dare ask and whose answers we simply can't know for sure. Faith – at its best a noble, humble and often luminous quality in humans – can never be rooted in certainty. It evaporates under the pressure of rigid dogma, which is why there seems such a gulf between religion as expressed in the simple faith of a believer and religion as expressed in the panoply and power of an institution.

Take the widespread belief in an afterlife. This is the most unknowable of all our beliefs because it is, by definition, untestable. The one thing we can say for certain is that no one can possibly know whether there's life after death or not, and it is this opacity that fuels the faith of those who believe in an afterlife and of those who don't. Faith is at its strongest, after all, when there is no objective evidence to support it beyond the intensity of human hope fuelled by imagination.

Certainty denies the very essence of faith. It is the impenetrability of life's mysteries that encourages our leaps of faith not merely into the unknown, but into the unknowable. That's why doubt is the engine that propels and sustains faith. We believe (in anything) precisely because we doubt. This is the great paradox of faith: we yearn to know but cannot know, so we construct or accept, ready-made from an established institution, a set of beliefs to satisfy our need to make sense of what's going on. If it's not religious belief, it might be astrology, the free market, feng shui, superstition, science, a particular psychological or philosophical orientation – Buddhist, Freudian, Jungian, humanist – or a moral code we believe will make for a good life and, by extension, a better world. (None of those categories is exclusive: plenty of religious believers are advocates for other political, economic or cultural ideologies as well.) But if we knew as objective facts the answers that faith supplies, there would be no need for faith. And if faith – that mystical, clouded, elusive yearning – is corrupted by the arrogance of certainty, it ceases to be faith and becomes mere delusion.

Enter the fundamentalist: the person who wants to transform faith into certainty. You can recognise the religious fundamentalist, or any other sort of fundamentalist, by their self-satisfied swagger: *I know best; my beliefs are correct; if your beliefs are different from mine, then you are wrong.* Such arrogance relies on absolute certainty, which is why it is so infuriating to those who don't happen to share that particular set of beliefs. It is also a caricature of faith.

When I was a university student, I was taken aside by one of the elders of our church and told that studying philosophy was not only a waste of time but potentially dangerous. 'Everything you need to know is in the Bible', he told me. Deadly serious, he was.

When the British biologist Richard Dawkins criticises religion for the fanaticism or cruelty of some of its followers, or for their blind embrace of scriptures riven with contradictions, this sounds less like a criticism of religious faith, per se, and more like an attack on fundamentalism. (Ironically, Dawkins is himself something of a fundamentalist, with his relentless one-note samba, his rigid dogma, his deification of science, his unshakable resistance to mystery or ambiguity and his unwillingness to acknowledge the value of religious faith for millions of people.) The religious truth-seeker, the pilgrim, yearns to see with the eye of faith but constantly falters. The plea from the father of a sick child healed by Jesus, quoted in Mark's gospel, captures the idea perfectly: 'I believe; help my unbelief'. That is the tension on which faith relies. Yet fundamentalists, including Dawkins, want you to develop a conviction so strong that you lose the capacity for doubt. They don't want you to believe; they want you to *know* you are right, with the same conviction you might have when you get wet and declare that it is raining.

I grew up in a fundamentalist church where every other version of Christianity was regarded as pretty suss. We even thought the Methodists were too liberal – they did things like dancing and wearing make-up. And the Roman Catholics, well, they were practically heathens. We used to have lessons about 'false cults', and I seem to recall that included just about everyone but us. As a young person, it made you feel pretty special, I can tell you, knowing you were right and everyone else was wrong. Even the Anglicans were off the track because of infant baptism, which we were taught was unscriptural.

If you adopt a rigid world view – religious, anti-religious, political, economic, academic, aesthetic or otherwise – you tend to see everything through the filter of your convictions, and, not surprisingly, you see what you're looking for. The more you use a particular theory for making sense of things, the more things seem to fit that theory. That's why fundamentalists feel so sure of themselves and why they can't understand how other people could fail to see things the way they do (though everyone's beliefs look weird to the person who doesn't share them). It's why they eschew the mystical: they don't want to marvel as Einstein did or to rest with mysteries; they want to wrestle them into submission. It's also why, puzzled that their beliefs are not more widely accepted, they feel entitled to try to impose them on others – believers with different beliefs and non-believers alike.

Take the case of marriage. In the midst of a community and parliamentary debate over the issue of same-sex marriage in 2012, the Anglican archbishop of Sydney Peter Jensen wrote a letter to all the churches in his diocese urging parishioners to lobby their members of parliament to oppose any change to the Marriage Act that might permit the legal marriage of same-sex couples. This opposition was to be based on a particular view of marriage not shared by all Christians, or even by all Anglicans, but dear to the heart of evangelical fundamentalists.

A spirited response to Archbishop Jensen's letter came from a fellow Anglican priest: Andrew Sempell, rector of St James' Church in the centre of Sydney (a church with a history of dissent from the prevailing orthodoxies of the diocese in which it rather uneasily stands). Sempell's letter pointed out that as a mere 5 per cent of Australian marriages were at the time being conducted by Anglican clergy, 'we must not overestimate our importance in this area, nor be arrogant'. Sempell went on to suggest that Australia would do well to adopt a variation of the Napoleonic Code (in which legal marriage is entirely a matter for the state) and proposed that couples who had been married in law might 'then seek religious recognition of their marriage if they wish'. Needless to say, such views carried no weight with the fundamentalists, who have a sense of impermeable certainty on their side and regard 'compromise' as a dirty word.

Being called upon to justify your beliefs has a bracing effect. You don't have to defend your observation that it's raining (if it is); nor will you be attacked for making it. But when your conviction is faith-based, you might well be asked to explain and defend it. When you do, your certainty will become even more deeply ingrained: nothing reinforces our convictions like the process of having to defend them against attack.

Fundamentalism, religious and otherwise, is like a steel trap that imprisons the soul and inhibits its freedom to wonder. It sucks the doubt out of faith and leaves a rigid shell that acts like armour. No wonder it's so hard for a fundamentalist's beliefs to evolve and mature: if you crack the shell, it falls apart and you're left with nothing. Yet fundamentalism is on the rise in all three of the Abrahamic traditions – Judaism, Christianity and Islam – with the potential for divisive and disastrous consequences. Why now?

This is one mystery we *can* penetrate. Fundamentalism (whether religious, political, economic or cultural) thrives at times of social upheaval and insecurity. When we are at our most perplexed or bewildered, gripped by moral panic and baffled by ambiguity, that's when we are also most vulnerable to promises of black-and-white simplicity that offer us certainty. Given our current anxieties over global warming, international terrorism, the world's growing refugee population and the threat of economic meltdown, it's not hard to see the appeal in any set of beliefs that offers stable reference points in a shifting geopolitical landscape. A period marked by rapid and unpredictable change is therefore bound to be a breeding ground for fundamentalism. A deepening sense of uncertainty only whets our appetite for certainty, and the quest for certainty in any context comes to feel like a search for some version of the Holy Grail.

Religious fundamentalists are soft targets. Because their faith has typically morphed into certainty, they hardly count as believers at all. Yet they would generally regard themselves as living the good life. They can easily conflate the idea of virtue with their own version of faith, and that is just as true in politics as in religion. The smug social democrats *know* theirs is the only defensible position. And so do the joyless, hardline conservatives, and so do the wild-eyed extremists on the left. The wets and the dries both have certainty on their side, just as the Germans and the Allies both believed they had the very same god on their side in World War Two. In the United States, conflicts between Democrats and Republicans are so visceral precisely because of the gulf between the philosophical certainties involved, always reinforced, like religious convictions, by the strong ties of tribalism. (The bandwagon is a powerful symbol of how right we are: *Look at all these other people who agree with us!*) Certainty is a social as well as an intellectual and emotional phenomenon.

When we turn to science, we assume that here, at least, our certainties are warranted. But are they? Most of us recognise the equation $E=mc^2$, even if we can't quite remember what the symbols stand for. We know it has something to do with Einstein's theory of relativity, and perhaps we know he revolutionised scientific thought by challenging the accepted wisdom that mass and energy were separate phenomena. Today, that theory is being tested and challenged, and it may well turn out that, contrary to Einstein's conviction, it is possible for particles to travel at speeds greater than the speed of light. No, I don't get it either, but I do get the underlying point: certainty in science, like certainty in everything else that relies on assumptions, interpretations and theories, is more slippery than we might care to imagine. Scientific proofs are, by their nature, always provisional. In *Religion and Science* (1935), the British philosopher Bertrand Russell expressed the uncertainty that empirical scientists must learn to live with. He wrote that science is 'always tentative, expecting that modification in its present theories will sooner or later be found necessary, and aware that its method is one which is logically incapable of arriving at a complete and final demonstration'.

Thomas Kuhn's *The Structure of Scientific Revolutions* (1962) challenged the ideas that scientific truths, once established, are immutable and that scientific theories evolve via an orderly progression of thoughts. His point was that any scientific theory is a subjective construction based on either constantly shifting data or perceptions of the data (or both), and on occasional startling, revolutionary insights that spark great leaps in scientific knowledge, which he called 'paradigm shifts'. To assume certainty or stability at any given point in this process is to ignore the long history of science. The integrity of any theory, Kuhn argued, lies in its falsifiability – that is, its openness to the possibility of repudiation in the light of more evidence, fresh insights or a more creative interpretation of data whose significance was not previously understood.

As we moved through the twentieth century, labelled the Age of Uncertainty by many philosophers, psychologists, economists, political scientists and social analysts, we came to realise that, as Australian social analyst Richard Eckersley wrote in *Well & Good* (2004), 'scientific knowledge is never the whole truth or an absolute, immutable truth. And what science is done, and how its results are applied, are powerfully determined by its cultural context'. Indeed, as Stephen Trombley put it in *A Short History of Western Thought* (2011), 'Any claim to absolute knowledge is questionable, and that knowledge is dependent on the perspective of the observer'. In other words, we interpret what we see in the light of our existing knowledge, our existing convictions, or faith, and even our existing prejudices: the viewer is indeed part of the view.

According to Brian Schmidt, co-winner of the 2011 Nobel prize for physics, for his team's work on the expanding universe, scientific theories should be regarded as predictions. Much of what we regard as scientific knowledge, he says, is mere hypothesis that allows scientists to get on with their work until the hypothesis is proved right or wrong. For example, some of the work of Schmidt's own team is based on the assumption that about 97 per cent of the known universe consists of dark energy and dark matter, and that only about 3 per cent consists of the atoms scientists can directly observe. Dark energy and dark matter? Schmidt lets us in on a trade secret: astronomers always use the adjective 'dark' to describe something they don't understand. 'If you think this means we don't know what we're talking about', he said in a 2012 lecture to the Royal Society of New South Wales, 'then you might have a point' (though a Nobel laureate's hunch about such things is likely to be more reliable than yours or mine).

The French philosopher of science Bruno Latour, among others, has taken the uncertainty principle one step further. In his provocative book *On the Modern Cult of the Factish Gods* (2011), he reiterates the conventional scientific wisdom that scientific facts are mere human constructions just like any other human construction and claims that, like those other constructions, scientific facts appear real and stable to us at a given time, even though they might be subject to future revision or reinterpretation in the light of new understandings. However, Latour departs from conventional scientific thought when he goes on to say that these scientific constructions are not significantly different from the artefacts of a religion, in which we construct beliefs (the religious equivalent of theories), icons, fetishes and even gods out of our understanding of the world as we experience it. Embracing scientific knowledge strikes Latour as being rather like a leap of faith based on fresh revelation.

Presumably, one implication of this would be that religious truths, precisely like scientific truths, should evolve and mature in the light of new understandings that emerge in new contexts. To some extent, this happens as theologians and historians shed more light on the origins and meanings of ancient texts, and in the shifts between literal and metaphorical interpretations of scripture. Nevertheless, religious institutions tend to behave more like defenders of immutable truths than custodians of evolving revelations – a charge less likely to be levelled at scientific organisations and institutions, though the powerful combination of self-interest and money can certainly inhibit the spirit of open scientific enquiry.

Latour writes that scientific knowledge 'is not a direct grasp of the plain and visible . . . but an extraordinarily daring, complex and intricate confidence' that we place in a long and gradually evolving series of theories, challenges and proofs that have reached the point where they 'force us to break away from the intuitions and prejudices of common sense'. For Latour, a churchgoing Roman Catholic, this could as easily be said of religion as of science. (When you read that Latour is a churchgoing Roman Catholic, did you think, *Ah, so that's why he's trying so hard to find some equivalence between religious faith and scientific knowledge*? If you did, then that's a neat example of how your own prejudices and predispositions can influence your response to new information.)

What, then, of love? Don't we all need the security, the certainty, of love that endures? Yes, Love with a capital *L* endures. But we all know, some from bitter experience, that declarations of undying love are more like predictions than firm undertakings. Romantic love is fraught with and, indeed, thrives on uncertainty. We may, in the long run, stick to a partner 'for better, for worse', but the 'worse' sometimes means that love has gone, and only grim duty and a cold, unremitting loyalty remain.

It might even be true that relying on the certainty of another's love for us breaks all the rules of the good life. If we are to live for others; if we are to give without thought of what we might receive; if we are to love unconditionally, then, by definition, we can't demand any of that in return. If we did, we'd be back in the old loop of reciprocity: *I'll love you as long as you'll love me.* Many romantic, sexual relationships do work like that in practice, but love at its shining best – pure charity – doesn't place those kinds of conditions on the people we love. An act of charity loses none of its value for being met with ingratitude.

Certainty is the enemy of reason and of reasonableness. It fuels our complacency and arrogance, wrapping us in a cocoon of self-confidence, perhaps even self-righteousness. In personal relationships, it diminishes our capacity for empathy and tolerance, so it is also the enemy of the good life.

In the good life, we take nothing for granted. We don't crave certainty or black-and-white simplicity, even in love, because we know it might distract us from the challenge of facing and accepting things the way they really are, in all their chaos and unpredictability, their mingled joy and sorrow. No wonder Carl Rogers suggested the good life is not for the faint-hearted. Whatever else you may say of it, it's a life for realists.

Let the final word on this topic be from the poet Alfred Tennyson's 'The Ancient Sage':

> For nothing worthy proving can be proven,
> Nor yet disproven: wherefore thou be wise,
> Cleave ever to the sunnier side of doubt.

The future

In *Against the Gods* (1996), Peter Bernstein tells a story about Kenneth Arrow, an American Nobel laureate in economics, who worked as a weather forecaster for the US Air Force during World War Two. Monitoring the accuracy of the forecasts, statisticians discovered that long-range forecasts for weather just one month ahead were no more reliable than numbers pulled out of a hat. Faced with this evidence, the forecasters asked their superiors to be relieved of their duty. The reply came: 'The Commanding General is well aware that forecasts are no good. However he needs them for planning purposes'. No doubt partly as a result of that experience, Arrow later wrote, 'Our knowledge of the way the world works comes trailing clouds of vagueness'.

Given the uncertainty inherent in so much of our knowledge of how the world works – especially the human aspects of it – the conclusion we're forced to is that in most of the important ways the future is unknowable, and the unknowability becomes more apparent the further into the future we try to peer. Who, for instance, correctly forecast how social media like Facebook and Twitter would revolutionise the way people communicate with each other, or the extraordinary impact digital tablets like Kindle and iPad would have not only on our reading habits but on our lives? Who predicted the profound effect on the American psyche of the 9/11 terrorist attack on the World Trade Center or the long-term consequences of that attack for innocent civilians in Iraq and Afghanistan? Who foresaw the scale of the global financial crisis or imagined the world would take so long to respond and recover? And which economist has been able to predict interest rates, unemployment levels, inflation or terms of trade with any consistency? Marketing companies spend millions of dollars on product research and development as ways of forecasting future success, yet about 80 per cent of new products fail in the market, including those introduced by some of the biggest, smartest and most sophisticated corporations, Coca-Cola's New Coke and Ford's Edsel being two of the most spectacular examples. Even with all the seismological skill and equipment now available, we are still taken by surprise by earthquakes and tsunamis.

We can't even predict the future of those we know the best. Who has ever correctly anticipated the direction of their children's lives? And who knows where love's impulses might take us?

There's an old Jewish joke that says if you want to make God laugh, tell him your plans. The reason God laughs is because planning feels to us like prediction. We all must plan, to some extent, or we'd run out of food, we'd never make appointments and we might get knocked over every time we tried to cross the road. Many jobs are *about* planning. Managers are obliged to plan the workflow of the organisations they manage. Politicians live by planning: how else would policies be developed and legislation passed? Engineers must plan their construction schedules, surgeons their operating procedures, accountants their spreadsheets, editors their content and layout, teachers their lessons. Yet things often turn out differently from the way we expected – sometimes better, sometimes worse. The weather intervenes; people become unexpectedly ill, or die; they complete tasks sooner or later than we thought they would; power failures and machinery breakdowns occur; people forget things; passion for a project may wane; we are distracted.

What if we *could* accurately anticipate the future? What if we knew what next week held for us? Or next year? If we knew we were facing unavoidable hardship or tragedy, would that prior knowledge make us feel better or worse? If we knew something wonderful was going to happen, how would we contain our impatience to get to it? If we knew trouble was around the corner, would we become hesitant and fearful?

Brenda and the missing invoice

Every office has its resident astrologer – the person who can explain everyone's personality in terms of their star sign, who can relax about whatever today's crisis happens to be because it's 'written in the stars', and who might even venture the odd prediction. In the office of Jerry's Smash Repairs, the resident astrologer is Brenda. Against all his instincts, Jerry has come to depend on Brenda's assessment of customers and even prospective employees. Seated at the reception desk, Brenda sees them all coming and going, and doesn't hesitate to give Jerry the benefit of her opinions. Though he is often irritated by her rather smug, superior attitude, as if she alone has access to some eternal wisdom, and though he'd be happier if she would keep her small collection of crystals hidden from the customers' view (he has finally banned the burning of incense in the office), Jerry has to admit that Brenda is right about people more often than she's wrong.

If called upon to describe Brenda, Jerry would say she was 'laid back', sometimes to the point of reckless disregard for the crises swirling around her. Her faith in the stars is completely mystifying to Jerry: he might find her character assessments fascinating, but he is often at his wits' end when it comes to deadlines. Brenda is unmoved by the present: her eye is always to the future. Though the accounts system has been computerised for insurance jobs, Brenda has been slow to transfer everything else to the new system: she seems to like handling manila folders and flipping through the grease-marked assessments, quotes and reports. Jerry once observed her holding a file to her forehead as if to seek telepathic inspiration from it.

Ron McIntosh is due to collect his car this afternoon, and Jerry wants the final report and invoice to be ready for him when he arrives. The McIntosh file is missing. No record in the computer. No folder in the hard-copy filing system.

'Come on, Brenda. We have to find it. *Now.*'

Brenda just shrugs. 'Mercury is in retro', she says, as though that explains everything and settles the matter.

'What?'

'Mercury is in retro. Things are bound to go missing. Happens every time. Be patient. It will turn up.'

'I'll tell you what will turn up. Ron McIntosh will turn up, at five o'clock on the dot, wanting his car.'

'And his car is ready.'

'But his paperwork isn't. He's not driving away without paying. This isn't an insurance job. He's paying for this one himself.'

'I can assure you it will all be okay. The file will turn up. He'll pay. He's an honest man.'

'So what do I tell him? "Mercury is in retro and we can't find your file"?'

Brenda shrugs again. 'That's the truth. You can make up something else if you like. You can say I lost it.'

'So when does Mercury come out of retro?' Jerry asks with mounting impatience, scarcely able to believe he is actually saying these words. 'When might the file reappear?'

Brenda smiles her ghostly smile. 'Next week. Mmm . . . Tuesday, most probably.'

'It can't wait until Tuesday. We need the paperwork now. Haven't we got some kind of back-up?'

Jerry is a highly skilled panel-beater – none better – but he is out of his depth with administration. Life was easier when Mel, his wife, worked in the office and covered for him, but Mel is at home full time with the twins, and Brenda doesn't have quite the same protective instincts.

Jerry pulls on his cap and returns to his office, in the corner of the factory. He is wondering whether Brenda's time might be up, entertaining and intriguing though she may be.

The phone rings at reception, and Brenda puts the call through to Jerry. 'Wendy McIntosh here. My husband was due to pick his car up this afternoon, but he's been called to an urgent interstate meeting for tomorrow and he's already on his way to the airport. I could come over myself, but—'

'No worries, Mrs McIntosh', says Jerry. 'We can lock it up here and look after it until your husband gets back. We can even keep it over the weekend if that would help.'

'Oh, would you? It wouldn't be in the way?'

'Not at all. Just get him to ring when he wants to come and pick it up.' Jerry bites his tongue to prevent himself from saying, *The paperwork's all ready to go.*

He walks back out to reception. 'We have until Monday for the McIntosh file', he says to Brenda.

Brenda smiles that infuriating smile. 'Tuesday', she says.

Over the weekend, Jerry describes this little episode to Mel and she offers to go in to the office to hunt for the file. She returns an hour later, holding the folder aloft. 'It had slipped down behind the filing cabinet. I had to pull the cabinet out to find it. It's happened to me before.'

On Monday, Jerry places the file on Brenda's desk.

'A day early', she says, incuriously.

There actually is no future. We imagine it, and we know what we mean when we talk about it. In some extreme circumstances, anticipating the future, maintaining faith in the idea that the future will be better than this present, is a way of preserving our hope and our sanity. Viktor Frankl, in *Man's Search for Meaning* (1946), wrote of the sense of hopelessness that overwhelmed some of the prisoners in the German concentration camp where Frankl himself was incarcerated during World War Two. His observation was that prisoners who lost their faith in the future – their hope – were doomed. Writing in *The New Yorker* in 2012, the neurologist Oliver Sacks put it in a more universal context: 'To live on a day-to-day basis is insufficient for human beings; we need to transcend, transport, escape; we need meaning, understanding, and explanation; we need to see overall patterns in our lives. We need hope, the sense of a future'.

And so we do. But there's a big difference between living with a sense of the future and living in constant reference, almost in deference, to the future. Some anticipation of the future, even some faith in the future, is natural and even desirable, but we must eventually learn to live with the fact that the future is one place we can never go. It's simply impossible (unless time machines do eventually come onto the market and usher in an era of unimaginable chronological chaos). There was a past, though it doesn't exist now, except in notoriously unreliable memory. But there is always, only, a present: we are living in it, and nowhere else, moment by moment.

The danger is that as soon as you reach for the future and try to anticipate it, you may think of it as if it somehow coexists or even competes with the present. Yet when it arrives, it arrives only as a new and different present. There's no way to jump that barrier, which is why so many philosophers, psychologists and theologians urge us to develop a mindfulness that allows us to engage fully with each moment of life, including the unpleasant ones. The same awareness leads wise parents to warn their children against wishing their life away. A sense of the future is a useful context, a theoretical reference point, for our moment-to-moment engagement with the present, but if we are preoccupied with the future, we may miss some of the most important moments of our lives.

> One of my kids was always worrying about what might happen. She didn't seem able to relax and enjoy the present at all. Even as a child she was a real worrywart. *What will happen if this or that happens?* That was always her approach. I tried to encourage her to stop worrying about the future and enjoy the present, but she never seemed to be able to let it go. She could never even see the point of studying – she always thought something would happen to derail her plans. Then she met this boy who was into meditation and the whole thing changed. She was crazy about him and started doing all the things he did. He had a huge influence on my daughter and I'll always be grateful to him for that. They broke up eventually – I think he became a monk of some description – but she never went back to the old way.

The art of living in the moment is an important aspect of the good life, because it ensures that we are fully aware of and engaged with the people around us, sensitive to their needs and open to the unfolding demands of each new experience. We are also more likely to be attuned to our own emotional responses and what can be learnt from them. Every meditative practice, every mindfulness discipline, every contemplative religious exercise is focused on this same goal: learning how to keep the mind fully in the present – this breath, this moment of looking at this page.

Why do we fret so much about the future? Why are we so easily distracted from this moment by thoughts of the next? Why do we spend so much time in fruitless speculation, even over the outcome of a football match, the result of which will be known soon enough? Some of it is harmless fun. We enjoy the excitement, the tension of seeing whether our predictions will come true. That's the appeal of many forms of gambling as well, especially betting on the outcome of horse races or other sporting contests. It's not because we imagine we have supernatural powers, but simply because we all feel a tiny surge of satisfaction at having a hunch proved right. *I told you so!* is great fun to say (though deeply irritating to hear). And a degree of future-consciousness – saving for a rainy day, buying airline tickets well in advance of a trip to take advantage of low fares or taking out insurance on a house or a car – is simply prudent in a world of uncertainty.

But planning for the future ceases to be either harmless or prudent if the future becomes the focus of our life, as it does for people who find themselves living in a state of perpetual anticipation, such as those addicted to betting on outcomes (at the racetrack or on the stock market); those obsessed with a concern for their personal legacy; and those who are, more grandly, so gripped by end-of-the-world theories that their most serious thoughts are devoted to the possible interpretations of predictions from the ancient world, including biblical prophecy. If you're constantly on the lookout for signs that the end is nigh or concerned that the Four Horsemen of the Apocalypse are waiting in the wings, it's hard to concentrate fully and respond wholeheartedly to the demands of those who need you in this moment. In fact, it's difficult to take much interest in the present at all if you have allowed your thoughts to become too future-focused.

The New Testament's highly controversial Book of Revelation (a book that, incidentally, very nearly failed to make the cut, the bishops of Rome having rejected it in the second century as blasphemous) has always been the subject of intense study among those who believe it contains hidden messages about the way the world will end. Modern scholarship challenges such interpretations: Elaine Pagels's *Revelations: Visions, prophecy and politics in the Book of Revelation* (2012) makes a persuasive case for the proposition that the text of Revelation is indeed a series of coded references, but not references to the end of time. Its author, John the Divine (a different John from the gospel-writer), was instead, according to Pagels, describing and complaining about the contemporary situation – political, religious and otherwise – at the time of writing: the fall of the Temple in Jerusalem, the power of Rome ('the Whore of Babylon'), the eruption of Mount Vesuvius, tensions among the early Christians. In particular, Pagels argues, Revelation was a vehicle for John's furious concern about what would happen to the embryonic Jesus movement, essentially a Jewish movement up to that point, if it were flooded with Gentiles, or non-Jews, as seemed in danger of happening. Viewed in this way, Revelation is a giant whinge. (Incidentally, Pagels's analysis takes a lot of the sting out of the book. The scary 666, for instance, the 'mark of the beast', is, according to Pagels, a numerological reference to the emperor Nero, and 'the seven heads of the beast' is a reference to the seven Roman emperors from Augustus to John's own time.)

Revelation has had a huge cultural influence on the Christian era, even for people who have never read it, because, like the prophecies of Nostradamus, it offers the intriguing possibility that we just might catch a glimpse of our own future. Right up to the present, there's a thriving end-times branch of theology and, in the secular world, a similarly healthy industry in books, TV programs and websites that attempt to read the future and see only bad news for this or that civilisation. The German historian Oswald Spengler set the tone in 1918 with his first volume of *The Decline of the West*, a book *The New Yorker*'s Adam Gopnik describes as the 'summit of declinism'. That theme has persisted right up to *Civilization: The West and the rest* (2012), in which historian Niall Ferguson links the decline of Protestant religious faith to that of Western democracies and predicts the eclipse of the West by China.

While prediction is always intriguing, the only things we know for sure about the future – apart from our death – are that it will throw up unexpected ideas, inventions, events and disasters, and that present trends may be little or no guide to what will happen beyond tomorrow or the next day. That may be even truer today than it ever was, thanks to the speed of change, especially in geopolitics, economics, technology and climate.

> We had such a marvellous time in London, I was already planning our next trip during the long flight home. Martin seemed less enthusiastic than I was, but I knew this would be the trip of a lifetime for him. I collected all the brochures and pored over the maps. I went on Google and started investigating hotels to stay in. We were going to spend a minimum of three nights in each place. I wanted to include a week in France, driving, but Martin seemed strangely reluctant about the idea of driving on the wrong side of the road, even though he'd done it many times when we were younger.
>
> One night, I had all the maps and my draft itinerary out on the dining table, and I noticed Martin didn't seem to be concentrating. Out of the blue, he said to me, 'I want a divorce'.
>
> I was so shocked, I didn't know what to say. I even wondered if he was joking. He wasn't.
>
> 'Is there someone else?' I asked him. A friend once told me a man never leaves a marriage unless it's for another woman, even if they keep it hidden for a while.
>
> He shook his head. 'You don't live with me any more. Not really. Your head is always somewhere else – mostly on some grand plan. If it's not this trip, it's the new kitchen or the next dinner party. You live in the future. I need to live in the here and now.'

> We didn't divorce. I persuaded him to stay, and I dropped the plans for that big trip. We never went anywhere after that. I think Martin knew he didn't have long to live, and he just wanted some peace. He was dead within six months of that conversation, and I felt as if I'd robbed us of years of our marriage.

The only certainty for each of us is that we will die. Beyond making appropriate preparations for that, we might do well to heed the advice of almost every sage or mystic who has ever given this a moment's thought. Socrates, Buddha, Jesus, Mohammed, the Jewish psalmist: they all had the same idea. Worrying about the future only diminishes your quality of life in the present. That applies even if your heart is set on an afterlife, with or without a Day of Judgement (though, there is no weaker basis for living the good life than the belief that you'll be eternally punished if you don't, since this takes the focus away from the intrinsic value of what you are doing and shifts it to a concern for extrinsic rewards and punishments).

Perhaps we need to keep reminding ourselves that, when we reach the end of our life's brief mortal span, the world will not have become Utopia, despite all our worrying and all our striving. Nothing will ever be perfect. We will have helped shape the future, though, mainly by the way we've lived moment to moment: by the example of kindness and compassion we have or have not set, by our commitment or lack of it to living a life for others, by the extent to which we have sought to promote goodness in ourselves and those around us. The good life is one that's lived realistically, and that includes living with a modest assessment of your likely influence. Your greatest and most enduring influence, for good or ill, will be upon the people closest to you, regardless of the grandeur of your dreams or the height of the monuments you might hope will be erected in your honour. Few of us are granted an enduring place in the pantheon, but we all contribute to the society we are becoming.

This is not to discourage us from dreaming of ways to make the world a better place; it is not to diminish the importance of responsible planning; it is not to overlook the need for warnings about the direction in which we may be heading. It is only to remind us that if we live with an eye too keenly fixed on the future, especially if we are concerned about its judgements on us, we will miss the richness of the present. The good life can only be lived here and now. The English poet Philip Larkin puts it graphically in 'Next, Please':

> Always too eager for the future, we
> Pick up bad habits of expectancy,
> Something is always approaching; every day
> *Till then* we say.

Finding yourself

Standing in line with my son in the cafeteria on the day I helped him move in to his university college, I overheard two women behind us in the queue discussing their own sons' motivations for being there.

'He told me he wants to find himself', said one.

'Oh yes, mine tried that on me, too', said the other. 'I told him he can go and find himself at his own expense. He's here to work hard and pass his exams.'

'They're all into finding themselves these days. I'm not sure I've ever found myself, whatever that might mean. I found a husband and had three gorgeous kids. Does that count?'

You can waste a lot of time trying to find yourself, especially if you're looking in the wrong place. Not that it isn't interesting and useful to know ourselves: humans have been exhorting each other to do that since at least the time of the ancient Greek philosophers. The problem arises when finding yourself becomes a preoccupation, perhaps even a reason for being, or when you expect to derive too much benefit from it, as though self-knowledge will, of itself, open a magic door to a satisfying and successful life. The truth is less grand than that: for most of us, finding ourselves is incidental to the process of living and maturing.

Over the years, we experience a gradually unfolding awareness of the person we are, warts and all. Along the way, we may question whether we can accept ourselves as we are – our values, our motives, our priorities – or whether we need to change in ways that will bring us closer to the person we wish to be. That process may involve occasional periods of deliberate reflection on the subject of self.

Self-absorption is the characteristic state of the adolescent who has begun to explore 'self' as a conscious concept, perhaps unconsciously driven by awakening hormones that raise the possibility of reproduction of the self. But if we're too enthusiastic about the quest for self-knowledge, we may become locked in to the adolescent stage of our development that, if prolonged, can encourage self-indulgence and even narcissism.

The journey towards self-knowledge can be hastened by moments of disciplined self-examination, even an occasional reflective celebration of the self on a birthday or other anniversary, but maturity gradually carries us into something richer and deeper: the sense that our identity is social at least as much as personal. It eventually dawns on us that we are part of a greater whole: a drop in the ocean, a grain of sand on the beach, a star in the sky, as many poets have suggested. *Who am I?* turns out to be a less interesting and less significant question than *Who are we?*

When the process of finding yourself is allowed to evolve naturally, it is likely to lead to an examination of your relationships, your social context, rather than being too intensely concerned about yourself as an individual. The psychotherapist Carl Rogers, for all his emphasis on the need to become who we really are, acknowledged that when a client is 'completely engaged in the process of being and becoming himself' he will discover that 'he is soundly and realistically social'.

The Greek philosopher Socrates never wrote anything down, so we have to rely on one of his pupils, Plato, to relay what he is supposed to have said. Perhaps the most famous statement attributed to Socrates is this: 'the unexamined life is not worth living'. Note those last three words carefully: *not worth living.*

For all his wisdom on so many subjects, for all his rich legacy transmitted to us through the writings of Plato and for all the heroism of his death as a martyr to philosophy (drinking hemlock after being convicted of corrupting the young and not believing in the Athenians' gods), Socrates, like all of us, was a prisoner of his cultural circumstances. As a young man he was a soldier, but he devoted the rest of his life to philosophical enquiry. Though personally poor, he lived among the privileged intellectual elite of Athens, a society starkly divided by class. Some of his attitudes hint at misogyny (in *The Apology*, Plato quotes him as describing people who plead for their life in court as 'no better than women'), and, like his peers, he regarded slaves as a lower form of life – he conceded they were capable of enjoying pleasure, but they were not, he thought, capable of experiencing the gratifications of the examined life; therefore, by implication, their lives were not worth living.

Even allowing for context, Socrates's famous proposition seems a little harsh. Think of people not intelligent enough to engage in self-examination or intellectual discourse about concepts like identity. Think of people in primitive or war-torn circumstances for whom every day is a desperate struggle for survival, and contemplation of anything else is not an option. Think of a person philosophers call the 'virtuous peasant': uneducated in a formal sense, no training in the life of the mind, yet raising children lovingly and responsibly, and fully engaged with the life of the community. A life not worth living?

The examined life may be something to aim for – indeed, to make an integral part of our daily moral journey – provided we have the cognitive skill to undertake the examination and the luxury of circumstances that permit it. As the British philosopher and novelist Iris Murdoch writes in *The Sovereignty of Good* (1971), 'It must be possible to do justice to both Socrates and the virtuous peasant'. Murdoch argues that an unexamined life can still be a good life, and who would disagree?

The unexamined life of Arthur

Arthur was known, from early childhood, to be not very bright. He struggled to learn to read; he coped well enough with simple arithmetic but not with any higher maths. His poor eye-to-hand coordination led to many humiliations in ball games. He sang beautifully and enjoyed being in the school choir more than anything else. Though he was sometimes mocked by the brightest pupils and by those who excelled at sport, he was a generally popular boy. The other children recognised him as a gentle soul: kind, reliable and generous.

He left school halfway through Year 9, on his fifteenth birthday, and took a job in a department store in the city arranged by his rather stern and aloof father. He travelled to and from the job by train each day, often working a six-day week.

The job was wonderful. Arthur felt fully useful for the first time in his life, and he threw himself into whatever was asked of him. He began in the mail room and was later trained to take his place, proudly, as a junior sales assistant in menswear. He did well. Customers appreciated his courtesy, reserve and conscientious attention to their needs. He was slow with the paperwork, though, and was relieved when all transactions and records were later computerised via the cash register.

Over the years, Arthur was twice offered promotion. He accepted the first offer, though it quickly became obvious that he was out of his depth with the increased responsibility, and he returned to his former post with great relief. The second time, he simply declined the offer and was grateful to receive a generous pay increase for continuing to do what he loved doing.

Arthur never married. He was a shy man in social settings, and though he had a serious crush on a girl in his final couple of months at school, he wasn't sure if she was interested in him or simply being kind, and they lost contact once he left. Though he occasionally envied the married couples he knew, Arthur adjusted to living alone in the house he inherited from his parents when they died. He never travelled, not being confident enough to attempt even an interstate trip. Every August, just after the store's mid-year sale, he rented a beach flat for two weeks, revelling in long walks, eating out at a favourite café where the staff greeted him warmly each year, and going to the local cinema, which had somehow escaped closure.

A community choir was formed in the suburb where Arthur lived, and, rather to his neighbours' surprise, Arthur was one of the first to join. All the joy of singing came back to him with a rush, and he often found himself humming items from the choir's repertoire on his walks to and from the station.

Arthur worked every Sunday for a local charity that provided free lunches for needy people. Sometimes he waited on the tables; sometimes he did the washing-up. He was always surprised and saddened by the number of people who turned up in need of a meal, including, he noticed, entire families. He also mowed the lawn for an elderly woman who lived two doors down, and generally made himself useful if anyone in the neighbourhood needed anything doing – mail taken in or garbage bins put out or pets fed – while they were away. He hadn't lost his reputation for kindness and reliability.

Once or twice, sitting on the train after a busy day at the store, Arthur caught himself thinking about his life. He never reached the stage of asking, *Who am I?* but he did sometimes idly wonder whether things might have turned out differently if he'd stayed at school longer, or what it might have been like to have had a brother or sister, or wife. But he banished such thoughts when they came to him.

He had been powerfully influenced by three pieces of advice he had been repeatedly given by his mother, a woman whom Arthur had loved with fierce filial devotion. Treat everybody with respect, even if they don't treat you well: you don't know what they might be going through. That was his mother's first piece of advice. The second was, Make yourself useful and keep yourself busy. The third, the advice that came to him whenever he felt he was drifting towards self-examination, was, Don't dwell on things and don't feel sorry for yourself. He wasn't necessarily feeling sorry for himself when he was occasionally tempted to reflect, but he was sure such reflections could be described as 'dwelling on things', and so he forced his rather simple mind back to the newspaper he always carried on the train with him, reading having become gradually easier for him once he was relieved of the pressure of the classroom.

Arthur died at the age of fifty, after a melanoma removed from his head turned out to have spread. At his funeral, held in a packed church, his beloved choir singing his all-time favourite song, 'All Through the Night', many people spoke about him with great warmth and affection. The young woman who lived alone in the house directly across the street from Arthur's and who had been the recipient of his kindness from the day she moved in, summed it up best: 'I think Arthur was the nicest man in the entire world'. Everybody wished they'd thought to say so before he died.

Arthur's life not worth living? This is not to denigrate the inward journey of self-discovery, but only to remind ourselves that it can easily become a false lead, a distraction, if we devote too much time and effort to it. Indeed, Iris Murdoch is sceptical about the whole idea of self-knowledge and its potential contribution to the good life:

> 'Self-knowledge', in the sense of a minute understanding of one's own machinery, seems to me, except at a fairly simple level, usually a delusion. A sense of such self-knowledge may of course be induced in analysis for therapeutic reasons, but 'the cure' doesn't prove the alleged knowledge genuine. Self is as hard to see as other things, and when clear vision has been achieved, self is a correspondingly smaller and less interesting object.

There's another reason why we might resist the idea of spending too much time on the pursuit of self-knowledge: so much of the 'self' is hidden from conscious view that we are never likely to uncover it. You don't have to be a Freudian or a mystic to recognise the role of the unconscious mind. As Timothy Wilson writes in *Strangers to Ourselves: Discovering the Adaptive Unconscious* (2002): 'Freud's view of the unconscious was far too limited. When he said that consciousness is the tip of the mental iceberg, he was short of the mark by quite a bit – it may be more the size of a snowball on top of that iceberg.' There are many readily observable aspects of human psychology to support that contention: lower-order mental processes (especially involving perception) that occur outside of awareness; the fact that our mind can be divided between conscious activity (like reading) and unconscious activity unrelated to the text, perhaps processing some unresolved issue; the phenomenon of 'automatic' thought, familiar to any driver who repeatedly traverses the same route; the experience of not being sure how we feel about something or someone – *Do I really love him?* – as though our true feelings somehow lie hidden too deep within us to be easily accessed.

Wilson points out that the 'adaptive unconscious' should not be thought of as a single entity but as a collection of modules or processors that do such unrelated things as facilitate our acquisition and use of language, allow us to recognise faces instantly or react 'unthinkingly' to intuitive assessments of our environment. These are examples of what Wilson calls the 'pervasive, adaptive, sophisticated mental processes that occur largely out of view'. When we set out on a determined course of self-knowledge, we might do well to prepare ourselves for the frustrating discovery that not all the wellsprings of human behaviour are accessible to introspection: we might only ever be able to find bits and pieces of the whole.

In *Intimacy & Solitude* (1991), Stephanie Dowrick writes of the need to separate ourselves occasionally even from those we love the most, in order to take time out for emotional and spiritual rest and recovery, and to nurture our sense of who we really are. But all such explorations need to be undertaken in the full realisation that we are not isolated individuals working out our personal destiny; other people are integral parts of our destiny and they need us to be part of theirs, as well.

If you're looking for reliable, well-trodden pathways on which to take that inward journey, many people find meditation classes helpful, but almost everyone who ever tries some form of creative self-expression – writing, painting, singing, dancing, acting, photography, gardening – reports that this is where you most reliably find yourself. Another of those classic paradoxes: we are most likely to find ourselves when we lose ourselves in a creative or performance activity that fully absorbs us.

To repeat: a preoccupation with *personal* identity can isolate us from full engagement with our *social* identity, the identity that springs from our roles as members of families, friendship circles, neighbourhoods, organisations, communities. We are, by our very nature, social creatures. We are in this thing together. It is our recognition that we belong to each other, our common sense of connectedness rather than our unique sense of separateness, that preserves society from descending into the chaos of anarchical self-interest.

If we all stuck to the independent path of finding ourselves without proper recognition, at every turn, that we are part of the social whole, everybody would be crashing into each other's goals, ambitions and desires; bruising each other; offending each other; trying to outdo each other; fighting each other; determined to be Me at all costs. That's not us at our best. That's not the pathway to the good life. Back to the Greeks – Aristotle, this time: 'He who is unable to live in society, or who has no need, because he is sufficient for himself, must be either a beast or a god'.

Intelligence

If you're in the market for a non-religious idol, none is less deserving of your devotion or more futile as an object of worship than intelligence. Intelligence is not an achievement to be admired, or a goal to aspire to; it is mainly an accident of birth, plus or minus a bit of training and encouragement. We all have it, and some people have more than others, but intelligence in no way predicts the kind of person we are likely to become, the level of contentment we are likely to attain or the influence, good or bad, we are likely to exert on the lives of others.

Yes, it seems like good news if your child happens to be intelligent, though seriously high intelligence carries some challenges you might not wish on a child or its family. But if you think intelligence guarantees a good life, think again. If you think intelligent people are more likely to be sensitive, kind, considerate, helpful to strangers, or more likely to take up the cause of human rights, think again. If you think intelligent people are more likely to be creatively brilliant in art, music, literature, sculpture or dance, think again.

Roy Baumeister, the professor of psychology at Florida State University whose work on the moral muscle of self-control we touched on in chapter 1, acknowledges that intelligence is widely regarded by psychologists as one of the most important and desirable human traits, 'the thing you would most like your children to have and your rivals to lack'. But what are we supposed to do with that information? Intelligence, like height, is part of our basic equipment: it comes to us via our genes. What we do with what we've got is the issue, which is why the techniques of modern education place such stress on tailoring teaching to the capacity of the child, not assuming that every child has the same intellectual potential, and recognising that there are many other worthwhile traits apart from intelligence that shape the person we become.

I always wanted to be a police officer. But I did so well at school, everyone said I was too smart to be a cop; I had to do law. So I did law, and hated it. I eventually went to police college and here I am – a cop – and loving it.

Most parents get excited when told they have a gifted child. Who wouldn't? But think carefully about that word 'gifted': intelligence is indeed a gift from nature via our genes, to be nurtured, certainly, but not to be celebrated as though the person with this particular gift is inherently superior, more valuable or more special than someone with another gift – a kind and caring disposition, for instance – that also needs to be nurtured.

Year 5 goes to the museum

Flora is obviously the brightest child in the class. She writes beautiful compositions: sometimes descriptions of nature that seem quite poetic, sometimes exciting stories that have the other children leaning forward in their seats when she reads them out to the class. She always tops maths exams and is the last person standing in spelling bees.

Matt is obviously not the brightest child in the class. He struggles in most subjects, though he excels at art. If the school had had the resources to provide special teaching for children with learning difficulties, Matt would have been in that group.

On class excursions, the teacher sometimes cautions Flora against speaking too loudly on the train to the city ('airing your knowledge' is a no-no in Mrs Palmisano's class), but she encourages Flora's habit of drawing the other children's attention to interesting sights from the train window. Mrs Palmisano can usually trust Flora to be the navigator when they get off the train and find their way to their destination, which is what happens on the occasion of their visit to the museum. Two parents are also in attendance to help Mrs Palmisano keep an eye on the children, but it is Flora who seems most confident about the best route to the museum. She had studied the map beforehand and now brandishes it confidently.

Matt always brings his sketchpad on these excursions, keen to record everything he sees. Sometimes, he amuses the other children by sketching their faces during train and bus trips, often rendering them as cartoon characters. When they have their routine debriefing sessions on the day after an excursion, Matt's sketches are always a highlight.

Flora is excited by the museum, rushing from one exhibit to another, with a small knot of similarly enthusiastic children accompanying her. Mrs Palmisano assigns one parent to keep a close eye on that group in case they get too far ahead of the others. Matt is dragging behind, pencil in hand, pausing to capture some impression, some angle, though not showing much interest in the printed descriptions of the contents of the display cabinets.

There's a park beside the museum where the children go for lunch. Mrs Palmisano's three rules for lunch in a public place are that everyone must remain seated, people may speak only to the person next to them, in a quiet voice (no squealing), and there are to be no exchanges of items from each other's lunches: eat only what your mum gave you.

Matt finds himself seated beside Flora, a girl to whom he can normally find nothing to say. He notices she seems agitated, rummaging in her backpack. 'What's up?'

'I must have left my lunch box on the train. I took it out of my bag when I was looking for the map, and I must have been distracted and left it on the seat. Silly me. Don't tell Mrs Palmisano, okay?'

Silently, Matt hands her a sandwich and an apple.

'You can't do that. What about your own lunch?'

'My mum always gives me too much and then complains when there's stuff left in my lunch box when I get home. Take it – you're doing me a favour.'

'Really?'

'Who needs two apples for lunch?'

Flora takes the surreptitiously offered food with as much nonchalance as she can muster. 'Thanks, Matt.'

Embarrassed, she turns to the girl on her other side and ignores Matt for the rest of the lunch break. He finishes his half-lunch quickly and is happily sketching again by the time Mrs Palmisano asks them to put their scraps in the bin 'in an orderly fashion'.

People of high intelligence can do wonderful things for humanity, serving the common good, perhaps as teachers, scientists, counsellors, medical practitioners, inventors, visionary politicians or providers of care and guidance for the dispossessed and marginalised. Others, with comparable levels of raw intelligence, develop weapons of mass destruction, or become criminal masterminds, corrupt politicians, ruthless tycoons or glazy-eyed drop-outs. Some highly intelligent people have diminished emotional lives and are accused of 'thinking too much'; others are able to love as deeply as they think.

Intelligence is no predictor of mental health. People at any point on the scale of intelligence can yield to crippling mental disorders like depression or bipolar disease, while others, of equally high or low intelligence, can remain untouched by such illness.

My mother won the university medal for history and she became a brilliant high school teacher. But none of that saved her from the tragedy of alcoholism, estrangement from her family, and premature death.

Insofar as it can be measured, intelligence has long been assumed to be distributed through the human population in what statisticians call a 'normal' pattern as represented by a symmetrical bell-shaped graph; that is, very few people have extremely high or extremely low intelligence: a larger minority are well above or well below average intelligence, and most are clustered around the midpoint. The IQ, or intelligence quotient, measure was developed in 1912 by the German psychologist William Stern when he was attempting to measure general intelligence, which he defined as 'a general mental adaptability to new problems and conditions of life'.

A person's IQ is derived from a formula that divides mental age (as measured by a series of tests) by chronological age and then multiplies the result by one hundred; effectively, it's a way of relating the intelligence of an individual to people of the same age. IQ scores therefore treat one hundred as average intelligence – that is, the level of cognitive functioning which is right in the middle of the range of human possibilities. Scores above one hundred and fifty or below fifty are extremely rare. Half fall between ninety and one hundred and ten, and the vast majority within the range of eighty to one hundred and twenty.

But we need to be sceptical about IQ scores. Such measures are dangerously simplistic, and performance on them can be influenced not only by cultural factors but also by coaching for the test, which rather defeats the purpose of the exercise. Nevertheless, the IQ measure, rough as it may be, continues to serve as one of the ways of assessing general intelligence in children. Traditional IQ scores correlate quite well with children's performance in school exams, though recent research suggests that simple tests of memory are actually better predictors of exam success, since so much of a person's performance in an examination is a function of memory rather than intelligence per se. Researchers are constantly looking for ways to measure intelligence that bypass pencil-and-paper tests and are not influenced by culture – for example, tests conducted on the structure and physical functioning of the brain.

A good education can help sharpen the faculties we were born with, and indolence, neglect and cultural deprivation (no inspirational music and no encouragement to read at home, for instance) can mask our potential and make us seem less intelligent than we are.

Filling in forms, reading instructions and maintaining concentration, to say nothing of managing money or making decisions about relationships and employment, are obviously great challenges to people of limited cognitive capacity. Yet one of the cruellest attitudes in modern society, arising directly from the tendency to idolise intelligence, is the prejudice against those of low intelligence, as though they were inferior people, as though it were their fault and as though they were not part of who we are. 'Stupid' is a particularly nasty epithet when it is applied to someone who is well below average in their capacity to think clearly.

What's really stupid is praising someone's intelligence as if it's an achievement rather than a genetic and cultural product. We're strange about height, too: among men, taller applicants have a greater chance of getting a job, and in white-collar occupations taller graduates tend to receive higher starting salaries. *Oh, she's formidably bright*, we say of someone who displays startling intellectual gifts. But, as Daniel Goleman has shown in *Emotional Intelligence* (1995), some kinds of intelligence that lie outside the conventional boundaries of cognition are nevertheless fundamental to a well-rounded, satisfying life and, in particular, to the formation and nurturing of stable personal relationships. Sometimes, *she's formidably bright* is used as an excuse for bad behaviour. (*He might be a rogue, but he's bright. She might lack tact or sensitivity, but she's so clever. He might not have much common sense, but he's scarily intelligent.*) We never say such accommodating things about height (*She might lack tact or sensitivity, but she's so tall*), so why say them about intelligence? What is it about this characteristic that inclines people to forgive bad behaviour? If she's so formidably bright, shouldn't she have been able to figure out for herself that mere intellectual capacity is no excuse for insensitivity, bullying or failure to recognise and respond to other people's needs?

In any case, what's the big deal with intelligence? It doesn't determine our ability to love one another and, when it comes to tasks often associated with 'thought', we have already developed machines with so-called artificial intelligence that can outstrip us in their speed and capacity. The development of artificial intelligence with even greater cognitive abilities is just around the corner, lightning-fast robotic trading on the stock markets of the world an early sign of what happens when humans willingly cede control to machines and then find they can't keep up. We might already be in the process of creating the life-forms that will supersede us, creatures that have not had greed and violence programmed into them, that can withstand more natural catastrophes than humans and can reproduce by building their own replacements.

People who experience the joy of participation in the creative arts don't need superior intelligence; nor do those who enjoy the richness of their emotional response to music, movies or well-played sport, or those who offer loving care and support to their families and friends, and to people in need who happen to lie beyond their social circle. No, intelligence is not the place to look if you're trying to decipher the codes of human behaviour: it is neither interesting nor significant as a discriminator of anything except people's ability to perform particular tasks.

The thing to strive for – the thing to nurture in our children – is not only the maximising of our intellectual potential, but the maximising of our potential for goodness. Together, intelligence and goodness form a powerful combination, but if you had to choose one for your children, which would it be?

Power, wealth, status and fame

One of the most oft-quoted remarks about power came from the pen of the British historian Lord Acton: 'Power tends to corrupt; absolute power corrupts absolutely'. That was written in 1887, in a letter to Bishop Mandell Creighton, in which Acton also wrote, 'Great men are almost always bad men, even when they exercise influence and not authority'. These observations were no doubt based partly on Acton's study of history and partly on his close encounters with so-called great men. They form part of a long and remarkably consistent verdict on the hazards of power.

The first-century Roman historian Tacitus claimed that 'the lust for power, for dominating others, inflames the heart more than any other passion', while the eighteenth-century English writer Samuel Johnson said that 'power is always gradually stealing away from the many to the few, because the few are more vigilant and consistent'. Edmund Burke, the great Irish statesman and philosopher, stated that 'power gradually extirpates from the mind every humane and gentle virtue'.

Needless to say, there's a counterview among those who actually wield power. They were well represented by the unidentified wit quoted on BBC radio: 'All power is delightful – and absolute power is absolutely delightful!' And Cecil King, the English newspaper proprietor, said, 'I see nothing wrong with power as long as I am the fellow who has it'. (It would be hard to find anyone who has power, or wishes they had it, who would disagree with King.)

The more we lust after power, the more we make ourselves vulnerable to its corrupting influence. At its extreme, power imbues us with the dangerous idea that we have the right to exert control over others. Landmark experiments conducted by social psychologist Stanley Milgram at Yale University in the 1960s and replicated at Santa Clara University in 2009 by Jerry Burger illustrated this in a frightening way. Milgram showed that if people are instructed by an authority figure to inflict pain on others via an electric shock, they will tend to do so. In his experiments, 62 per cent of participants (in Burger's study, 70 per cent) gradually increased the intensity of the pain to the maximum possible, in spite of howls of protest and cries of pain from the victim strapped into a chair in the adjoining room but invisible to the person administering the shock. (The victims were actors, and the shock was not real, but the participants in the study knew neither of those things.) The experiments are often interpreted as being about obedience to authority; more chillingly, they seem also to demonstrate that being given significant power over another person tends to bring out the worst in us.

Power doesn't have this distinction on its own: great wealth can corrupt us, too, and in roughly the same way, especially when it is wielded as a symbol of power. So can a preoccupation with social status, whether based on inherited position, money, education or any other criterion we imagine has placed us above the common herd. Fame, that great thief of humility, is another potential corrupter of our better nature.

Why 'corruption'? What kind of corruption are we talking about? Though some wise and mature people resist their blandishments, power, wealth, status and fame have the potential to corrupt us in three ways. First, they encourage a sense of entitlement based on an assumption of superiority. *I'm the boss, so that makes me a more important person than you. I'm richer or more famous than you, so I'm entitled to more privileges than you. I hold high office* – a term with the potential to corrupt anyone – *so I expect to be treated like royalty. I* am *royalty, so I expect to be treated better than everyone else.* (A friend of mine working for a member of the British royal family once received a severe reprimand for scribbling a note on the bottom of a piece of paper on which the royal personage had previously written.) These are not universal attitudes among the powerful, wealthy or famous, and, it must be added, such people are often fawned over by the rest of us in ways that leave them in no doubt that *we* think they're superior. Henry Kissinger, former US secretary of state, famously described power as the 'ultimate aphrodisiac'. Whether he meant that it worked for the powerful or for those in awe of power was never made clear.

Though it's difficult to withstand the temptation to abuse one's power, wealth, status or fame, many fine people manage to do so. There are humble politicians who strive to do no more than represent their electorates conscientiously and contribute to public debate with as much integrity and impartiality as they can muster. Nothing could be further from the minds of such people than the exercise of power. Neil Armstrong, the late US astronaut who lives in human history as the first man to walk on the surface of the moon, could have relished the fruits of the global fame thrust upon him by his role in that mission. But he was almost equally famous for eschewing fame and all its trappings: he declined most requests for media interviews and appearances, preferring to live quietly and modestly, always insisting that he was only ever doing his job.

Similarly, there are wealthy business people who, perhaps having created a product or service that has been hugely successful in the market, have been surprised and even humbled by their success and make no claims for special treatment, either from the tax office or from their fellow citizens. Indeed, some wealthy people systematically distribute large chunks of their fortune in ways calculated to contribute to the common good. They do it without a backward glance, as if to say, *What else would I do with all this money?* Others let their wealth support them so they can devote their time to acts of charity, fostering neglected children, working in refuges for the homeless, mentoring disadvantaged young people.

There are people who hold positions of leadership who are there not because they actively sought, plotted or connived to achieve it, but because they were assessed by others as being the right person for the job. I'm with Plato on this: the best person to take a position of power and authority is the person who doesn't seek it. The very seeking of power ought to disqualify anyone from being given it, because the power-seeker – the person who dreams of holding the reins and exerting great influence – is the person most likely to be corrupted by the experience. Ambition is at its most dangerous when it's focused on the acquisition of power, status and influence, precisely because these fuel the sense of entitlement. A particularly stark example of the entitlement and superiority mentality emerges among some individuals with vast personal wealth who combine the bedrock minimisation of personal income tax with acts of significant philanthropy, believing that they, rather than the government, should be able to decide how their money is spent.

'Entitlement.' It's a curious word. We understand it easily enough when it refers to benefits people are entitled to as a condition of their employment or in compensation for their disadvantage or misfortune, via social security arrangements or other government support. But when it comes as an accessory to power, wealth, status or fame, it can too easily generate a delusional sense of being titled, in the aristocratic sense – a person of superior rank to others.

> I've done well, and I make no apology for that. My kids will do well, too. Others won't have the same opportunities. That's just the way it is. There are winners and losers in every society – drop-kicks, drop-outs – I accept that.

This all sits rather oddly with the cultural heritage of countries like the United States, Australia, New Zealand and Canada that have been built on the dream of egalitarianism (though that dream may be evaporating under the pressure of increasing socioeconomic inequality in those countries). Certainly, an explicit sense of entitlement has begun to emerge among members of Australia's burgeoning wealth class, suggesting egalitarian principles are being strongly challenged.

> Every society on earth has a social class system, whether they admit it or not. Thank God ours is not based on birth. You can move up in Australia by a combination of education, hard work and a modicum of luck.

This comment conveniently overlooks the fact that this is precisely how class structures are created and maintained: when great wealth is acquired and passed on within a family, what else does that do but foster an economic class system based on birth?

Consider the insidious effect of the bizarre term VIP. Can you imagine the cast of mind that allows a person to be comfortable with being described as a 'very important person'? And can you imagine the long-term effects of being labelled like that, particularly on a person's attitudes to the rest of us, the hoi polloi, the great unwashed? Can you imagine the extent to which a person's social attitudes have been corrupted if they've reached the point where they *expect* to be treated like a VIP?

This has nothing to do with the fact that every society, every community, every organisation needs its leaders – people who are prepared to take on the mantle of responsibility for others' wellbeing; people capable of inspiring and encouraging others to become the best they can be. Self-sacrificial leadership is a social good, and leaders deserve our respect and gratitude for taking on that onerous role. At its best, leadership is a textbook example of the life lived for others, because, as any truly effective leader knows, leadership is the ultimate form of service to an organisation, community or society. Leadership therefore calls for a larger than usual dose of humility. Arrogance fuelled by a sense of entitlement is the mark of a person who has not yet grasped what leadership is about. If part of your notion of the good life involves achieving a position of power, wealth, status or fame because that entitles you to a sense of superiority, then the entire good-life project will have collapsed before you've even engaged with it.

The second way power, wealth, status and fame may corrupt us is by fuelling our greed. Any form of addiction is corrosive, because it takes control of our priorities away from us. The person helplessly addicted to drugs, for instance, may lie, cheat, steal and commit acts of violence in order to get the money necessary to feed the habit, even though before succumbing to the addiction they might well have regarded all such behaviour as morally repugnant. Problem gamblers, similarly, may experience a dangerous corruption of their capacity to manage their money, or to act responsibly towards those who are financially dependent on them. They may abandon family and lose their friends in the endless quest for the big win that will save them.

If we allow ourselves to become addicted to the pursuit of power, wealth, status or fame, we become greedy for more,

more, more of whatever will bring us closer to the summit of our ambition. The truth, obvious to everyone except the person corrupted, is that such summits are unreachable, because the addict can never get enough. For the person corrupted by greed, one trophy, one conquest, one prize only whets the appetite for more. On history's big canvas, this has been true of leaders like Alexander the Great, Genghis Khan and Adolf Hitler, all of whom were driven by dreams of world domination. On a more modest scale, it's true of any worshippers of corporate power and status who, having been appointed to one board, seek appointment to more and more boards. (In Australia, corporate regulators have finally begun to wonder just how attentive and conscientious it's possible for multi-board directors to be.)

The former New South Wales Labor minister Rodney Cavalier once described parliament as an inherently unhappy place where all the members of the opposition want to be in government, all the backbenchers want to be on the front bench and all the ministers want to be premier. That was a caricature, an exaggeration, but when power is your goal disappointment and frustration are your constant companions: no amount of scratching will make that itch go away. This helps to explain the 'relevance-deprivation syndrome' described by some retired politicians and others who have previously enjoyed the trappings of power and the sense of being close to the action. People addicted to the limelight as performers or celebrities, similarly, tend to find the post-career adjustment to life as ordinary citizens difficult to make. Addiction of any kind is hard to kick.

You can't have too much power, wealth, status or fame if you are pursuing those things for their own sake. On the other hand, if they are mere by-products of your work and you've learnt to regard them with scepticism, suspicion and perhaps even some amusement, then you're probably safely inoculated against such corruption.

But even if our feelings of avarice are not powerful enough to pitch us into unrestrained pursuit of the goals of great wealth or power, they may still disturb us enough to distract us from the ideals of the good life. I recall, as a young person, attending a church where materialism was frequently denounced from the pulpit and scriptural exhortations were invoked to discourage material greed. A favourite was 'Lay not up for yourselves treasure on Earth, where moss and rust doth corrupt; but lay up for yourselves treasure in heaven'. Afterwards, we would go outside and admire each other's new cars. That was partly because there's much to admire about the look, smell, sound and feel of a new car, but it was mainly about sheer envy: we hankered after owning those cars, too.

Where are they now, all those shiny new Ford Zephyrs, Morris Minors, Austin A40s, Volkswagens, Holden Specials and Standard Vanguards – or even that one memorable Mercedes-Benz? Rusted-out wrecks, no doubt, corrupted by moss or possibly recycled as refrigerators and washing machines. The scrapyard is a perfect symbol for the good life conceived as what we own.

There's nothing wrong with loving cars; nothing wrong with power that is sensitively and selflessly exercised in the interests of the common good; nothing wrong with wealth, fame or status, either, depending on how you acquired them and what you choose to do with them. The hazard is getting hooked on all this stuff, wanting these things so desperately that they become not merely distractions but idols we worship. 'Money is the root of all evil' is a popular misquotation: the wise original says that 'the *love* of money is the root of all evil'.

The third way we can be corrupted by the lust for power, wealth, status or fame is that we come to judge other people by the same criteria we use to measure our own success. The evidence of this form of corruption is all around us: people who assign status according to the accumulation of the trappings of wealth and power, and sneer at those they judge to have fallen short; people who rate a person's worth by their material success, equating poverty with inferiority, inadequacy or even failure; people who operate on the assumption that 'every man has his price'. We know, intuitively and instinctively, that it's ridiculous to think like that, and most resist it. But if we're worshipping at the altar of power, wealth, status and fame, we run the risk of being blinded to the real worth in other people, to the social inequities (in educational opportunity, for instance) that persist in a society supposedly committed to egalitarian principles, or even to the needs of the marginalised, the disadvantaged and the distressed. And what could be more corrupt than that?

You might recall the story of the evil Roman emperor Caligula, who outraged everyone by the way he indulged his horse, dressing it in lavish clothing, providing it with a palace with servants and even, it was said, planning to appoint the animal to the high-ranking post of consul. It sounds like an obsession with power and status gone mad. But perhaps there's more to the story than meets the eye. In *Caligula: A biography* (2003), the German-born classicist Aloys Winterling casts a quite different light on this strange episode in Roman history. According to Winterling, the emperor's absurdly extravagant treatment of his horse was intended as satire. Reviewing a new translation of *Caligula* in the *London Review of Books* in 2011, Mary Beard writes that the emperor 'was satirising the aims and ambitions of the Roman aristocracy; in their pursuit of luxury and empty honours, they appeared no less silly than the horse'.

Molly King was my teacher in Years 5 and 6 of primary school, and I have been in her debt ever since. Here is an extract from the obituary that appeared in *The Sydney Morning Herald* following her death, in 1996:

> In no doubt about her vocation, she went from school to teachers' college and [then to teach at] Bundanoon in rural NSW and at suburban Warrawee. When asked to teach an 'OC' class of gifted children at Artarmon Public School, her response was typical:

> 'Oh, I don't think I could do that'. 'We think you could', was the reply, and so she did and stayed for 36 years. She couldn't retire because, she said, she'd have to make a speech.
>
> She was a natural teacher – warm, intelligent, creative, meticulous – but there was something more. She empowered children by believing in them so they came to believe in themselves. She set high standards of behaviour – old-fashioned courtesy, respect for others.
>
> She had a rare ability to adapt – to be content. She never said 'I wish I had . . . ' or 'I wish I were . . . '. She never envied anybody. She found interest and pleasure in each moment, encounter and conversation but could be still and content with herself.
>
> King held no high office; she neither travelled nor aspired to be a leader. Her life – one of integrity, faith, humour, kindness and courage – is a reminder that depth counts as much as breadth.

Albert Einstein would have approved of Miss King. 'Try not to become a man of success', he said, 'but rather a man of value'.

The simple life

I have nothing but admiration for people who choose to sup lentils from an earthenware bowl while sitting cross-legged on a jute mat. I'm similarly impressed by people who decide, usually late in life, to give away most of their possessions and retreat to one or two spartan rooms in which they give themselves up to the thinking of noble thoughts, become focused on the moment by gazing relentlessly into the flame of a candle and possibly devote themselves to good works that demonstrate their new-found piety or zeal – creating their own hand-painted greetings cards made from organic materials, for instance. I'm sounding cynical, but, seriously, I am impressed by such asceticism, just as I am impressed by people who enter a religious order and devote their life to praying for the rest of us. Impressed, but unconvinced.

I'm more convinced by people who pursue simplicity in more practical ways: avoiding food products that have clocked up too many food miles in reaching their tables, only eating fruit and vegetables in season, exercising restraint in their spending habits or their reliance on technology, taking initiatives that encourage people to live in ways that benefit their social and physical environments.

Activist Huw Kingston's passion for reducing damage to the environment led him to start a successful campaign in Bundanoon, in the Southern Highlands of New South Wales, to eliminate bottled water from the town. Chosen by *Time* magazine in 2009 as one of their twenty-five Worldwide Responsibility Pioneers, Kingston has selflessly dedicated himself to educating the community and organising the installation of free-water stations around the town.

There are people like Kingston all over the world, interpreting 'the simple life' in imaginative and productive ways that benefit their local communities while exposing some of the more absurd examples of modern material excess (none more absurd than the mass marketing of bottled water – our own water, sold back to us at a higher price per litre than petrol, and about a thousand times the price of equally pure tap water).

However they are expressed, the motivations for the simple life are usually pure. People become disgusted by the culture of materialism and their complicity in it. They sometimes realise this only when they find their own children conforming to the patterns of a consumerist society and are no longer able to blame the media.

> I was standing in the bathroom shaving one morning and I heard my kids arguing over some product in a TV commercial. I suddenly thought, *How did my kids become such little materialists?* Then I looked at myself in the mirror. Yep – they were only following our example.

Sometimes, the moment of truth comes when people are renovating their home or packing to go on holiday and are suddenly confronted by the extent of their possessions.

> Too much stuff! Where did all this stuff come from? Why did we ever think we needed all this junk? I looked at my husband one day and said, 'We must be mad. I can't even remember buying half this stuff'. Time to de-clutter!

Others have a moment of insight when it suddenly dawns on them that they have spent half their life saying one thing and doing another.

> It's all about your values. People say they're not into materialism and still clutter their lives with material possessions. That's just hypocritical. If you keep saying your family is your highest priority and yet you work such long hours that your relationship with your spouse or kids is suffering, there's something seriously wrong. You've got to stop pretending. You've got to do something about it.

The simplicity-orientated messages of the green movement have appealed to many people, providing them with ways of making a personal contribution to the campaign to clean up the planet: use less energy, recycle every possible thing, adopt a more natural lifestyle. Others have responded to appeals by international aid organisations on behalf of the millions of people living in poverty and hunger: 'Live simply so others may simply live'. Whatever the specific trigger, a passion for the simple life is usually based on the belief that there is something inherently virtuous in the decision to live more simply: not only will it reduce our carbon footprint, but we may become better people as a result of our concern for the natural environment and our determination to be more faithful stewards of this fragile planet. Hard to argue with any of that.

The simple life is often motivated by the same impulses that impel us towards the good life. In *Zen Mind, Beginner's Mind* (1970), Shunryu Suzuki suggests that 'the most important thing is to express your true nature in the simplest, most adequate way and to appreciate it in the smallest existence'. Goodness, whether in the sense of our moral behaviour towards others or in the more private sense of a wish to live a more virtuous, less self-indulgent life, has much in common with the idea of simplicity. But they are not the same thing. The extent to which the simple life is good depends partly on our motivations, and they may range from helping to save the planet to feeling better about ourselves or getting away from it all, as described by Harry Ruby and Rube Bloom in their classic hit:

> I don't believe in frettin' and grievin'
> Why mess around with strife?
> I never was cut out to step and strut out
> Give me the simple life.

Some devotees of the simple life may pursue simplicity as a way of purifying themselves and their way of life, regardless of any contribution they may or may not be making to the common good. Others undermine their position by developing a supercilious attitude towards those who don't follow the prescribed path of simplicity, almost as if they see themselves as having evolved into a higher life-form than the rest of society. Simplicity as a lifestyle seems rather less attractive when it is combined with arrogance.

> My sister and I grew up in a household with parents who were very into the idea of living simply. We didn't have a lot of stuff – we only had one car when most of our friends' families had two – and we went on really primitive camping holidays where Dad taught us all kinds of things about living in the bush. So I guess we were Greenies before they were called Greenies. But Mum and Dad were very into being connected to the community, as well. So it's interesting how the two of us have turned out.
>
> I'd say my partner and I lead a pretty simple life: we live economically. We shop carefully. We turn lights off when we're not using them and we only put as much water in the jug as we need to boil. We grow a few

vegies but, actually, we believe in keeping fruit and vegetable growers in business. We try to buy organic . . . the usual things. But we don't go overboard and we certainly don't preach about it.

My sister? Different story. Totally. She's gone right over the top. Her kids drink nothing but water. They grow heaps more stuff than we do; their place looks like a dump, actually: it's just one big vegie patch with a lot of weeds. No pesticides or herbicides, of course. And no lawn – they're always lecturing their neighbours about the carbon emissions from lawnmowers. They refuse to own a car or a TV. And they're so holier-than-thou about it all. I think it's cut them off from their neighbours and most of their friends, except the few who are like them – they're like a weird little cult. My sister will hardly speak to me; she refuses to let her kids come to our place in case they're contaminated. There's simple and then there's obsessive. I know what's going to happen to her kids in the end: they'll become TV addicts and chocaholics once they're off the leash.

Asceticism, whether in the name of religion or the environment, can easily lead to a withdrawal from social networks, either for fear of contamination or because of a veil of mutual suspicion that cuts the austere purist off from encounters with the less pure. The arguments in favour of a simpler, more environmentally sensitive life are clear and powerful, but they don't encourage a blind devotion to simplicity at the expense of our social responsibilities to the people on our doorstep.

The meaning of Life

What is the meaning of Thursday? (Don't laugh. Stay with me.) There are many ways of answering that question. You could say, *It's named after Thor, the Norse god of thunder; Thor's Day became Thursday*. Or you could say, *It's the day before Friday, so I always start gearing up for the weekend on Thursday*. Or you might say, *Excuse me, but days of the week don't have meanings. Days of the week are whatever we make of them. You wouldn't ask, 'What is the meaning of rain?' or, 'What is the meaning of sunshine?' So why are you asking for the meaning of a day of the week?* If you were a scientist with an interest in the weather, you might say that both rain and sunshine mean something, as symptoms of weather and climate patterns. Or you might explain how they each come to exist. But there's a big difference between *What does it mean?* and *How does it happen?* For most people, rain is just water falling out of the sky and, like Thursday, is something we experience and respond to in many different ways.

My point is that, philosophically speaking, asking about the meaning of Life with a capital *L* is a bit like asking about the meaning of Thursday: the question is based on a misapprehension about the subject of the question. Yes, cosmologists, biologists, geologists, physicists and other scientists may have plenty to say about the origins and evolution of life on earth, about how it happened, but when we ask questions about the *meaning* of Life, those are not usually the answers we're looking for.

So what answers are we looking for? And do those answers exist? Some philosophers like to talk about category mistakes – that is, discussing one category of objects, events or ideas as if they belong to another category entirely. We are making a category mistake when we ask, *What colour is forty-two?* or, *What does the soul eat?* or, *How fast are streets?* or, *What is the meaning of Thursday?* Questions about colour, diet and speed are simply not appropriate for numbers, souls and streets. Nor are questions about meaning appropriate for days of the week.

What if questions about the meaning of Life are like that, too? Perhaps Life is not something about which you can reasonably ask, *What does it mean?* You can ask how it originates, or why it exists on this particular planet, or how to establish its presence or absence, in trees or rocks, for instance, but not what it means. *Why are we here?* is a popular variation on the theme of *What is the meaning of Life?* and it's a similarly inappropriate question to ask; a similar category mistake. Scientific curiosity about the origins of our species is natural, but *Why are we here?* is a very different question from *How did we get here?* Whether we're talking about our existence on this planet, the earth's place in our solar system or our solar system's place in the universe – or, indeed, about finding ourselves in any situation not of our making or choosing – the only sensible response is, *We are here; what now? How shall we make the best of the situation in which we find ourselves?*

If you accept that Life itself doesn't have any inherent meaning, one conclusion that certainly does *not* follow is that our lives are therefore pointless. We know that isn't true: we don't have to tap in to some vast eternal plan to see that what we do, day by day, has great consequences for us and others, and while we sometimes do pointless things – standing in a queue and then finding all the tickets have been sold, for instance – much of what we do is designed simply to keep us alive. If we wish to live, then earning an income, eating, drinking, breathing, sleeping, excreting and exercising have a great deal of point. And if we wish to thrive as social beings, then everything we do to foster and nurture our personal relationships has meaning.

To say that Life itself is not something to which we can properly attach any meaning is therefore not to say that your life and my life have no meaning. We can certainly live as if they don't, but we can also live as if they do: we invest our own life with meaning whenever we define a purpose for ourselves that makes sense to us, if not cosmically then at least personally.

When we were students we used to sit around discussing what we called 'the meaning of Life'. It was mostly about politics or what we were going to do on Friday night, but occasionally someone would say something like *Why do you think we're here?* or *Why do we all think our own lives are so important?* We could never answer the first one, but the second one used to get us going – we soon realised it was all down to us and there were no answers waiting for us somewhere out there in the cosmos.

Each life has the meaning we ourselves choose to invest in it, whether we make that investment consciously or not. This is not as radical an idea as it might sound: we do it all the time with language. Words are, of themselves, meaningless. We invest them with meaning and, over time, come to feel as if certain words mean certain things. We construct dictionaries and then think they tell us what words mean, but dictionaries are mere historical documents, museums of meaning, telling us how, at certain times and in certain places, people have used particular words to convey particular ideas. Any lexicographer will tell you that every new edition of a dictionary must incorporate hundreds of new words and must also reflect the hundreds of changes in the ways existing words are being used. We made up these words to help us communicate with each other, and we'll use them any way we like – look at the recent shifts in the ways we use the words 'wicked', 'gay', 'enormity' and 'disinterested'.

I imagine you have no trouble living with the idea that Music as an art form has no inherent meaning, even though you may have strong emotional responses, positive or negative, to particular pieces of music, and some music may have special meaning for you. Music is something we experience and interpret without feeling as though we have to crack the code that will reveal some mystical, deeper meaning of Music to us. Life is like that: we interpret it in our own ways, through the experience of living our own life. We are the authors and directors of the purposes that give meaning to our lives. Those purposes may change as we age and mature: as we acquire more insight into our capacities and potentialities, we may well rethink our priorities and goals, just as our musical tastes may change as we mature and are exposed to new and different musical forms. But this grand thing we call Life? Fascinating, glorious, puzzling, horrifying – and meaningless. A flickering candle, likely to burn for a tiny fraction of the existence of the planet that supports it.

Here is a list of goals by which people throughout history have invested their lives with a sense of meaning:

Make as much money as possible. (*Richest person wins!*)

Persuade as many people as I can to conform to my beliefs.

Live in a way that ensures I will go to heaven.

Never harm anybody, even wrongdoers or sworn enemies.

Give pleasure to as many people as possible.

Make the world, or at least my corner of it, a better place.

Expose hypocrisy wherever I encounter it.

Destroy my enemies.

Be remembered for my achievements.

Always act rationally.

Be as kind as I can be to everyone I meet.

Live in ways that will nurture my personal relationships.

Help people in need.

Be surrounded by beautiful things.

Contribute.

Learn to love my neighbours, whoever they may be.

Be as honest and open as I can be in everything I do.

Be left alone to live my life the way I want.

Be admired for my accomplishments.

Have fun.

Always be in charge.

Live in ways that are true to my religious beliefs.

Minimise my carbon footprint.

Become famous.

Glorify God.

Acquire as much knowledge as possible.

Make people laugh.

Get married and have kids.

Have it all.

Be really good at just one thing.

Die at peace.

If you ran through that list mentally ticking off every item that applies to you, you may have caught a glimpse of some of the purposes that give meaning to your own life, though a better way of examining your life's meaning might be to look at what you actually do – in particular, how you spend your time and money.

A friend of mine used to irritate his boss, a person much given to airy and pompous mission statements, by insisting that 'our policies are what we *do*'. He was making the point that what we do can be very different from what we say we'll do, or what we aspire to do, or what we might idly dream of doing. The meaning of our lives lies in none of those things.

4

A good life or a good time?

For twenty years, Vanessa has been reading about the Sandwich Generation and now, at forty-five, finds herself in the thick of it: young teenage children still heavily dependent on her; her own increasingly frail parents relying on her for advice, support, reassurance and even companionship; a recently widowed father-in-law who seems rather at a loose end planning to move into the spare room while he sorts himself out; a husband, Adrian, who adores her and expects his fair share of adoration in return. With the children's schedules becoming even more complicated than her own, Vanessa finds running the household a daily challenge. Adrian tries to be supportive but has never been fully domesticated, though he has finally mastered the art of school lunches. Oh, and she has a full-time job in events management that she wouldn't give up for anything.

Raised by an enlightened mother to be a truly liberated woman, Vanessa revels in the knowledge that she is living a rich, full (if slightly over-complicated) life, and that life has bestowed many precious, magical moments on her. But her energy levels are depleted and she's beginning to feel desperate. There are times when her so-called liberation feels like just another form of enslavement.

She's becoming almost obsessed by the thought of escape: a Buddhist retreat, perhaps, or a spa resort; even a short stay in hospital seems attractive (provided it was nothing serious, obviously). A conventional family holiday wouldn't do the trick: that's usually more work than staying at home. She loves them all, of course, even the rather doddery father-in-law, who finds it easier to confide in her than in his own son. The kids can't wait for him to move in, and Vanessa knows one reason why: he has plenty of time for them and affects blithe ignorance of the house rules about . . . well, about anything, really.

One thing Vanessa wouldn't say about her life is that she's having a good time. She and Adrian go out occasionally and always enjoy themselves, though he falls asleep in movies, and if they have dinner they seem to have trouble sustaining a conversation about anything other than their kids or their parents. *Life isn't meant to be like this,* Vanessa sometimes mutters to herself. *I never expected happily ever after, but I did expect to be getting more fun out of life. I expected to have more time for me. I suppose I assumed I'd feel more content, more settled at this stage of my life: gorgeous kids, a loving husband, my parents still with all their marbles (or most of them). I just didn't think it would be so relentless.*

When she and Adrian were young, they and their friends had a slogan that often buoyed their spirits: 'We're not here for a long time; we're here for a good time'. Looking at her parents' passage into a prolonged old age, Vanessa now thinks she, too, is probably genetically programmed to be here for a long time, but she wonders if the good time is already behind her. She hopes not.

Someone needs to explain to Vanessa the difference between a good life and a good time. Yes, she needs to sort out her schedule to allow a little more time for rest and recreation. Yes, she needs to exercise regularly, perhaps also to meditate. She needs a creative outlet. She and Adrian need to discuss a more equitable division of household and parenting duties, and she probably needs more paid domestic help. (In fact, as soon as she reveals to Adrian how ragged she's feeling, that's the first thing he'll suggest: *Why don't we pay someone to do more of this stuff? We can afford it.*) But there's a deeper question for Vanessa that goes beyond all those sensible suggestions about organising her life so she's not overwhelmed by it. The idea that life is meant to be more fun than this, that she's not happy often enough or that other people are making too many demands on her might mean that she hasn't yet thought through the idea of the good life.

A life lived for others

The good life is a life lived for others. Much more needs to be said, of course, to explain and justify a statement like that: many qualifications still to come, many ways to interpret that phrase 'for others'. We'll get to all that in chapter 5. The starting point is the recognition that we are all inseparably part of each other and that our human destiny is to accept and nurture our connections. We are each part of a larger whole: a family, a friendship circle, a neighbourhood, a community, an organisation, a world. Each of us is a player in the same big human drama. This does not mean we should lose ourselves in these connections or deny our individuality. But it does mean that, if we take a look at the big picture, we will come to recognise that our identity is defined by our context even more than by our essence. It's more a case of *Who needs me?* than *Who am I?*

Vanessa is actually the kind of person who makes the world go round. She is a heroic figure. Hers is indeed a life lived for others: she takes seriously her responsibility to the organisation she works for (and not all employees do). She is devoted to the wellbeing of her children (and not all parents are); she is attentive and responsive to her elderly parents (and not all children are); she is concerned about maintaining some private magic between herself and Adrian (and not all spouses are). She finds time to be a good neighbour (and not all urban-dwellers do). She sees a need and she responds to it. She is at the opposite end of the spectrum from people who feel socially isolated, marginalised or alienated and who, as a result, are at greater risk of depression, despair and even suicide. Friendship, connectedness, engagement, community: these are the great life-savers, the great sources of human fulfilment. We are by nature social creatures – herd animals – and we cut ourselves off from the herd at our peril.

If we don't interpret it sensibly, 'the life lived for others' can sound like an encouragement to become a doormat. That's quite the wrong metaphor, because it's quite the wrong way to live. This is not about being servile, subservient or subjugated. This is about being fully engaged in a spirit of equality with the people we encounter, wherever we encounter them. The life lived for others is lived as an open doorway, not as a doormat.

Vanessa might well be attempting too much: having it all rarely turns out well when it means 'all at once'. But many of her frustrations stem from a view of the world that is simply unrealistic: she has failed to grasp the crucial idea that a good life, a valuable life, isn't the same as a happy life, a fun-filled life or even a life that feels good all the time. The good life is a loving life, and when was love only about having a good time?

Ask yourself this: what is the most powerful, creative and fruitful force for good in the world? Answer: Love. (Do you have a better answer?) Love, in all its many manifestations – kindness, care, compassion, generosity, tolerance, encouragement, support – is the source of everything we admire and appreciate most in human behaviour.

Next question: how can we make any sense of love without putting it in the context of a relationship or a community? Love, given or received, is about our engagement with others.

The answers to those two questions lead us logically, inescapably, to the proposition that lies at the heart of this book. If love is the ultimate source of goodness in our lives, it follows that the good life is primarily about others. What else could it be about?

In everyday speech, when we say 'the good life', we usually mean to convey the simple idea that we're having a good time; we're feeling contented; we're doing well – perhaps materially, perhaps emotionally, perhaps in some other way.

> My mate Herbie has cashed in his super and moved to the Gold Coast. He reckons it's time to lead the good life.

'Good' is one of those tricky words, like 'love', that carries many possible connotations. 'Good time', for instance, has almost no connection with the idea of being good. Nor does 'good girl' when used as praise for a child who has mastered the art of walking or talking, or eating without covering her face and hands in debris. Good food, good party, good job, good journey, good conversation, Good Friday: same adjective, many shades of meaning. Some of our uses of the word are ambiguous: 'a good woman', for example, might refer to anything from a virtuous wife to a good-time girl, and 'Good luck!' can be heartfelt or ironic, depending on your tone of voice.

The English poet, novelist and critic G. K. Chesterton once remarked that 'the word "good" has many meanings. For example, if a man were to shoot his grandmother at a range of five hundred yards, I should call him a good shot, but not necessarily a good man'.

So what do I mean by 'good' in the context of this book? To repeat a sentence from the Preface:

> When I say 'the good life', I'm referring to a life that is characterised by goodness, a morally praiseworthy life, a life valuable in its impact on others, a life devoted to the common good.

Having spent most of my career listening to people in research projects talking about their lives – their dreams, their passions, their joys and their sorrows – it strikes me that though most of us know deep within ourselves what constitutes a good life, we spend much of our time barking up a succession of wrong trees. Perhaps we are genuinely unsure of how to put our convictions into practice. How would you actually live by the so-called Golden Rule, even if you really wanted to? 'Do unto others as you would have others do unto you'? It sounds like the recipe for a good life, but how in practice do you stifle your perfectly natural urges towards greed, ambition, competitiveness or revenge, the very things likely to leach goodness out of your life? How do you shed grudges you actually enjoy carrying? How do you find the emotional wherewithal to forgive someone who's wronged you? How do you let go of stuff you've done in the past?

Perhaps we are simply distracted by glittering baubles that offer variations on the themes of self-indulgence and self-satisfaction – money, pleasure, status, possessions – that have the power to seduce us. Or perhaps we've made a calculated decision to go for the good time before embracing the good life, just in case we miss some of the fun. Saint Augustine is supposed to have prayed this ruthlessly honest prayer: 'Grant me chastity and continence, but not yet'.

In chapters 5 and 6, we shall see just what living the good life might entail. But first, think about this: aren't we all capable of quite remarkable displays of goodness in our lives?

Everyday altruists

At its most attractive, the good life involves that wonderful human quality we call 'altruism', the precise opposite of selfishness. Altruism involves doing things that benefit others without any thought of a reciprocal benefit to ourselves. It sometimes involves acting in ways that are actually against our own interests.

Ah, the cynics may say, *there's really no such thing as altruism. We never do things only for the benefit of others. There's always something in it for us, too. Humans are selfish creatures and we're always looking out for Number One. It's the Darwinian principle: survival of the fittest. Life's a contest and we all want to win. We disguise it with a civilised veneer, but self-interest is never far below the surface.* If that's your line, you haven't been looking at the big picture. There's simply too much evidence to support the opposite view, too many signs that these same humans who visit the most violent and destructive mayhem on each other have nevertheless managed to create and sustain stable and cohesive communities for aeons and have proved themselves capable of acts of genuine altruism, large and small, that simply don't fit the self-interest model.

Perhaps the most celebrated examples of altruism are the extraordinary sacrifices made by those who have fought wars, just and unjust, on behalf of the societies they represent, so ordinary people like you and me can go on leading our ordinary lives in peace. Similarly, some people's altruism has led them to suffer torture and even death for the sake of a principle they believed in or to save someone else's life. Such people display heroic virtues of courage and self-sacrifice beyond the call of duty. But a nation's character is not defined by exceptional cases like these; it is defined by those who are prepared to get on with lives destined to be lived out of the spotlight, who stick to the often tedious tasks they have been saddled with, who accept the responsibilities that go with being ordinary.

So we might do well to ponder another type of courage found in another type of hero: those who plug away, year after thankless year, doing their best to be faithful partners, loving parents, good neighbours and responsible citizens. These are the unsung heroes, the everyday altruists, who maintain the heartbeat of a civilised society and demonstrate that the good life is not beyond our reach, after all:

> The parents of a child with severe health problems or learning difficulties, who have to find the resources to cope with the crushing demands of caring for someone with special needs. It's not just the physical demands; it's also the emotional challenge of watching so-called normal kids and their parents get on with lives that seem like a breeze by comparison.
>
> The woman whose husband suffers from dementia and who has finally, reluctantly, admitted him to a nursing home. She visits him every day, usually finding him in a state of ignorance of who she is or why she's there. Like thousands of sad spouses in this situation, she is only occasionally rewarded by a flicker of recognition but is driven by the powerful combination of

love and duty to attend to his needs and maintain the closest possible contact with him.

The man who once had aspirations to be a leader in his profession but who finally realises that, in the eyes of his peers, he is an also-ran. Having a wife and children to support, he sticks gamely to his job, year after year, seeing his kids through university and hearing his wife lavishly praised for re-establishing a glittering career in her fifties.

The married couples, countless in number, who learn to swallow their disappointments in each other but maintain marriages that ultimately help them discover the rich meaning of 'for better, for worse'.

The mothers (and occasionally fathers) who sacrifice their careers to care for young children, hoping they'll find a way back to work in the future but happy to know they are nurturing the next generation first hand, in spite of the mystified disapproval of their peers.

The couples who foster other people's children, sometimes for weeks or months, sometimes for years, because those children's parents, for whatever reason, are unable to care for them.

The men and women who wish they had a partner but find themselves living alone, through bereavement, marriage breakdown or simply the luck of the draw. They learn to find their completeness by enriching the lives of their families, friends, colleagues and neighbours.

Those who welcome refugees into their homes, befriending and supporting them through the early difficult weeks of orientation to their new surroundings and helping them meet the challenges of mastering the language and finding work.

Volunteers of every kind, feeding the poor and homeless, visiting the sick, repairing furniture and toys for under-

> resourced families, performing household tasks for the frail and elderly, driving people with disabilities to the shops or to appointments, teaching sporting or life skills to kids from deprived backgrounds, cheerfully undertaking all such tasks for the benefit of people who could not manage if they had to pay for the services.
>
> Those who patrol surf beaches as volunteer lifesavers, and those who devote hours of their spare time to coaching sporting teams with no thought of personal gain or glory.
>
> Those who were looking forward to the freedom of having the children off their hands but whose aged parents have become increasingly dependent on them and who, on top of that, find they are expected to care for their grandchildren two or three days a week. They love everyone involved and confess only occasionally, and then only to each other, that they'd expected life to be a little easier than this by the time they reached their sixties.

That is merely a small selection of the many varieties of everyday altruist: people who just get on with it without complaint, who neither seek nor receive praise for what they do, who put others' welfare ahead of their own and who make quiet but heroic sacrifices every day of the year.

None of this has much to do with happiness, as popularly defined. According to Harvard psychologist Daniel Gilbert, research shows that parents are less happy interacting with their children than they are exercising, eating and watching TV. Similar results have emerged from other studies suggesting what is intuitively obvious: parenthood is a powerful source of meaning and purpose, but because it calls for a high degree of self-sacrifice, it is often associated with low levels of 'happiness' in the popular meaning of that term.

Contemporary research evidence only confirms what ancient wisdom has always asserted. In a 2013 article in *The Atlantic*,

'There's more to life than being happy', New York writer Emily Esfahani Smith expressed it succinctly: 'By putting aside our selfish interests to serve someone or something larger than ourselves – by devoting our lives to "giving" rather than "taking" – we are … expressing our fundamental humanity.' Smith quotes psychologist Roy Baumeister: 'Partly what we do as humans is to take care of others and contribute to others. This makes life more meaningful but it does not necessarily make us happy.'

Perhaps we'll grow out of the need for war heroes, one day. Perhaps we'll reach the stage where we'll look back on war and it will all seem like a grotesque carry-over from a primitive and brutal past. But heroic sacrifice in the name of everyday altruism will always be needed, and heroes will always be found. They will be no more visible then than they are now, and no more likely to expect recognition for their sacrifice and goodness.

Good people, bad people?

Evolutionary biologists, neuroscientists and psychologists are becoming increasingly interested in the question of altruism. For years, the accepted wisdom was that all altruism is, in effect, reciprocal; that is, people always expect to receive some benefit (practical or emotional) in return for performing good deeds. But recent research has suggested otherwise: in *A Cooperative Species* (2011), US economists Samuel Bowles and Herbert Gintis suggest that it is part of our nature to be cooperative. Their argument is that we act altruistically not because that will benefit us personally, directly or indirectly, in the short or long run, but because humans are programmed to act that way. Where is the evidence for this? Just take a look at the kind of people we are. We are members of a species that relies on cooperation, tolerance, altruism, harmony and acts of grace for its very survival.

Unfortunately, that is not the whole truth about us. We humans are also capable of behaving in ways that contradict each of those admirable qualities. We go to war over territorial disputes or, even more bizarrely, over conflicting religious beliefs; we lie, cheat and compete ruthlessly with each other; we lose our temper; we commit acts of violence and abuse, even against children; we take advantage of our fellows; we fail to keep our promises; and we often fall short of the ideals we claim to espouse. In other words, we're selfish by nature, as well as selfless; we're competitive as well as cooperative; we're flawed.

So another truth about us is that we are all born with the capacity for goodness and evil within us. We are all at war within ourselves: many of the desires that drive us are in competition or even conflict with each other. We want to maintain loving relationships, but we often let our desire for control interfere with them. We want to cling to our deeply held values and beliefs, but we sometimes jettison them in response to our aspiration to belong to a particular group or tribe with a different set of beliefs and values.

'Do you really believe all that dogma?' a friend of mine once asked someone who had recently converted to Roman Catholicism.

'Oh, I don't worry too much about all that', they replied. 'I just love being part of the institution. It's like a great big family, as well as the most powerful tribe on earth.'

The question my friend really meant to ask was, *How could you give up so much of what you previously believed in order to become a Catholic?* Perhaps the answer would have been the same.

We sometimes want to be good, and we sometimes want to be bad. As a species we have shown ourselves capable of murder, rape and pillage as well as startlingly selfless acts of charity. Our racial, religious and cultural prejudices can overwhelm what Abraham Lincoln described as the 'better angels of our nature' and lead us into hideous expressions of intolerance, injustice and hatred, spiralling all the way down to war and genocide. Yet we can overcome those prejudices and learn to love and care for those who have utterly different religious or cultural perspectives from our own.

Why, then, do some people seem inherently bad? Given that the capacity to act badly is within us all, it takes only a particular set of circumstances to bring out the worst in us: a tough, brutal childhood; formative years spent in a state of perpetual fear of persecution or humiliation; a level of disadvantage and deprivation that leads to behaviour designed to ensure survival, regardless of its other consequences. All the way from stealing a loaf of bread to avoid starvation to killing an intruder who is threatening the lives of your family members: none of us knows how we might behave if the circumstances were challenging enough or how we might have turned out if our upbringing had been different.

We can learn to hate, because the capacity for hatred is within us all. We can learn to nurture prejudice, because the capacity for prejudice is there, too. Put a child in a sufficiently horrifying situation for the formative years of its life and it will be hard to pull it back from the brink of evil. But there is no formula here: plenty of people have risen from the wreckage of unfortunate and damaging childhoods to become worthy citizens and loving companions. It's just that a relentless reinforcement of the dark side of our nature increases the potential for bad people to emerge.

Hitler, Stalin, Pol Pot: the names of notoriously evil leaders roll so easily off the tongue it's easy to forget they could have achieved none of their aims without veritable armies of supporters willing to do their bidding and share their passions, and, of course, to elevate such people to positions of leadership. Equally, we forget that the people we might want to think of as good guys can also commit acts of alarming recklessness and barbarity. (We don't have to go back as far as the Crusades: who would dare say, now, that the 2003 invasion of Iraq by Western allies was morally good?) Most good people do bad things. Most bad people do good things, too. That doesn't excuse their crimes or misdemeanours: it simply reminds us that a thoroughly bad person is hard to find, and when we speak of someone as 'the embodiment of evil' we are almost certainly oversimplifying. Some forms of madness, such as megalomania and paranoia, can distort a person's view of the world so that any propensity towards goodness is stifled. When that happens, terrible deeds may follow, but in time the consequences are always bad for the perpetrator. In our day-to-day existence, the bad behaviour of other people might disappoint us, but it should not astonish us, since we know that we, too, have the capacity to act badly.

'Charity begins at home'

Proverbs are often subject to such change in their usage that their original intention can be obscured or entirely lost. 'A rolling stone gathers no moss', for example: half the population thinks that describes shiftless ne'er-do-wells who will never accumulate any wealth; the other half thinks it means that if you keep on the move, you won't atrophy or decay by becoming clogged with moss. (If you're interested in which version is historically correct, it's the first. 'Moss' was once slang for 'money', rather as 'bread' later became.)

'Charity begins at home' is a particularly striking example of the phenomenon of meanings being tailored to suit ourselves. Today, when quoting this proverb, most people mean that we should first look after our own – our families, our inner circle – before extending our charity further afield. That's a very convenient and self-serving reinterpretation that entirely misses the point of the original. Ponder the essential idea of 'the good life' for a moment; think about the strands of ancient wisdom that have been woven into the moral fabric of our society. Could 'charity begins at home' ever really have meant that we should look after ourselves first, and only then think about responding to other people's needs?

The origin of the proverb (which, like many others, is biblical) suggests a quite different interpretation. In the King James translation, the writer is urging that 'children should learn first to show piety at home'. Don't get too hung up on that word 'piety':

newer translations use different words, and in any case the proverb that sprang from this idea connects piety to the broader and more secular notion of charity. So the original intention of 'charity begins at home' was to remind us that the lessons of charity – how to be kind, generous, respectful and compassionate towards others – need to be learnt at home, while we are young.

No one needs to be told they have a responsibility to care for their own. That comes naturally to most, and we don't need to harness the wisdom of the ages in support of such an obvious proposition. What we *do* need, as children, is for someone to nurture our altruism, to teach us from an early age to take other people's rights, needs and wellbeing into account. We need to be taught from the very beginning how to cooperate rather than compete.

In other words, our most civilising impulses need to be encouraged when we're young: if it doesn't happen at home, it might never happen at all.

The common good

The history of the human race tells us that communities survive when the cooperative aspects of our nature prevail. Having evolved as social creatures who typically thrive in familial and other communal groupings (isolates and hermits clearly being the exceptions), we are born to relate to each other and to foster communities by acknowledging and responding to each other's needs. You could still argue that there's a benefit for each of us in maintaining our communal way of life by serving the common good, but Bowles and Gintis suggest that this has become such a well-established tendency in human behaviour, it may be being transmitted both genetically and culturally. In fact, we don't need to know whether it is being transmitted genetically: cultural transmission is powerful enough on its own.

Writing in the online journal *New Matilda* in 2012, Australian economist Ian McAuley described a revealing case of altruistic citizenship drawn from Michael Sandel's book *What Money Can't Buy: The moral limits of markets* (2012). When the Swiss government announced the site for a nuclear-waste storage facility near the village of Wolfenschiessen, 51 per cent of local citizens supported the idea. Given Switzerland's reliance on nuclear energy, they acknowledged that they should accept their share of responsibility for dealing with the waste. Because the result of the plebiscite on the issue was so close, the government then offered residents a substantial cash incentive (almost nine thousand dollars) in the hope of increasing the level of support. To the surprise of no one who understands the deeply embedded nature of altruism, support for the proposal collapsed, with only 25 per cent of the citizens subsequently in favour. As McAuley wrote, 'Politicians may have been surprised, but behavioural economists weren't. What had been a duty, a social obligation, became just another "what's in it for me?" market transaction, devaluing the villagers' sense of citizenship'.

We shouldn't be surprised when individuals are sometimes overwhelmed by uglier motivations or when the very instincts that lead us to form a cohesive community flip over into hostility towards an out-group. But nor should we be surprised when we show ourselves capable of harmonious and even charitable cooperation.

Michael and the vomiting baby

Everything seems to be against Michael as he stands in the crowd of bleary-eyed people milling around the baggage carousel at Heathrow. After such a long flight (Brisbane–Singapore, Singapore–London, twenty-four hours all up), he is in no mood for complications that might stand in the way of his schedule. A meeting at nine, lunch with the managing director, another meeting at the Dagenham plant at four. It is now well after six-thirty, and he barely has time for breakfast, a shower and half an hour on his back before that first meeting.

He knew the schedule for this trip was madness. His wife knew it was madness and said so. His PA knew it was madness but restrained herself from saying it out loud. She spoke more discreetly of the need to schedule a buffer day while he was here. He said he might do that next time.

He's done trips as quick as this on several previous occasions. He's done worse than this – he once flew from Brisbane to London for an all-day meeting and got straight back on the plane that night to fly home. He felt . . . what? Exhausted, of course, but also strangely elated. Important: that's how he mainly felt, though he wouldn't admit it to anyone. He often feels important, and that is a good, good feeling. At the centre of things. In demand.

His doctor has warned him about the hazards of his lifestyle and insisted on a stress test and a series of other examinations. The results clearly disappointed the doctor, who was hoping for evidence to back up his warnings. But all the tests proved that Michael is as strong as an ox, apparently thriving on this way of life. He still has a problem with asthma and psoriasis, and his reflux is getting worse, but his heart is in excellent shape and his general fitness is good. He could afford to lose a few kilos, but that isn't urgent. 'Badge of rank, that gut of yours', one of his colleagues, similarly overweight, is fond of saying.

The only downside of all this scooting back and forth to London is its impact on his marriage. Jenny is tolerant, and she's busy with her own life. But they both know there's strain at the centre where real intimacy should be. They don't discuss it.

The crowd at the carousel is dwindling and there is still no bag. Michael looks at his watch. Almost seven o'clock. He has his briefcase with him and could just about manage the day's work with that. But his spare suit, toiletries, clean shirts and underwear are in the bag, along with some papers he'll need later in the week.

And then his bag appears, just before the carousel stops. *I paid good money for this business class fare, and I'm bottom of the luggage pile*, he thinks with irritation (not actually having paid for the ticket himself: it's the principle of the thing).

Out to the cab rank. More trouble: an accident of some kind. A mother, distraught, with two young children, one screaming in her arms and the other sobbing beside her, clutching her mother's skirt. A small, battered bag burst open on the footpath and a policewoman taking particulars. Michael stands a discreet distance away, not wanting to get involved yet unable to ignore this woman's obvious distress. The line of cabs is moving steadily, soaking up the queue.

The policewoman shakes her head, pats the woman on the shoulder and walks away.

Michael steps forwards. 'Is she getting you some help? Is everything all right?'

The woman turns to him and looks him full in the face, silent tears streaming down her cheeks. She is in despair.

Michael bends down and begins to gather up the loose clothes, shoes and baby items, and stuffs them back into the tiny bag. One of the catches seems to be damaged and the lid won't close properly. Impulsively, he slips his belt from his trousers and wraps it around the bag to hold it closed. The belt is only decorative anyway; his expanding girth is well able to hold his trousers up. Another, larger suitcase seems to be intact.

'Where are you going? Can I drop you off somewhere in my cab?' He hears himself saying it before he has decided what to say.

'I'm afraid my handbag was stolen. Ripped off my shoulder, somehow. I thought I had hold of it. They must have cut the strap. Two young men. They were gone before I'd realised what had happened. No one else saw anything. Everything was in the bag – cash, cards, passports. And my mobile, of course.'

'Where are you going?'

'To my sister's in Norwich. I'm to call her and she'll explain about where to catch the train. We've never been here before; things have rather fallen apart. That broken bag is kind of symbolic, I'm afraid.' She manages a smile.

'Did the thief do that, too?'

'No, I did it all by myself. I dropped it trying to stop Sam from running onto the road.'

'Is that policewoman getting you any help?'

'I'm not sure, really. I was a bit distracted. But I think she said there is somewhere I can go for assistance. Some travellers' aid type of thing, I assume. She was called away to something that was obviously more urgent than another boring old bag snatch.'

Michael looks dubiously about him. They are the last in the queue. One final cab is waiting. 'Come with me', he says, putting the woman's luggage in the boot of the cab with his own. 'You can come to my hotel to get cleaned up and call your sister from there.'

Michael has never much liked children, and he and Jenny long ago decided not to have any of their own. Now this woman is appealing to him to hold the baby while she straps the toddler into the back seat of the cab. He takes the child from her and holds it rather awkwardly while the woman settles herself beside her daughter and fastens her own seatbelt. The baby chooses this moment to regurgitate some warm milk, which Michael can feel seeping through his shirt.

When the woman is settled, she reaches out for the baby and notices the stain on Michael's shirt and tie. 'Oh, I'm so sorry. They know how to time it, don't they?'

Michael hands her the baby, grins reassuringly and climbs into the front seat. As they drive towards London, the conversation is exclusively between the woman and her daughter. No personal details are exchanged between Michael and the woman: they are all from Brisbane, which seems like a sufficient bond. Later, he hears her announce herself on the hotel phone to her sister as 'Suze'. The baby's name is Josh and he remembers the toddler is Sam, a girl. He makes no attempt at conversation with Sam, nor she with him, though when they reach the hotel, she spends a lot of time staring silently at him.

The hotel finds a strap for the broken suitcase, and Michael, with the baby's vomit roughly sponged off his shirt and tie, takes them in another cab to Victoria Station, where he buys their tickets and puts them on the train to Norwich. He gives Suze a few pounds to see her through the journey.

He returns to his hotel, strips and showers, changes into fresh clothes and flops onto the bed, with ten minutes to spare and still no breakfast. He sends Jenny a text message, knowing she'll be asleep. He tells no one of the incident until the following day, when he confides to one of his English colleagues that he obtained the phone number of Suze's sister from the hotel records and had been unsuccessfully trying to call her, to make sure everything turned out okay.

His colleague looks at him as if he's mad. 'What were you thinking of? That could all have turned very nasty.'

'I don't think I was thinking at all. You'd have done the same if you'd been there.'

His colleague looks sceptical. 'You some kind of saint, Michael?'

Michael is not some kind of saint. He is actually pretty typical of humans when they know someone needs help and there's no one else around to offer it. His assistance to that young mother in distress might seem a rather noble example of human nature, but the psychology is the same whenever we act from a charitable impulse that overrides our self-interest. Of course, Michael would rather have had breakfast and a more relaxed start to his busy day, just as you might prefer not to jump off a jetty fully clothed to rescue a swimmer in distress, but you'd do it without a second thought. People who have actually been in such situations typically say, *Anyone would have done it*, and they're right. That's the kind of people we are.

I was on a train in Paris and I left my mobile phone on the seat. When I realised what I'd done, I thought, *Oh no – that's the end of that*. But I was wrong. A businessman picked it up, rang one of the programmed numbers in it, which happened to be my sister-in-law who lives in Scotland. He explained who he was and what had happened, and he

> found out from her where I was staying. He dropped the phone in at the reception desk at my hotel – didn't even wait for me to come down and thank him.

As a species, we're rather good at altruism. It's certainly not an activity confined to the eccentric fringe; in fact, it's the cornerstone of any civilised society and the foundation of any coherent moral code. In a way, it's expected of us: *failing* to help someone who needs help is the more peculiar response. Notice how instinctively appalled we are when we hear stories reported in the media about people's failure to realise a neighbour had died or the indifference of bystanders to someone in distress in a city street. We're appalled because we know that's not us at our best – it's not even us acting normally. Such events make the news precisely because they are exceptional. Perhaps it's the knowledge that altruism is part of our nobler nature that makes us disinclined to crow about it, though some branches of the modern philanthropy movement are putting that attractive tendency at risk by suggesting that if you do good you should make sure everyone else knows it.

It might not be fair to say that altruism ceases to be altruism if you brag about it, or that philanthropy ceases to be philanthropy if it's publicly acknowledged; after all, the beneficiaries of your generosity still benefit. But if Michael had called people's attention to the way he had helped that woman and her children, the focus would have shifted to him as hero; and wouldn't it then be arguable whether his action should count as compassion or kindness at all? If I seek praise or recognition for a charitable action, is it still pure charity or has it also become a vehicle for personal aggrandisement?

Professional fundraisers and the people who devise clever schemes to encourage rich people to give more to charity would reject my argument. They would think that philanthropy should be as public as possible, to encourage other potential donors to follow suit. And perhaps it does work like that. Perhaps you *can* have your cake and eat it: make piles of money by any means you like, give big licks of it away, benefit the poor or the disadvantaged, get tax breaks, enjoy the potent combination of a private thrill *and* attract some public recognition for your gesture. Giving a million dollars to a charitable enterprise is a wonderful thing, no doubt; but it's slightly less wonderful, considered purely from the point of view of altruism, if you'd hardly miss it or if it's as much about the benefit to your ego and reputation as the benefit to the recipient.

Many people, rich and semi-rich, report a warm inner glow from making grand charitable gestures. Indeed, that's often part of the pitch: *This will make you feel good about yourself!* But isn't that a challenge to the very notion of kindness, charity and compassion?

There are other ways to praise a life

When we reflect with satisfaction on our own life or admire something about the lives of others, we don't always talk in terms of goodness. Many labels are popularly attached to lives that may seem, in some way, to be worthy of praise or admiration without necessarily contributing to the common good. Any of these admirable lives might also happen to be good lives, but they might not. Only the people who live them could tell you that.

A full life

Sounds attractive. Sounds worthwhile. No wasted time here. No meandering. No loose ends. These are the people who, in addition to holding down a job and raising a family, belong to so many organisations, sit on so many committees and seem to achieve so much in a single day that their friends and colleagues can only marvel: *How do they fit it all in?* Rather annoyingly, such people also manage to take thrilling vacations during which so many activities are packed in to the tight schedule that lesser mortals are left gasping. *Don't waste a minute!* is their rule of life. *Life is for living!* is another of their favourite aphorisms, as if 'living' can only be equated with constant activity.

Being around people like this can be exhausting, but it's hard not to be impressed by their energy and pace. These are the people who led the trend towards greeting each other by asking, *How are you – busy?* as if busyness should be our default position, the only acceptable sign of a life being well lived.

In the rush to live life to the full, it's easy to lose sight of the point of all this activity, let alone know whether it's contributing to the common good. Incessant activity has always been an effective strategy for avoiding mindful reflection: as long as we keep running, we don't have to stop and ask ourselves, *Why?* or, *Who is this for?* Painful as it can be to admit, an overly busy life – rushing here, rushing there – can be a highly effective insulation from engagement with the very people who may need you to stop rushing, listen to them and take them seriously enough to spend time with them.

A charmed life

Wouldn't it be fun to live one of these? Everything clicking into place for us. Forever falling on our feet. Being in the right place at the right time. Meeting just the right person at just the right stage of your life, falling in love and sticking together in a storybook marriage. (I was about to say, *through thick and thin*, but in a charmed life there's no place for thin.) Being born into a family that gives us wealth, perhaps, or sufficient status to guarantee access to a network of fruitful contacts. Or receiving favourable treatment for no reason other than having been born with a beautiful face. Finding you have the knack of enchanting people.

A charmed life is a life largely dependent on accidental factors – genetics, inheritance, lucky timing – that have propelled us into a place of comfort, prosperity and perhaps even power. Plenty of people live a charmed life, and some of them live the good life as well, recognising their advantage as a matter of luck rather than entitlement and still managing to live for others. But a charmed life is not the most sympathetic environment for virtue to blossom.

A productive life

A life devoted to the fulfilment of our potential to make things or make things happen. A life of achievement. Output. A life rich with accomplishment and gratification. Nothing to criticise there, surely, and plenty to admire.

But being productive says nothing about being virtuous or leading a life characterised by goodness. It's perfectly possible to lead a productive life that brings you great personal satisfaction, and perhaps even great fame and wealth, but heaps misery upon those around you. Plenty of creative people, including artists, scientists and philosophers, as well as high-flyers in business and the professions, have lived like that: wonderfully productive output, huge personal rewards and generous public recognition, but intensely frustrating, infuriating or destructive to those close to them, their personal relationships sacrificed on the altar of productivity.

Of course, some highly productive people happen to lead wonderfully virtuous lives as well – lives characterised by kindness, generosity and compassion. But there's no necessary connection between the two.

A fortunate life

A book with that title, published in 1981, has become something of an Australian classic. It's the autobiography of Albert Facey, and the title is often regarded as ironic, since so much of Facey's life was dogged by hardship and misadventure. He was itinerant, illiterate and in many ways unfortunate, yet his tale of a simple man's struggle to overcome massive disadvantage, from the harsh Australian outback to the military landing at Gallipoli, has inspired many.

It's a well-known theme in literature and in life: apparent disadvantage eventually comes to be recognised as advantage, because it throws up challenges which, when met, stiffen the sinews and strengthen the character. So an unfortunate life might actually lead to the development of a nobler nature, a more compassionate attitude and a greater willingness to offer a helping hand to those in need: all signs of a good life. But some people who overcome terrible adversity might also be embittered by the experience and decide to exploit the system that disadvantaged them: turn to a life of crime, develop a victim mentality, become ruthlessly self-serving. Positive consequences from hardship and struggle are not guaranteed.

When we use the term 'a fortunate life' colloquially, we sometimes mean a lucky life, perhaps getting a break at some point or enjoying a run of luck that leads on to success, if not fame and fortune. Such lives may well be thrilling to live, at least in retrospect, but whether they are also good is a separate question entirely. Fame and fortune are not to be equated with goodness, and neither is a stroke of luck, no matter how enjoyable it is to be on the receiving end. We congratulate lottery winners as if they've done something praiseworthy, but they, and we, know that luck is unrelated to good behaviour. If it's lucky, it is by definition not earned or deserved; nor is it an expression of any virtuous impulse.

An authentic life

'Authenticity' has become the buzzword of the early twenty-first century, right up there with 'self-esteem', as if to be authentic is the best thing you can possibly be. You don't have to be loving, kind, generous, compassionate, tolerant or respectful of others: authenticity is the thing!

Obviously, being inauthentic – insincere, artificial, deceitful – is usually undesirable: no one likes a phoney. But a bit of inauthenticity might occasionally seem like a good idea. If you're interested in the common good and in promoting the wellbeing of others, it's not always appropriate to match your behaviour to your mood: reining in your grumpiness, for instance, out of respect for other people, will sometimes be a better plan than letting it all hang out. (Is self-control inauthentic, then? Are courtesy and good manners inauthentic? Yes, sometimes; but they are also the oil that lubricates our social machinery.)

Authenticity guarantees nothing about goodness. By 'authentic' perhaps we mean a life lived in accordance with a recognisable set of values, a life in which people can claim to have been true to themselves, a life in which, as the British writer E. M. Forster put it, 'the passion and the prose connect'. And that sounds rather attractive, at least as a starting point. But I can be true to many values that don't benefit anyone but me. I can adhere absolutely to the pleasure principle, making sure everything I do is calculated to bring me the maximum possible advantage. That's authentic. I can be gripped by blind ambition and act in ways that serve that ambition. That's authentic, too; it might be ruthlessly self-serving, but it's authentic. Plenty of criminals, to say nothing of historical ogres like Hitler and Stalin, could say their lives were consistent with their values and beliefs. Except in the narrow sense of being true to some aspect of my nature, my authenticity guarantees nothing about the goodness of my life.

An exciting life

Sounds like fun, doesn't it? A life lived at a fast pace. A life of adventure, mountain-climbing, perhaps, or on the trading floor, on the stage or screen, on the sporting field or at the frontier of biotechnology. We all need excitement in our lives; that's why some people go on adventure holidays, take up extreme sports or behave recklessly with alcohol, sex or cars. Some take their excitement more vicariously, at the movies, online or curled up with a good book. But everyone needs to feel that there's something exciting to look forward to: the birth of a baby, a family wedding, a party, a vacation, a special night out, a significant purchase, a promotion at work, the closing of a deal, the completion of a project or even an action-packed weekend.

We tend to admire people who can claim to have had an exciting life. We might even envy them. We're certainly inclined to wonder whether they have had a more thrilling life than we have. Yet 'exciting', like all these other labels, implies nothing about goodness. At its extreme, an exciting life may simply be a sign of a person trapped in an uncontrollable addiction to the adrenalin buzz.

There are people who do important work in dangerous places as journalists, doctors, diplomats or peacekeepers, and who display an extraordinary ability to cope with the inherent stress of such situations. But whether they are leading the good life actually has nothing whatever to do with the level of excitement, danger or stress involved. You can live badly in those situations, by acting selfishly, insensitively or exploitatively; or you can live well, as you can in any situation, by acting with kindness and compassion. The level of excitement might add to the glamour of your life, but it will say nothing about its goodness.

A blameless life

This is generally meant as praise, but doesn't it sound rather dull? It sounds like a life with no risk, no edge, no real purpose beyond obedience to the dictates of the law and conscience. *He led a blameless life* sounds unutterably bland, even rather sad. In any case, it's unlikely to be true. Who among us can say we could never be blamed for anything? Never a cross or hurtful word? Never a vengeful thought? Never a selfish act? Never a failure to recognise and respond to someone's need for help? Never a refusal to listen attentively and sympathetically to someone who's taking too long to say something? No, 'blameless' sounds rather suspect to me. Personally, I prefer passionate, red-blooded humans who err occasionally and need a bit of forgiveness.

A passionate life

We admire passion in artists, athletes, pioneers, inventors, explorers, innovators and activists. People who are restless, driven, enthusiastic and highly motivated. People who want to get on with it, change the world, overturn convention. Iconoclasts. People who manage to see things in a new and exciting way, to recognise opportunities the rest of us have overlooked. We love to see passion in our children. We admire its power to stimulate them and to drive out apathy. We watch eagerly to see if their passion will translate into a life that will satisfy them and perhaps inspire others. What a dull place the world would be without passion! We associate it with creativity, visionary leadership, revolution, leaps of progress, radical reform.

Whether passionate people live a good life is a question only they can answer, since it is bound up with private and personal motivations. Some people channel their passion into righting society's wrongs, campaigning for peace and justice or responding to the needs of the poor, the sick, the disadvantaged or the marginalised. Some devote their passion to the raising of children, as parents, teachers or carers. Some pour their passion into charitable work in their local community. Some create beautiful works of art or performance that inspire, entertain, amuse or unsettle us. All are clearly contributors to the common good. Others use their passion in finding new ways to make lots of money, or indulging themselves in ways that give them intense pleasure and satisfaction. In those cases, the good life is still a possibility, even if it isn't the focus of those passions. How they relate to those around them, especially to those who need their love and support, is, as always, the acid test of goodness.

A creative life

Lives that are passionate and productive are often associated with creativity, but 'creative' is a tricky adjective. It is sometimes clearly intended to imply permission to live recklessly, behave badly or be outrageous, impatient, rude or arrogant, as though all will be forgiven in the name of Art. (We're less forgiving in the case of creative accounting.) While it's true that many painters, composers, writers, poets and creative people in fields other than the arts have acquired a reputation for treating people shabbily, others have managed to maintain stable and loving relationships and to treat people with respect while still producing remarkable work.

In his great satirical essay 'The Harm That Good Men Do', the British philosopher and anti-nuclear campaigner Bertrand Russell wrote of the poet Wordsworth:

> In his youth he sympathised with the French Revolution, went to France, wrote good poetry, and had a natural daughter. At this period he was a 'bad' man. Then he became 'good', abandoned his daughter, adopted correct principles, and wrote bad poetry . . . It is difficult to think of any instance of a poet who was 'good' when he was writing good poetry.

It all depends what you mean by 'good' (as applied to both poets and poetry). Russell presented a whimsical caricature in which 'good' was equated with a person who 'does not drink or smoke, avoids bad language, converses in the presence of men only exactly as he would if there were ladies present, attends church regularly, and holds the correct opinions of all subjects'. By all such criteria, Russell himself was immeasurably bad while he was producing good mathematics and philosophy. Here's another take on it, from Mae West: 'When I'm good, I'm very, very good. But when I'm bad, I'm better'.

The question that always arises in the case of eccentric and antisocial artists is whether their creativity would have been inhibited and their output diminished if they had been kinder and more considerate in their personal and social lives. Would the poems have been as good if the furniture had not been smashed in a drunken, jealous rage? Would the novels have read so well if their author had managed to remain faithful to her spouse? Would the paintings have had the same evocative power if the artist had not beaten his wife senseless and run off with the maid? No one can answer such questions. Some creative people are eccentric to the point of madness; others remain mild mannered, saving their wild creative impulses for the page or the canvas. Some artists appear to have sacrificed their personal lives and perhaps even their sanity to their art; others have turned to the creative life as a way of retaining their sanity in what they see as a crazy world.

Does all this creative output contribute to the common good? In *What Good Are the Arts?* (2006), the Oxford scholar and critic John Carey contends that the arts do not 'improve' us any differently or any more than other forms of entertainment or recreation, including exposure to nature, that give us pleasure. Carey is particularly sceptical about what he regards as the overestimated cultural value of art galleries (as though gazing at pictures is somehow good for us), though he believes literature can contribute to our moral development. There's no doubt that some music, plays, movies, poetry, artworks and novels raise our spirits, inspire us and challenge us to see the world in a new light: we are certainly cultural and emotional beneficiaries in this respect. Creative work, especially writing, can sometimes benefit us in ways that go beyond entertainment or distraction: many people say their lives have been transformed through the reading of particular books.

In such ways, the lives of creative people may radiate goodness. Whether their private lives are good is an entirely separate question, answerable by no one but them. Countless biographies attest to lives of struggle, in which neither a good life nor a good time figures as prominent concerns. It's hard to avoid the conclusion that some of our greatest works of art, music and literature have been the products of tortured souls who lived for their art rather than themselves. But let's not over-romanticise this: some artists might conceivably have been in it for the money.

Charmed, authentic and productive lives are attractive at some level; all seem desirable and in many ways worthwhile. But none is necessarily built on goodness in the richest sense of that term, implying moral value; none is necessarily virtuous, though any of them might be. The good life can be lived – *is* lived – by millions of people whose lives will never attract labels like any on that list. The good life is about something else entirely.

Jack fell down and broke his crown

Returning home from her second visit to the LOL Club, Jill Thurkettle finds Jack slumped on the floor, pale and frightened, unable to speak. She calls an ambulance immediately and, after a night of almost unbearable anxiety, learns that Jack has suffered a stroke. The prognosis is good, they are assured, provided he submits to a strict regimen of rehabilitation, including regular physiotherapy and speech therapy.

Three months later, Jack is back at work part time. His stay in hospital and rehab finally convinced him to go ahead and acquire a dog – not only for his own benefit; it's a dog that can also be used to visit nursing-home patients. At his lowest ebb, he personally experienced the therapeutic effect of interacting with an animal, through a dog that visited the rehab centre, and he saw many other patients similarly comforted, reassured and encouraged by canine affection. Twice a week, he takes his dog to a local nursing home and does the rounds of patients who have been identified by the staff as likely to benefit most. They don't just interact with Horrie (so named by its previous owner because it had such a horrible face as a pup); Jack finds himself increasingly drawn into these encounters.

Horrie also introduces him to a group of dog-owners who congregate in a local park and chat while their animals romp. Jack is amazed by the intimacy of some of these exchanges and by the level of tragedy people from his own suburb are dealing with in their private lives. Already, he and another man from the group have organised themselves to do some simple home maintenance for a single mother, Beth, who, another woman in the group confided to them, is 'struggling a bit'. Until they visit her home and share a cup of tea with her, they have no real idea what 'a bit' means. It turns out that Beth's husband and younger son were both killed in a car crash, and she and her surviving seven-year-old are still dazed by the loss.

Jack has never imagined himself as a volunteer, never wanted to join a service club, never had much interest in community affairs. Horrie has changed all that. As he gets to know the dog-walkers better, Jack learns that two of the women in the group routinely look after each other's pre-schoolers, to allow visits to elderly relatives, shopping trips, medical appointments and the like: one has a mother with advanced dementia, and the other has a brother who is in and out of hospital with a rare blood disease.

Jill, meanwhile, has become deeply immersed in the life of the LOL Club. She and Jack sometimes marvel at the dark complexity of other people's lives and the relief that can be given through simple friendship and support, and occasional bits of practical help.

Their daughter Sally has been staying with them for another of her wound-licking retreats from a painful relationship. (There's a larger truth: Sally is worried about her father and wants to see, first hand, how he has been coping since the stroke.) She notices both Jack and Jill are more attentive to her, more willing to listen, more interested in her story and less inclined to gloss over the awkward bits or simply urge her to cheer up. They both seem rather busier and livelier than last time she stayed with them. There's a new energy about the place.

In the three months since the stroke, neither Jack nor Jill has initiated any further conversations about the state of their lives. A previously mooted move to an apartment has not been mentioned again, and they have found themselves, just once or twice, explicitly acknowledging how much they value each other and their marriage (though Jill can't yet claim to share Jack's devotion to Horrie). When they are watching TV together one night, Jill falls asleep and her head falls onto Jack's shoulder. He can't remember the last time that happened. (It's usually

Jack who falls asleep.) He sits as still as possible, not wanting to wake her, wanting only to smell her hair and listen to her breathing.

'Good' times often come in heavy disguise

Jack and Jill are not the first people to discover that a crisis – health, financial or otherwise – can precipitate a complete reordering of priorities, the reassessment of a relationship, a determination to enrich time spent with loved ones and to put a little more goodness into their lives.

When I was twenty-eight, I thought the only thing that mattered was my next overseas trip, or possibly getting the 'right' handbag. I cringe now, but I didn't get a reality check until the baby came along, my partner vanished, and I realised this was what my life would be about from now on.

At every point in the life cycle, we are vulnerable to the impact of unexpected events that tear off our mask, shake us out of our complacency and propel us into some serious thinking about what matters. People who have lived through life-changing events can often be heard to say, *Why did it take a crisis to bring us to our senses? We always knew what was important, but we didn't act as if we knew.*

We used to be like strangers in our own street. Didn't even know our neighbours' names. We waved occasionally, coming and going – that was it. All our friends were elsewhere, and we were just marking time here, really, waiting until we could afford to live somewhere better. Then the storm hit, we lost our roof, and everything changed. People were amazing. We discovered we were living in the middle of a real little community and we hadn't even realised it. I never knew such support could come from people who were virtual strangers. They certainly didn't owe us anything. It's very different now, of course. We're part of the place. We could never consider moving from here. Why would we?

5

Do unto others . . .

It takes only a moment's reflection to realise that if you caught the bluebird of happiness and kept it in a cage for your own personal pleasure, it would rapidly become the bluebird of misery and frustration. William Blake captured that idea in his poem 'Eternity':

> He who binds to himself a joy
> Does the wingèd life destroy
> But he who kisses the joy as it flies
> Lives in eternity's sun-rise.

Once we focus on the idea of a good life as being a valuable life, a life that contributes to others' wellbeing, worries about our personal level of contentment or our material prosperity will fade into the background. The good life is not about being smart, rich, famous or sure of yourself. You don't have to be the life of the party to prove you're having a good life. You don't even have to *be* at the party.

It's true that many people who live the good life will experience moments of overflowing happiness. Some will enjoy prosperity, contentment, deep satisfaction in their personal relationships or even fame. Some will have a rip-roarin' good time, at least part of the time. But some won't. And here's the point: none of those pleasant possibilities actually has much to do with whether yours is a good life or not.

The whole idea of a good life will evaporate if we focus on ourselves and what we're getting out of it. In particular, if we allow ourselves to become preoccupied with how we're feeling about our life, whether we're up or down on particular days or whether people are treating us well or badly in a particular situation, we may lose sight of what goodness really is. Self-absorption is not a recognised pathway to goodness, let alone to enlightenment or fulfilment. Of course, if people are consistently treating you badly or if you find yourself persistently depressed, these are warning signs that you may require professional help. But even people in desperate circumstances can still be living the good life.

How could that be? Let your mind drift around the idea of goodness for a moment: goodness and evil, good and bad, right and wrong, doing the decent thing, behaving well, doing good, being good, virtue, kindness, those familiar words of the twenty-third Psalm: 'Surely goodness and mercy shall follow me all the days of my life', good deeds, a good ear, a good person, a good home, the common good.

The more you think about the idea of goodness in this way, and about the proposition put forward in chapter 4 that the good life is a life lived for others, the more you'll be drawn to the conclusion that the good life is, inescapably, an ethical concept. It's about the moral value of a life.

It's not an emotional concept: *How do I feel? Am I enjoying myself?*

It's not an economic concept: *Have I done well in financial terms? Am I reaping my reward for working hard?*

It's not even a time-management concept: *Am I getting the balance right between my work and my personal life? Am I spending too much time glued to my smartphone?*

There's nothing wrong with enjoying yourself, of course, any more than there is anything wrong with prosperity, as long as you haven't achieved your wealth unfairly or dishonestly, or broken the law, or exploited people or diminished anyone else's wellbeing in the process of acquiring it. And the management of your time can certainly be the key to leading a productive life. It's just that those things are not what the good life is about.

The three Rs of morality: recognising, respecting, responding

Morality is based on a very simple principle: it is only when we recognise, respect and respond to each other's rights and needs that it becomes possible for us to live together in relative peace and harmony, minimising the tensions and divisions that arise from social exclusion, unfairness and inequality. At its heart, that's all morality is about: cooperation, mutual respect, a sense of community, a spirit of egalitarianism, taking each other's wellbeing into account, acknowledging each other's point of view.

In practice, it's about the strong supporting the weak, the haves sharing their prosperity with the have-nots, the able offering guidance and support to the less able. Metaphorically speaking, it's about finding ways of bringing everyone with us on the journey, carrying those who can't walk by themselves, giving guidance to those who are lost, throwing an encouraging arm around the shoulders of those who seem bewildered, confused or spent.

Morality doesn't ask questions about whether the poor or needy deserve our support. People who are sick, distressed or disabled in some way don't need to justify their appeal for our help: their situation is its own justification. The mere existence of a need defines our moral duty. Refugees need a home. The disadvantaged need compensation. The marginalised need to be brought back into the fold. The incompetent need our encouragement and good counsel. No question.

Morality takes for granted that we shouldn't break the law (unless the law itself is unjust and needs to be challenged), but it goes further. Morality obliges us to be sensitive to other people's needs even when the law doesn't demand that of us.

Morality can never be a solo performance. You can be comfortable on your own; you can be rich on your own; you can have bright ideas or tinker with inventions on your own; you can sail around the world or cross the Sahara on your own (though if you get into trouble, you might be glad to know other people think your survival matters); you can even be happy on your own. You can lead a blameless, exciting or passionate life on your own, but you can't lead a good life on your own, because morality is about our interactions with each other. It makes no sense to consider the good life in isolation.

Morality is like a blueprint for managing our relationships with those we love and those we don't – especially those we don't, since it's easy to respond well to those we love. In fact, for many philosophers, the real test of our moral worth – our goodness – is how we respond to the needs of total strangers, including those who are quite unlike us socioeconomically, ethnically, culturally or religiously.

Harry's little secret

(If you have a squeamish disposition, please skip the following little story about Harry and his sexual proclivities.)

Harry, aged sixty-four, lives alone. No one, including Harry, is quite sure what went wrong with his marriage, but his wife left him a long time ago. Harry is a good man. Everyone says so. He is a member of his local church and an enthusiastic volunteer at a nearby school where he reads to the children and does some coaching of slow readers. He's kind to strangers. He has a part-time job as an auditor, having retired from full-time accountancy on his sixtieth birthday – a move long planned.

His tastes in reading are broad. He has a fondness for the classics but loves a good detective yarn, as well. He reads the daily newspaper and takes an interest in politics and sport. Harry uses email but is otherwise uninterested in the internet. He has never accessed pornography in his life. He is appalled by the whole idea of porn, actually. Harry is not an exploiter. He is not a sexist, a sadist, a psychopath or a narcissist. He suffers some loneliness, though. Even though he is a respected and even loved figure at his church, he is not a great socialiser. He yearns for some intimacy but finds himself relying on radio and TV for companionship.

Rather to his own surprise, Harry has developed a fondness for fresh chickens from the local supermarket. Not to eat, so much (though he does that, too), but as objects of sexual desire; a fetish. He eyes them off in the supermarket cabinet and is aroused by the very sight of them, knowing the pleasure they can afford him. He allows himself only one a week. Every Saturday night, he takes the chicken out of his refrigerator and, using liberal quantities of personal lubricant, has a form of sexual intercourse with it. The chicken is then returned to the fridge and after Harry returns from church on Sunday morning, he roasts it for lunch. On the rare occasions when he has guests for Sunday lunch, he changes the menu.

In the beginning, Harry occasionally used to wonder if this was wrong in some way, but he couldn't see any harm in it and still can't, except that he is sometimes distracted from his religious devotions by a tingle of anticipation of this ritual. (But then, when he was married, he was sometimes distracted by the thought of his wife's stockinged thigh beside him in church.) He is surprised by this turn of events in his life but regards it as a pleasant and harmless habit that eases his sexual frustration and gives him a secret thrill to look forward to every week.

Disgusting? Revolting? Yes, to some of us; perhaps to most of us. But has Harry done anything wrong? Even if you acknowledge that his actions are not immoral in the normal sense of that word, are you still left with the uneasy, queasy sense that what he has done seems so yucky that you are prepared to make a moral judgement about it?

It's a serious question. Many of our apparently intuitive moral judgements seem to be based more on gut instinct than on moral reasoning. In fact, the eighteenth-century Scottish philosopher

David Hume was of the opinion that moral judgements are rooted in the emotions and wrote in his *Treatise of Human Nature* (1739) that 'reason is, and ought only to be, the slave of the passions'. If Hume were right, then anything we found offensive or aesthetically revolting could be judged as morally wrong. It's easy to agree that we might want to avoid contact with things that strike us as unpleasant or even repugnant, but does that make those things immoral?

> I always think you just know when something's wrong. You feel it. I suppose it's your conscience, or something – and I suppose you get that from how you were brought up. But whatever it is, I don't think you really have to work it out; your gut tells you. I can't think of a single occasion when I ever sat down and really puzzled over whether something was right or wrong. I might have agonised over whether I was going to *do* the wrong thing or not, but I still knew in my heart it was wrong. We always do, don't we?

Perhaps there's not much emotional distinction between our reactions to behaviour that clearly breaks a generally accepted moral code and behaviour that strikes us as being so aesthetically repulsive, it simply *feels* wrong. But to conflate those two seems to be taking a bold and rather risky step. One is about the effects of our actions on others; the other has no impact on anyone else, but is purely about the effects of our actions on our feelings about ourselves: their impact on our self-respect, perhaps. You might be tempted to assume that people who act in ways that erode their own self-respect, people who persist in doing or viewing things they find distasteful, might also be more willing to act in ways that offend others, but you'd be hard pressed to find evidence for that connection. Media depiction of violence is a telling case in point: millions of people habitually watch violent material they find disturbing without ever behaving violently themselves.

Obviously, there's a huge range of individual differences when it comes to deciding what is offensive. Things that might offend me might not offend you. Some creators of offensive material or people who perform offensive acts may have to overcome their own revulsion to go on doing what they're doing; others may not. Harry worried about his little ritual in the beginning, but then he adapted to it and, as time went by, ceased to question it. Indeed, after some initial hesitation, he came to feel that his actions were not only harmless but actually beneficial, adding welcome colour to his private life.

The tale of Harry's sexual adventures with chicken carcasses is an embellished version of a story used in a research project conducted by the US social psychologist Jonathan Haidt, designed to test how people justify the moral judgements they make. His results, reported in *The Happiness Hypothesis* (2006), suggest that Hume's view is still popular: most people who took part in Haidt's study said the chicken man's behaviour was wrong, even though they couldn't quite say why. The yuck factor was so strong that his actions seemed *morally* wrong as well as aesthetically repugnant.

But shouldn't we be able to do better than that? Shouldn't we be able to justify our moral judgements on some more reliable basis than repugnance? It would be the ultimate form of moral subjectivity to say that if something offends my aesthetic sensitivities then it is wrong, and, conversely, to say that if I happen to like it, it's morally okay. What about people who don't share my aesthetic sensitivities? There's an echo here of the moral criterion said to have been adopted by the writer Ernest Hemingway, that if it feels good afterwards, it's right, which, being based on a judgement made after the event, is not much help as a form of moral guidance.

Isn't there an important difference between being merely disgusted and being morally offended? Jean Piaget, a twentieth-century pioneer in the study of the psychological development of children, believed that moral development depends on cognitive development, and that 'moral reasoning' therefore means what it says: it's something we can figure out rather than simply feel. *What will be the effect of this action on other people?* is a question that requires careful thought and sensitive estimation.

So where does this leave the sense of outrage many people feel when confronted by pornography, for example, or on-screen violence, or public nudity? Are they making a moral or an aesthetic judgement? Are they entitled to complain about such things on moral grounds when their reaction is based mainly on feelings of queasiness, disapproval, embarrassment or a vague sense of uneasiness? Haidt concludes that, however much we might dress them up in fine words, most moral judgements *are* simply rationalisations of our gut feelings. If that were the case, then the moral foundation of the good life is easy to define: to take a leaf out of Hemingway's book, the good life would be a life that made you feel good. And that's a slippery slope if ever I saw one: next thing, we'd be adopting personal pleasure as the measure of the good life, and where would that end?

Harry's behaviour might strike you as aesthetically repugnant, but think very carefully before you judge it to be morally wrong as well. It mightn't seem a nice thing to do (though it's only slightly different from other forms of masturbation that most people wouldn't find repugnant), and you may feel that Harry is a somewhat disturbed person who could possibly benefit from some psychotherapeutic investigation of his sexual preferences. You might want to take Harry aside and remind him of the joys of more conventional intimacies with a responsive partner. But, on our strict societal definition of morality, Harry is doing nothing wrong. He's not even doing it in public; we've only heard about it and perhaps tried to visualise him doing it.

What about the morality of smoking tobacco, then, another activity many people find aesthetically repugnant? We used to think there was nothing wrong with smoking per se; then we discovered it was a health hazard for the smoker and realised it was a foolish thing to do if you were interested in a long and healthy life. But it wasn't a moral issue. Then we learnt about passive smoking and realised it was indeed a moral issue, because *my* smoking could affect *your* health as well as my own.

> My dad smoked like a chimney all his life. We all hated the smell of it, and our mum hated him smoking in the house, but he always said, 'It's a free world'. Well, it was a free world for him, but what about us? My sister and I have both had problems with asthma that the doctor thinks are due to all that smoke when we were little. Dad died of cancer years ago – long before anyone had even heard of passive smoking. I don't mind people drinking themselves to death as long as they don't get behind the wheel of a car, but smoking can affect everybody around you.

Some health professionals would now go further and say that even smoking in isolation is a moral issue, because smoking contributes to many diseases that ultimately place strain on the health system and therefore on the public purse. And that certainly erodes the common good.

To take a more harrowing example, what about the morality of suicide? The argument in favour of suicide is usually based on the idea that it is up to each individual, and no one else, to decide whether to end their life. In fact, the French existentialist writer Albert Camus regarded the question of whether or not to end our lives as central: a perpetual agenda item, the ever-present option. Defenders of suicide see it as a personal, private decision that affects only the perpetrator. It certainly couldn't be a crime, because there's no one left to charge once the deed has been committed.

Suicide can indeed be regarded as a moral issue, however, as long as there are consequences for other people: family and friends who might be adversely affected by the suicide, for instance; children who might be traumatised; partners who might be devastated. But a person without friends or family or, conversely, a person whose friends and family support their wish to die may justifiably feel they can take their own life without moral consequences, since the moral issue is always about the impact of our actions on other people.

The public and private faces of virtue

That strict definition of morality still leaves many people feeling vaguely uneasy, as if there must be more to it than that. It doesn't seem to answer all our questions about goodness, and it doesn't settle the question of why so many people feel morally outraged by Harry's behaviour. If it's not wrong in terms of its effect on others, why do those people still want to describe it as wrong?

We can sometimes get more insight into a moral dilemma by asking a second, more introspective, perhaps more spiritual question: *Is this action consistent with my personal ideals, my sense of my own inherent goodness – my integrity, my self-respect – regardless of its effects on others?* This question is often answered in the gut rather than in any calculation of consequences: *This doesn't feel like the right thing for me to be doing.*

In *The Sovereignty of the Good* (1971), Iris Murdoch strongly advocated the two-question approach to moral decision making. She thought we could discern an ideal goodness by asking not only the classic utilitarian question about consequences for others (*Will this action cause more good than harm to others?*) but also the private virtue question (*Is this action in harmony with my ideal of virtuous behaviour?*).

Not all virtues are private, of course. Some of the qualities we typically describe as virtues – courage, justice, benevolence, fidelity, politeness, generosity, compassion, mercy, gratitude, tolerance, kindness, love – make no sense unless they are expressed in actions that benefit other people. But some virtues are more inward in their orientation: frugality, fortitude, prudence, restraint, self-discipline, simplicity. Some of those private virtues also seem to be about the common good; prudence and frugality, for instance, may help to husband the world's scarce resources with benefits flowing to us all. But as a group they are primarily about people's private sense of their own integrity.

Obviously, there is some overlap between these two questions about out-there morality and in-here virtue, and, in any case, not everyone is comfortable with the idea of private virtue. The British philosopher Bertrand Russell, for example, was sceptical of it: he believed goodness could be discerned only in our behaviour, not in our thoughts or motives. And in *The Language of Morals* (1952), the British ethicist R. M. Hare wrote, 'If we were to ask of a person "What are his moral principles?" the way in which we could be most sure of a true answer would be by studying what he *did*'.

Yet Harry's case illustrates why, for many people, the question about consequences or even the simple question about the behaviour itself doesn't seem comprehensive enough to settle the matter. They still want to know what's going on inside Harry's head. So let's see whether asking the question about private virtue might help. If you include restraint and self-discipline in the list of private virtues, as I have done, that may explain why so many people feel Harry's behaviour is wrong: perhaps they think such behaviour flies in the face of these commonly accepted ideals (though who knows how commonly accepted they are?) and that it is wrong for Harry not to rein in his chicken-fed impulses.

But even if Harry's behaviour offends your sense of what is virtuous, you might still be hard pressed to say it is doing more harm than good, even for Harry. Who knows what positive effects this little ritual might be having on his mental health and social disposition? Who knows whether it has any negative impact on his sense of his own integrity? After all, this is not child pornography we're talking about. Who, apart from Harry, knows what Harry's gut is telling him? In this case, private really does mean private.

Here's something most of us can agree on (or can we?)

Ask people the secret of a civilised society and most will tell you it's about people treating each other respectfully, courteously, fairly and kindly in the expectation that they will be treated well in return. Some will go further and say we should treat other people well regardless of how we are treated in return, simply because that's the right way to live. In either case, it's about the members of a community learning how to live harmoniously, cooperatively and in ways that respect each other's rights and needs and promote each other's wellbeing. That doesn't mean we all live like that, but we do seem to intuitively recognise it as the ideal.

(This is not a universal consensus, of course; there is a vocal minority that tries to adapt a biological principle to society by clinging to the primitive idea that it's all about survival of the fittest: each of us should therefore unflinchingly obey the dictates of self-interest. But the prevailing view in any civil society is more compassionate than that; more generous and more tolerant of weakness.)

If you ask people what being good entails, you'll receive a similarly consistent response. Apart from the idea of obedience to the law, people will typically talk about honesty, kindness, fairness, treating other people with respect, responding to the needs of the disadvantaged and never taking advantage of others. Again, we don't always do it, but we acknowledge it as the ideal.

It seems so obvious, doesn't it? We don't need philosophers, social theorists or religious leaders to explain it to us. We can discover the secret by simply giving it a moment's honest thought. Most people, without much hesitation, would come up with some version of the Golden Rule: do unto others as you would have others do unto you, or, in less archaic language, treat other people the way you would like to be treated. Some people find the principle easier to grasp if it is turned around to emphasise the negative – don't treat other people in a way you would not like to be treated – a variation sometimes referred to as the Silver Rule.

Some reflective thinking may lead us to formulate the rule for ourselves, but there's ample guidance on offer from virtually every religious and ethical tradition in human history. Versions of the Golden Rule appear in ancient Egypt, ancient China and ancient

Greece, and in religious traditions ranging from Confucianism, Taoism, Hinduism and Zoroastrianism to the three Abrahamic faiths – Judaism, Christianity and Islam – and newer religions such as Baha'i. You'll also encounter it in non-theistic religions like Buddhism, in Scientology and in every form of humanism.

No one owns the idea. This is not a principle that needs a god to ordain it or a religion to enshrine it: it is absolutely integral to any systematic attempt to work out how humans might best live together in peace and harmony. Six centuries before the Christian era, the ancient Greek philosopher Pittacus put it like this: 'Do not to your neighbour what you would take ill from him'. Socrates, quoted in Plato's *Crito*, went one step further: 'One should never . . . mistreat any man, no matter how one has been mistreated by him'. 'Never impose on others what you would not choose for yourself', said Confucius. In the Hindu tradition, the same idea appears in *The Mahabharata, Book 13*: 'One should never do that to another which one regards as injurious to one's own self. This is, in brief, the rule of dharma. All other behaviour is due to selfish desires'. The Old Testament book of Leviticus renders it as 'Love your neighbour as yourself', a sentiment echoed several times in the New Testament, most explicitly in the gospels of Matthew and Luke, and this same rule underpins the most modern attempts to define universal human rights.

If it's so easy to articulate and so widely acknowledged as a good idea, why is the Golden Rule so hard to put into practice? Is the standard it imposes on us too strict to encourage daily, routine implementation? Or is the Golden Rule's great competitor, the unwritten Law of Reciprocity, so powerful in human affairs that we can't resist it? *You scratch my back and I'll scratch yours. You listen to me and only then will I listen to you. You treat me badly and I'll treat you badly. You damage my reputation and I'll damage yours.*

The seductive appeal of revenge

As those examples suggest, the Law of Reciprocity often operates darkly and even malevolently. It drives the spirit of revenge, for example. Why wouldn't I want to vent my anger, my outrage, at the person who has wronged or offended me? And why wouldn't I want to give as good as I get? The Jewish teaching 'an eye for an eye and a tooth for a tooth' has instinctive, immediate appeal to us. It seems just. It seems fair. It seems natural. We tend to interpret it as permission for revenge, but in fact it was originally intended to convey an altogether different idea: that any punishment should precisely fit the crime – an eye, and no more than an eye, for an eye. It was a warning against over-reaction.

The ability to resist the urge for revenge is the acid test of our commitment to the Golden Rule. Revenge is the ultimate perversion of the rule: it amounts to saying, *I will treat you the way you've treated me* – the opposite of treating you in the way I myself would like to be treated. Revenge drags us inexorably down to the level of the person who has wronged or offended us. We are responding to bad behaviour with bad behaviour. That's one of the strongest arguments against the death penalty: to kill someone as punishment for their brutality simply legitimises brutality and makes brutes of everyone involved.

Oh, it feels great. What a surge of pleasure we get from exacting our revenge on someone. *He deserved that! Look what he did to me! Now we're equal!* And we are equal, in one sense: we've both behaved equally badly. We've corrupted the Golden Rule into a grotesque rephrasing: treat others the way they treat you, even if they have treated you badly.

There are other popular corruptions: treat others the way you think they might treat you, or, even worse, treat others the way you've been treated in the past. That's the variant that drives the perpetuation of bad behaviour through generations: *I was abused by my father/teacher/priest, so I'll abuse my son/pupil/acolyte*, or,

My people were persecuted in the past by someone else, so now we're going to persecute you – even if those now being persecuted had no role in the persecutions of the past. Revenge can make us feel as if the slate is now clean, whereas the opposite is the case. Not only is the slate still dirty; it's cracked and broken. We have defiled it.

Faced with the challenge of forgiveness, negotiation, rapprochement or reconciliation, we reject all those possibilities in favour of the rawest and most simple-minded reaction. There's plenty of symmetry in revenge, but no virtue. Revenge challenges the very idea of virtue. No one in their right mind embarks on an act of revenge in the belief that they are serving some virtuous purpose. No one thinks of revenge – from personal payback to war – as an act of goodness, kindness or compassion. We might say, *This will teach her a lesson!* but we never mean a lesson about virtue; we only ever mean a lesson about reciprocity.

In a Golden Rule world, what would we have to give up?

Some people don't want to live by the Golden Rule because to do so would curb their competitive urge, their ambition or perhaps their sense of personal freedom and independence. The rule calls for a highly cooperative approach, which works best when we think of ourselves primarily as members of a community rather than primarily as individuals with independent identities in competition with each other for a share of the pie. It's a rule that makes perfect sense to communitarians, humanitarians, egalitarians and peacemakers; it's more of a stretch for those who have been seduced by the Western fashion for rampant, self-indulgent individualism. If you think we are all competitive by nature and that the inevitable story of any society is about winners and losers, you might have trouble paying more than lip service to this rule.

If national leaders lived by the Golden Rule, no nation would ever invade another. There would certainly have been no unprovoked invasion of Poland in 1939 by Germany or of Iraq in 2003 by the so-called coalition of the willing (led by George W. Bush in the United States and Tony Blair in the United Kingdom, with Australia's John Howard and a few others meekly colluding), described by its perpetrators as a 'pre-emptive strike'. In the absence of any military or political justification for that invasion, beyond protecting the West's access to Iraqi oil, it was portrayed as morally justified by the rather vague demands of the war on terror (a war said to be morally unlike any other and therefore free from the constraints of the Geneva Conventions on war, including the treatment of prisoners). Such unprovoked invasions represent a breach of the Golden Rule so flagrant, it's hard to imagine how anyone could keep a straight face while claiming moral justification for them.

Knowing what war does to the innocent civilian populations on both sides of a conflict, to a nation's infrastructure and to the fomentation of hate, leaders committed to the Golden Rule would harness the power of diplomacy and negotiation and, when diplomatic solutions proved elusive, would accept mediation (from the United Nations, for example, or the International Court of Justice). There would be no more sabre rattling, because sabres themselves would have been rendered obsolete.

In a Golden Rule world, politicians would treat their political opponents as they themselves would wish to be treated. Political debates would be marked by a spirit of courtesy based on a proper recognition of each other's legitimacy as elected members of parliament and respect for each other's convictions, as well as a respectful appreciation of each other's human frailties and vulnerabilities. Politicians would take their opponents seriously, not as armies might take their enemies seriously, but as we all wish to be taken seriously in our day-to-day dealings with each other.

> I sometimes wonder if politicians realise the effect they have on the way we think about them. When they attack each other so viciously and so relentlessly, the voters are left to draw the obvious conclusion: they must all be as bad as each other.

Shane Hogan, the head of Sydney's St Ignatius College, once complained in his school's newsletter that Australian political leaders had failed to grasp that the art of debate was 'not to condemn your opponents but to point out why your arguments were more credible'. Hogan's point was that the political life can be entirely consistent with a life driven by respect for others – even our opponents – rather than by animosity.

Business leaders trying to live by the Golden Rule would rate respect for their customers, employees and suppliers as highly as their respect for family and friends. They would aim to treat all those people as they themselves wish to be treated. In a Golden Rule-driven marketplace, commitment to telling the truth would be as universal as the desire to be told the truth, and transparency would be the hallmark of all transactions. There would be no price gouging, manipulation, deception or exploitation; no place for personal greed or underpayment of employees or contractors. Prices would be fixed not on the basis of what the market will bear but on the basis of what generates a reasonable level of profit for all concerned and the fairest possible deal for the consumer. (There could be exceptions. In some product categories, there's a kind of compact between consumers and producers that acknowledges consumers' need for products to be overpriced: in the case of high-end cosmetics, for instance, exorbitant prices help to justify the hope consumers invest in the transformative power of the product; and price has always been a powerful cue in the market positioning of luxury cars.)

If marketing companies and retailers were to obey the dictates of the Golden Rule, how would some of the cutthroat practices of the commercial world survive? How, for instance, could a big and powerful corporation justify savage price-cutting or other measures specifically designed to drive smaller competitors out of the market? This is not an argument against competition; only against competitive strategies deliberately designed to damage competitors rather than concentrating on producing and presenting a superior product.

How could a retail giant impose such tough terms on its suppliers that their profits were cut to the bone in favour of inflated profits for the retailer? How could organisations give their lowest-paid workers an absolute minimum while offering their senior executives multimillion-dollar salaries and bonuses regarded as excessive, if not obscene, in the wider community?

Newspaper columnists, radio shock jocks and other media commentators bathed in the glow of the Golden Rule would feel obliged to make only truthful assertions and would carefully distinguish between the facts as they understood them and their opinions about those facts. Maligning and mocking people they happened to disagree with – the stock-in-trade of some commentators – would be seen as unworthy and unacceptable behaviour.

If athletes played by the Golden Rule, that would be the end of cheating. Sledging would be penalised as harshly as any other tactics designed to win an advantage over an opponent by means other than superior sporting skill. On a Golden Rule sporting field, all such behaviour would simply appear ridiculous (as it already does to many spectators), being so flagrantly contrary to the spirit of the game.

If as individuals we were to observe the Golden Rule, we'd never swing a punch (literally or metaphorically), deliberately give offence, behave in a way that exploited, deceived or manipulated others or cut moral corners that disadvantaged others commercially, professionally, politically or personally.

It's not hard to visualise that world, though my descriptions may strike you as being as Utopian as the dreams described in chapter 1.

But the point is both serious and simple: if we are prepared to endorse the Golden Rule in principle as the heart of our moral code, imagine what would happen if we adopted it in practice, especially in circumstances where it is challenged by less worthy impulses. Greed, for instance, is a great insulator from the spirit of the Golden Rule. If I can justify what I'm doing in terms of enhanced profits for my business, increased wealth for me or more trophies in my cabinet, then perhaps we can set aside the question of moral responsibility just for the moment. Or if I can justify what I'm doing in terms of the political advantage I'll obtain, then, in the words of more than one political operator, I'll do whatever it takes. Blind, ruthless ambition, whether driven by territorial, commercial, political or personal goals, is such a powerful urge that for those in its grip, kindness, fairness and compassion can seem a bit soft by comparison.

Qualifications, exceptions, modifications . . . is the rule flawed?

The ancient Chinese philosopher Laozi proposed that 'to the good I would be good; to the not-good, I would also be good, in order to make them good. With the faithful, I would keep faith; with the unfaithful, I would also keep faith, in order that they may become faithful. Requite injury with kindness'. These teachings contain powerful echoes of the Golden Rule and closely match the moral teachings of Jesus, five centuries later. But it was Confucius, rather than Laozi, who ultimately became revered as China's national sage, and he was not a turn-the-other-cheek kind of guy. On the contrary, Confucius said we should return good for good, but justice for injustice, a view which coincides with practice in Western countries, including nominally Christian countries, where Jesus' Sermon on the Mount is preached more often than it is practised.

A recurring problem with the Golden Rule is that it seems too easy to think of exceptions or ways in which it could be misapplied. A classic exception, proposed by the German philosopher Immanuel Kant, asks us to imagine a person convicted of a crime appealing to the sentencing judge to be lenient on the grounds that this would be treating the criminal as the judge would himself want to be treated. That seems absurd, and it is: the Golden Rule can't be applied as a universal guide to behaviour without some qualifications, especially when the question of justice is involved.

Here's another difficulty: treating people as we would like to be treated is not necessarily the same thing as treating them as they would like to be treated. The masochist loves having pain inflicted on him, so should he treat others in the way he'd like them to treat him?

No rule, not even the Golden Rule, can sensibly be applied without reference to the law (or, more broadly, to justice), to the principle of fairness or to the way in which particular circumstances might influence its interpretation. What, for example, should we say about workplace bullies, control freaks or narcissists who, in their various ways, make life miserable for the people who work with them? Should we just continue to be nice to them regardless, as the Golden Rule seems to imply?

Difficulties like these led Kant to decide that morally acceptable behaviour is behaviour that could provide the basis for a universal law, and we can test that by simply asking, *What would happen if everybody did this?* In the case of the workplace bully, Kant would presumably say it's not morally acceptable to indulge or humour such people, for two reasons. First, their own behaviour is morally unacceptable, because their behaviour could not form the basis of a universal moral law: 'bosses should always be bullies' hardly qualifies. Second, if everyone pandered to bullies, the world would be run by them, and the rest of us would have willingly made ourselves victims.

There's a strong argument for saying that in the case of bad behaviour we should treat others as we ourselves would expect to be treated if we had behaved as badly as they have. Yet, even here, the Golden Rule has something to offer: if we find ourselves in the position of needing to point out to such people the negative impact they are having on us and others, we should always do it with courtesy and respect. This is the justification for so-called tough love.

So we need to apply some qualifications to the Golden Rule. Perhaps it should be expressed like this: treat others the way you'd like them to treat you, provided that is just, fair and reasonable in the circumstances. It doesn't have quite the same ring as 'do unto others', and it leaves open all sorts of questions about the interpretation of 'just, fair and reasonable'. But it does remind us that moral dilemmas are not always simple and straightforward, and that the context needs to be taken into account.

There's another dimension to the Golden Rule that's easy to overlook. When we say 'treat others the way you would like to be treated,' it's important to acknowledge that 'others' might not be confined to the people we're dealing with most obviously and directly. Our actions may have consequences, however indirect, for people hidden from our view. This reminds us that the Golden Rule should not be applied selectively, as if to say, *I'll treat these people as I'd like to be treated, but not those people.* Commercial strategies sometimes involve selective application of the Golden Rule: we'll treat our shareholders and perhaps our customers as we ourselves would like to be treated, but not our suppliers or employees. The same selective application can be found whenever a teacher or parent favours one child over another: the favoured child (being treated the way the parent or teacher would like to be treated) feels terrific; the others in the class or family may feel neglected, marginalised or diminished. So a further qualification can be added to the Golden Rule: treat *all* stakeholders – people who will be directly or indirectly affected by your actions – the way you yourself would like to be treated, provided that would be just, fair and reasonable in the circumstances.

It goes without saying that there are many occasions in life when we can't treat others in quite the way we would like to be treated. Breaking off a romance may be the best thing to do in certain circumstances (such as the discovery that the beloved is less enchanting than we had first imagined or that we are not yet ready to commit to anyone), but in the short term it will involve treating someone else in a way you would not like to be treated if you were in their shoes. (Soon afterwards, of course, it may strike them that you vanished from their life in the nick of time.) Disciplining a child, terminating someone's employment, failing a student in an exam, saying no when someone badly wants you to say yes: all such circumstances involve pain for the other person, and no one but a sadist enjoys inflicting pain. Yet even in circumstances where we know we are going to disappoint someone else, perhaps unavoidably, the way we handle the situation can still reflect our commitment to the Golden Rule: we can still show respect for the person; we can still exhibit kindness; we can still treat them the way we ourselves would like to be treated in the circumstances.

None of these qualifications should discourage us from using the Golden Rule as our guide in trying to work out what's the best thing to do in every situation, assuming we want to introduce a little more goodness into our lives. It's a simple and elegant principle. Its implementation would transform the life of any community, whether a family, a neighbourhood, a workplace, a school, a university or a parliament, by fostering cooperation, willingness to compromise, an unyielding attitude of respect for others and concern for their wellbeing. As a guiding principle, it certainly beats revenge. It beats unbridled self-interest. It beats letting the competitive urge off the leash in ways that damage or diminish others. At least, it beats those alternatives as long as you're interested in goodness; as long as you'd like to see humans evolve in ways that make us less violent, less rapacious and more committed to living in harmonious communities.

Not everyone shares those aspirations. In any society, any organisation, there is always someone driven by such a powerful desire for personal power, wealth, status or fame that they are prepared to abandon the principles of civilised cooperation in favour of a ruthless determination to get their own way. In extreme cases, such people would be delighted to see everyone else living by the Golden Rule – being kind, sensitive and cooperative towards each other – so the ruthlessly ambitious one can slip through on the inside and claim the prize for themselves. Though such behaviour is generally despised, people who engage in it presumably regard that as a price worth paying, perhaps hoping to compensate with well-honed charm – the stock-in-trade of the political and corporate bully.

> I've learnt this in life: when someone playing by the Marquess of Queensberry rules is up against a street fighter, the street fighter always wins, at least in the short term.

Though we will sometimes have trouble living according to the Golden Rule, most of us are favourably disposed to be cooperative and to respect the rules of fair play. Deep in our psyche, perhaps even in our DNA, is the conviction that there is no other way to live if the species is to thrive.

> One of my kids only ever wanted to make money and the other one only ever wanted to change the world. The first one has made his money all right – he could buy and sell the rest of us many times over. The younger one is plugging away in a not-for-profit organisation helping juvenile offenders straighten out their lives and get back on their feet. He hasn't changed the world – yet – but he's doing an awful lot of good and, I'm sure, getting a lot of satisfaction out of it. Guess which one is nicer to be around.

Don't let the thought of a reward distract you

Anyone who's raised or cared for children knows how damaging a reward system can be. Once you've set up the reward, that's what the kids aim for. Before long, you find they've been hooked on the reward and might be reluctant to do anything that doesn't carry one. In *Punished by Rewards* (1993), American writer and teacher Alfie Kohn argues that the use of incentives is a counterproductive technique in management, teaching and child raising, and may do lasting harm. He points out that rewards and punishments are two sides of the same coin, both involving one person in a position of power making judgements about another person with less or no power; the reward or punishment exacerbates that power imbalance. But his central argument is simply that rewards distract us from the intrinsic value in what we are doing by focusing on the reward for doing it.

The same problem exists with the good life. As soon as you start wondering if you are going to benefit from being morally sensitive, cooperative rather than competitive or kind at some cost to yourself, the whole idea of the good life has slipped from your grasp. This is not an instrumental concept; it's not something you do as a passport or stepping stone to some benefit for yourself, either now or in the future, or even in some anticipated afterlife. This is something you do because it's a good thing to do; it's the only way communities can function properly; it's an end in itself. *Will giving money to charity make me happy?* Wrong question. *Will being a bit more patient with my poor demented mother make me feel better about myself?* Wrong question. *Will I receive some credit, some recognition, for all these hours I put into voluntary work in the community?* Wrong question.

The same wrong-headed way of thinking has infected the approach of many business leaders to the subject of corporate and commercial morality. *Good ethics is good business!* they declare, as though the financial bottom line might be a factor in deciding whether to behave ethically or not. Good ethics might be good for some businesses, some of the time, or it might not be; that is simply not the question.

The cardinal question, always, is this one: *Is this a good thing to do?* Not, *Is this a good thing for my commercial wellbeing?* or, *Is this a good thing for my public image?* but simply, *Is this a good thing in and of itself, an action motivated by a desire to contribute to the common good even if, this time around, there's no collateral benefit for me personally or commercially?* This is a better question, a higher question, than merely asking: *Is this the right thing to do?* Telling the truth is generally the right thing to do, but in cases where truth-telling might be damaging or hurtful, it's not always a good thing to do. In fact, there are many situations where 'good' and 'right' are not necessarily the same thing.

The emergence of so-called hate radio is a case in point. Presenters who transmit bile over the airwaves and foment hatred and prejudice in the community may build a large enough audience for the radio station that employs them to conclude that in a commercial sense it is the right thing to do. But is reinforcing hatred and prejudice a good thing to do?

> I sat with my wife in the doctor's surgery and listened while he told her every conceivable thing that could go wrong. I could see her becoming more and more agitated. I know they think they are doing the right thing – giving you the complete picture – and I know they have to protect themselves against litigation by spelling it all out. I understand that. But this doctor hadn't even done the biopsy and got a final diagnosis, so it was all quite inconclusive. Frankly, I think he could have gone a bit easier on her. What he said might have been true – I'm sure it was – but that wasn't a good time to be saying it.

Is this a good thing to do? is a question that can be posed in many ways. *Am I treating this person the way I would like to be treated in the circumstances? Will this action help make the world a better place? Will it set a good example to others, especially my children or my colleagues? Will it benefit the people affected? Will it harm anyone (anyone at all), and, if so, will the good outcome so heavily outweigh the bad that I can justify inflicting some harm?*

That last question captures one of the most difficult moral dilemmas we ever have to face. It can easily lead us into the embrace of that tawdry moral seducer, 'the end justifies the means'. A more solid proposition is that everything we do on the way to achieving a morally praiseworthy goal should itself be morally praiseworthy. Yes, that's a tough standard, and there are bound to be occasional exceptions that arise in extraordinary circumstances. But it's still a sound principle that discourages, for example, lying to get what you want, even if what you want happens to be a good thing in itself. It also discourages governments from treating asylum-seekers harshly as a way of dissuading others from arriving by irregular means: the goal might be achieved, but if the strategy for achieving it involves moral blindness to the plight of asylum-seekers being incarcerated in detention centres run like prisons, then the price is too high.

Most philosophical and religious traditions favour the idea of goodness for its own sake, the good life as an end in itself. Followers of Confucius, for instance, regard benevolence as the highest of all the virtues, and they value most highly the desire to seek other people's happiness. Buddhists, similarly, believe their highest goal is to develop an attitude of compassion to all without hoping for anything in return.

Many people do, in fact, receive a collateral benefit – a private sense of deep satisfaction – from living selflessly. Here is part of an address by Rowan Gillies, a former international president of the council of Médecins Sans Frontières, to the boys of Sydney Grammar School in 2008:

> We cannot claim ignorance of the fate of those less fortunate, either in this country or others. We cannot pretend that the

problems of the world are outside our purview and we cannot claim a lack of choice in what we do: our lives are our own, not decided by some militia force as it was in Liberia or is today in the Democratic Republic of Congo.

If you listen to the hollow promises and claims of parts of our society, you could assume ownership of an iPhone, a Ferrari and a waterfront home is all you need to be happy.

However, if you listen to your soul and maintain your own counsel, you will hear a more insistent voice urging you to enjoy the true fruits of what it is to be human . . . and first among these are the rewards of assisting those less fortunate than ourselves.

For, believe me, to assist someone to restore their own dignity, be it through respect, compassion or just keeping them alive is the most rewarding act I have experienced and can imagine.

That private sense of satisfaction is deeply rewarding to those who experience it. But the reward is not the purpose of the act. In fact, the good life offers no promises of reward, either public or private. It certainly offers no glittering prospect of praise or recognition. We don't live the good life at home, at work or in any of the settings of our life for any reason other than our recognition that this is the best way for humans to live. To do otherwise is to deny the nobler aspects of our nature. Yes, we humans are capable of all kinds of nastiness, ruthlessness and insensitivity; our innate potential for goodness can be undermined by negative formative experiences. But we were born to be good guys.

The role of religion

From a coldly clinical, ruthlessly rational point of view, the only way to respond to the idea of God, whether considered as an out-there creative force, an in-here loving spirit or a deity in any other form, is by remaining agnostic, committing yourself to neither theism nor atheism. To abandon that position by moving in either direction – towards theism or towards atheism – is to take a leap of faith.

To agnostics, any so-called evidence on this matter is so ambiguous that agnosticism seems the only defensible philosophical position. All they are prepared to say about the existence of God, an afterlife and any other supernatural concept is that such things are incapable of scientific proof and therefore unknowable – a position that strikes both theists and atheists as faintly pathetic, since, to people in both those camps, the evidence seems to lead directly to their own preferred conclusion.

'Unprovable' doesn't mean the same thing as 'false': if you're agnostic, then the proposition that God exists is neither true nor false. And 'unprovable' doesn't mean the same thing as 'useless': the idea of God has been an inspiration and a source of life-sustaining hope for millions of believers throughout history. God is a concept that has been around for as long as human imagination; even if it's not an idea that can be proven or disproven by science, believers say it makes sense to them, because of their intuition on the subject (their hunch or best guess), because of the ease with which they can imagine a deity of some kind or even because the idea of God meshes with their own experience of how the world works. Some believers will admit their faith is based on nothing more than a fervent *hope* that God exists.

Atheists assert the precise opposite of all that: *their* intuition, imagination and experience lead them to reject the idea of any supernatural being, especially one that is supposed to exert some control over the natural world, let alone human affairs. (*What about natural disasters? Epidemics? Mass starvation? What about war? What about pain and suffering? What about injustice?*) And yet, as long as the matter lies outside the range of scientific proof, atheists have to count as believers, too: they believe any God-based proposition to be false.

Some theists reach out to atheists and agnostics by claiming that the biblical proposition, 'God is love', can be interpreted literally:

That's all we mean by God – the spirit of love in the world. To this, the hardline atheist will respond, *We all acknowledge the existence of love and its beneficial effects in the world, but why do you need to call that God? Why can't love just be love?* Some theists will suggest, in response, that love is a sign of God's presence in the world. And so on.

This chapter – indeed, this book – is not the place for an argument about the existence of God. For our purposes, the question is not whether belief in God can be justified but whether religious faith and practice play a generally positive role in promoting the good life. We know that people who live the good life can be found in the ranks of atheists, agnostics *and* theists. And the reverse is true: people who lead a self-centred, dissolute and degenerate life can also be found in all three camps.

There are too many stories of self-serving priests, corrupt religious institutions and sanctimonious hypocrites for us to fall for the idea that religion necessarily promotes goodness. But that's not the end of the story. Much of the influence of religion in the world is benign, and even spectacularly beneficial, for individuals who are inspired or merely consoled by it; for communities that have been enriched by the activities of people motivated by religious impulses; for entire societies that have become more humane under the influence of religion. Examples abound: in the abolition of slavery; the US civil rights movement; the establishment of charitable organisations devoted to the care of the sick, disadvantaged and marginalised; the care of refugees; the promotion of mass education (though not, generally speaking, the promotion of gender equality). Revolutionary and charitable work is also done by people with no religious beliefs, however, so there's nothing uniquely good about the effects of religion on our behaviour, though twenty-three of Australia's twenty-five largest charities are run by faith-based organisations.

The Australian theologian Bruce Kaye is careful to point out that charitable works should not be regarded as the purpose but only as by-products of Christian faith: 'Christianity is about following Jesus Christ as a disciple', he says, 'and that implies some clear patterns of behaviour'. A similar point could be made for Judaism and Islam. The Christian New Testament contains the statement that 'faith without works is dead', and the Koran, similarly, praises practical expressions of Islamic faith: 'those who believe and do good deeds are the best of creation'. Most people whose faith propels them to act kindly or compassionately are as horrified as anyone else by corrupt, violent or otherwise offensive behaviour by those acting in the name of religion.

The most vigorous opponents of religion may regard it as an essentially evil influence in the world, in ways ranging from the enmity and hatred it spawns to its inhibiting effects on the intellectual and emotional development of children; but the more general attitude towards religion, among atheists and agnostics alike, seems benign. They typically regard it as irrelevant to them but broadly positive in its effects on those who embrace it and a generally positive influence in the community. They recognise that in spite of the obvious corruptibility of religious institutions, like any institutions that acquire power and devote themselves to maintaining it, most religious teaching advocates charitable behaviour.

The key points of Jesus' Sermon on the Mount, for example, seem to be that the quest for material prosperity and happiness is misguided and that human enrichment and fulfilment are to be found by putting the age-old Golden Rule into literal and sometimes painful practice: pass no judgement on others; if someone takes what is yours, don't demand it back; if someone hits you on the cheek, turn the other one; when a man takes your coat, let him have your shirt as well. (No one could accuse Jesus of being half-hearted about charity!)

Yet there's another side to this story. If a person is responding to the needs of others because they assume God will approve of their good behaviour rather than simply because those people are in need, is this not a rather tarnished, diminished version of goodness? Perhaps the German theologian Dietrich Bonhoeffer had such a thought in mind when he provocatively suggested that God wants us to live as if there were no God. Certainly, the good life requires no author or director but ourselves.

The role of luck

We don't always like to admit it, but luck can play a huge part in determining the life we end up leading. By 'luck' I mean circumstances or events that lie beyond our control: genetic luck, for instance, determining aspects of our appearance, health, height, weight, intelligence or even the intensity of our emotions or the urgency of our sexual appetites, any of which might, singly or in combination, affect the kind of partners we attract or the kind of work we are able to do. I also mean the luck of the draw with parents, siblings, friends or a particular teacher or other influential figure who enters our life at a time when we are open to what they are saying to us. Or the luck of being born at a particular time or in a particular place that either enhances or diminishes our opportunities for education or employment.

Then there are events entirely due to chance that might have a life-changing effect on us: the wave that carries one surfer to a world championship and shatters another's spine; our involvement in an accident that kills or incapacitates someone else, leaving us with a legacy of unwarranted guilt – the driver of a train, for instance, that kills a person who accidentally or even deliberately fell onto the track; war service that scars our mind and leaves us wondering why we were spared when others fell; a mysterious virus that saps our energy and reduces our zest for life.

When unexpected, unpredictable and uncontrollable events crash into our lives, we may initially flinch from them but, at a deeper level, many of us welcome them, partly as a source of stimulation (we all want something to happen), but partly, perhaps unconsciously, as a test of our personal resilience. The trajectory of some people's lives carries them, apparently by chance, into situations where they are called upon to help others in need; others' lives may not bring them into contact with many disadvantaged or marginalised people, leaving them wondering whether they would be capable of responding if called upon to do so. *Do I have what it takes to behave well in an emergency? Would I know what to do or say if someone in real distress appealed to me for help? Am I only good because I've had it so easy?* Reflections like these are unhelpful: they can best be banished by a firm commitment to the ideals of the good life: a determination to act unselfishly whatever situation Fate may throw in our path and to treat others as we would wish to be treated in the same circumstances. The good life does not imply sensational or spectacular goodness; it's simply a life lived for the benefit of others, a life of service to the common good.

The US philosopher Martha Nussbaum points out in *The Fragility of Goodness* (2001) that the philosophers of ancient Greece aspired 'to make the goodness of a good human life safe from luck through the controlling power of reason'. That's another way of saying that our devotion to the ideals and principles of the good life needs to be strong enough to withstand the contingencies of life. Luck will play its part, but bad luck cannot be allowed to undermine the strength of our commitment to goodness.

Nor should we ever be arrogant enough to take personal credit for a lucky break. The Australian writer Malcolm Knox expressed it like this in a *Sydney Morning Herald* essay: 'The consequence of acknowledging luck is that those who come out on its right side will humbly stop, look back, and give a hand to those who have not'. Knox also quotes the British writer Ed Smith who, in *Luck* (2012), argues that the stance we take on luck affects our stance on charity, personal responsibility and community: acknowledging the role of luck in each other's lives should deepen our sense of humility and our ability to recognise that the victims of bad luck are not to blame for it.

Training to be good

Like everything else worthwhile in life, goodness needs to be nurtured and developed. We are born with the necessary equipment to live an unselfish life revealed most clearly in altruism, but also revealed in our capacity to love our children (and sometimes other people's children) unconditionally, to listen attentively to someone's story when there are a million other things we'd rather be doing, to work harmoniously with colleagues we don't especially like, to perform spontaneous acts of kindness to strangers, to change our plans in order to help someone out, to love the unlovely. But goodness doesn't always come easily. Self-interest constantly lurks and occasionally overwhelms our best intentions.

Therefore, like an athlete with natural talent, we need to practise; we need coaching; we need discipline. We need the courage to 'go for it'. Watching goodness in action, in movies, novels, poetry and biographies, is inspiring for many people, and the opposite is also true: watching too much nasty stuff can erode your interest in goodness and diminish your attachment to virtues like kindness, compassion and tolerance. There's a useful biblical exhortation about this: 'Whatsoever things are true, whatsoever things are honest, whatsoever things are just, whatsoever things are pure, whatsoever things are lovely, whatsoever things are of good report . . . think on these things'. Hundreds of poets, from William Shakespeare and Robert Herrick to Christina Rossetti, John Keats, Gerard Manley Hopkins, Elizabeth Barrett Browning, Walt Whitman, Amy Lowell and Robert Frost, have encouraged the same sort of mental exercise by extolling the virtues of gazing upon beauty, contemplating all that is fine and noble in the human heart and reflecting on the boundless joys of love.

As Iris Murdoch put it, 'Where virtue is concerned, we often apprehend more than we clearly understand and grow by looking'. Murdoch was a great believer in the value of intense, focused contemplation, suggesting that 'we can all receive moral help by focusing our attention upon things which are valuable: virtuous people, great art, perhaps the idea of goodness itself'. Murdoch insisted 'there is nothing odd or mystical about this' and believed our ability to act well when the situation demands it depends partly, perhaps largely, upon the quality of what she called 'our habitual objects of attention'. In other words, train for the good life by having plenty of goodness in your mental diet. Stock up on goodness.

Murdoch's idea of growing by looking meshes with the contemporary thinking of sports psychologists and coaches who urge athletes to visualise themselves doing the things they are being trained to do. Winning in the mind, it seems, can be a useful precursor to winning on the track. Aspiring athletes also hang out with proven performers, watching and learning from them. Following that example, we can nurture the goodness in us by associating with people whose goodness we recognise and admire, avoiding the close company of those whose self-interest infects everything they do and may infect our own thinking in the same way.

Like the athlete's training, though, most of the training for the good life is not just in the mind. Merely thinking about the good life won't get us there: we need to *do it*. We need to master the art, through practice, of behaving respectfully towards everyone we encounter, whoever they may be. We need to tune in to the needs of people in our community and beyond. We need to become more alert to disadvantage and unfairness in the family, the workplace, the neighbourhood and the wider society. We need to find ways of showing our concern for others' wellbeing.

In the village where I live, one resident realised there were several men suffering from loneliness, some following a divorce or bereavement, some after retirement from the workforce. He began inviting them to gather at the local store for morning tea, and he watched their spirits revive as they began to focus on each other's circumstances and respond to each other's needs. Another local man instituted a state-wide program of counselling for farmers economically and emotionally devastated by prolonged drought. The men's shed movement has achieved a similar level of re-engagement for retired or isolated men (initially, Vietnam veterans having trouble reintegrating into their communities) who are feeling adrift or undervalued and who discover, through assorted community projects, the rich meaning of a life lived for others. In suburbs and towns all over the world, there are good-hearted people constantly on the lookout for ways to be good neighbours, responding to problems ranging from homelessness or social isolation to the pressure on carers, the anxieties of new mothers, the restlessness of kids with not enough to do, or the reluctance of men to discuss mental health issues.

When the ideals of the good life or the demands it makes on our time and energy seem daunting, it's worth reminding ourselves that goodness is not some extraordinary feat we're attempting; it's simply part of our nature waiting to be developed. As long ago as 1625, Francis Bacon wrote something that has been well and truly confirmed by the work of modern social scientists: 'The inclination to goodness is imprinted deeply in the nature of man'.

6

Living the good life

Once we embrace the modified Golden Rule as the guiding principle of our life, the next part should be easy. We should have no difficulty working out how to treat others, because their wishlist will be much the same as ours. The one item you'll find on practically everyone's list is *Please take me seriously as a person.*

> In my job, I see a lot of kids who've been on the wrong side of the law. Some of them are tragic cases but they all have this one thing in common – a real chip on their shoulder about not being taken seriously. I remember one young man said he was sick of always being spoken about, never spoken to.

In *What Makes Us Tick? The ten desires that drive us* (2010), a book about the psychology of human motivation, I suggested that the desire to be taken seriously is the most ubiquitous, the most pervasive of all our social desires (closely connected to our desire to belong to human herds and tribes, our desire for somewhere that feels like 'my place', and our desire for love). Each person wants to be acknowledged, respected, appreciated, understood, valued and accepted. Though we know we are all part of the same human story, we each want our unique role in it to be recognised. We each want our voice to be heard.

> You want to know the worst thing about getting older? People don't take you seriously any more. They don't ask your opinion about anything, and they don't listen when you have something to say. *Oh, that's just Gran raving on* – I'm sure that's what they think. Well, I'm not brain-dead

yet – I just wish they'd all treat me with as much respect as they used to. I'm starting to feel like an extra in a movie.

Considering that this is close to being a universal human desire, it is surprising how often we fail to acknowledge its importance. When someone's behaviour (including your own) puzzles or perplexes you or seems more irrational than usual, consider first the possibility that the desire to be taken seriously may have been frustrated and is now striking back. Frustration of any of our desires can bring out the worst in us (though most of us eventually learn to live with the idea that they won't all be satisfied all the time). The frustration of our desire to be taken seriously is the hardest to handle, because this is the desire that goes right to the heart of who we are: *If you don't take me seriously, if you don't respect me as a person, what else matters?*

Intense and sustained frustration of the desire to be taken seriously can boil over into anger, violence or even war: observe the behaviour of entire nations who feel their rights or needs are being ignored or, at the extreme, that their territory is being violated. Ethnic or religious minorities typically act badly when they feel marginalised or undervalued. We are all capable of becoming irritated, sometimes even affronted, by things as seemingly insignificant as a waiter's failure to notice our appeal for attention or someone's lateness for an appointment. (Lateness is not only discourteous but sends this unambiguous message: *I had something to do that was more important than meeting you.*)

When people are being cranky, sullen, withdrawn or antisocial, they are often expressing nothing more than the frustration of their desire to be taken seriously. That applies to children, adolescents, young adults, people in their middle years, the elderly – at every point in the life cycle, we are powerfully driven by this desire. That's why we react so badly to being mocked, exploited or humiliated: when we are made to feel we are not worthy of someone's respect, it feels like a sign that we are not being taken seriously. It's why we resent being lumped in with a category, as though we are mere stereotypes: baby boomers, single mothers, refugees, Jews, Muslims, the wealthy or the unemployed. It's why we hate other people making assumptions about us – what we're thinking or how we might act – without first consulting us. It's why we plead for space in a relationship when we feel we are no longer being taken seriously enough.

We know all this from our own experience, so why is it hard for us to acknowledge that it's the same for everyone else? If the good life is a life committed to treating others as we ourselves would like to be treated, then it's a life committed to taking others seriously . . . and showing them that we do.

A tale of two leaders, part 2

Kieran O'Toole sweeps in to the small conference room attached to his office and takes his place at the head of the table. Eighteen months into his new job as a junior minister at the Department of Recreation for the Ageing, he is not pleased with progress being made by Team O'Toole. His chief of staff has remained loyal (though 'loyal' might not be the right word: he has applied for several other jobs since the new minister arrived but has not yet been successful in securing a transfer). Three media advisors have come and gone, and that position is currently vacant. The political advisor is a new appointee, having arrived only a week ago, after a shake-up in his media organisation left him without a job.

Kieran rules his office by bullying and intimidation. The people who surround him have often discussed how they might best tell him what they believe he really needs to hear, but so far no one has tried it. His staffers prefer moving to another job to the prospect of standing up to him. Jon, head of the PR firm charged with making Kieran the most popular politician in the history of the world, needs the work. He is soldiering on in the face of mounting hostility and impatience from the minister.

The voters seem to like Kieran well enough when they are asked specific questions about him, though not all can place him, and he is frequently confused with a local actor with a similar name and an even more assiduous PR machine. Under intense questioning from the minister, Jon has reluctantly admitted that the name Kieran O'Toole is never mentioned spontaneously in the focus groups regularly conducted by his company.

Kieran reports to a cabinet minister who has become increasingly disenchanted with him and says so. But Kieran is undeterred. He still has his eye on a cabinet post and has managed to convince his factional colleagues that he is their best hope for higher office.

'So, Jon, any good news this morning? I certainly hope so.'

'Well, Minister, there's an opportunity for an extended talkback radio segment on a rural station. I have it right here . . . ' Jon scrolls down the screen on his iPad and eventually finds what he is looking for. 'It's actually a community FM station in the Central West; they are trying to build an audience and they think it would be quite a coup to have you on. It can all be done by phone, of course.'

'A community FM station that's trying to build an audience. Is that really the best you've got? Planning, Jon. Minister for Planning, remember? We're eighteen months into the two-year strategy, and you're offering me a talkback segment on a community FM station in the wilds of . . . where, exactly?'

'Gulgong, actually. It's a very professional outfit and I think we should do it. Every gig is a stepping stone to something else. Especially if you say something controversial.'

'Talk to Polly. See if she's got anything new for me to say. There might be a euthanasia clinic somewhere that's been modified for motorised wheelchair access. God help us.'

Just down the road, Kate Sherman is welcoming the chairman of the board to one of the regular Friday drinks meetings of her senior colleagues in the aged-care organisation. The chairman is complimenting them all lavishly on the work of the past year. Several mention their appreciation of Kate's leadership style, and he heartily endorses that sentiment.

Kate will have none of it. 'This is a team, and that's not a cliché. "A team" means what it says. No single person can take the credit for this – especially not me. You have all been marvellously supportive of the new girl, and I'm proud to have become part of the place.'

'By the way', says the chairman, 'I used to be summoned here once a month to hand out awards of various kinds. What happened to all that?'

Before Kate can answer, one of her colleagues jumps in. 'Oh, we dispensed with awards. We want everyone to feel valued and we want everyone to realise their job is important even if it doesn't attract front-line attention. Morale has improved dramatically since we abolished the awards. There are no losers any more; no one feels they are being overlooked or unappreciated.'

The chairman looks at Kate. 'This your idea?'

'We're all in this together, Chairman. If we didn't agree about things as fundamental as that, I couldn't work here. We really do believe in consensus, you know. The structure is as flat as we can make it. There's a hierarchy, inevitably, but positions are not about power, only about different roles and responsibilities. Everyone has their say. And I mean everyone.'

The chairman appears dubious. 'Well, I can't say I was ever a fan of consensus, but these results speak for themselves. I'll confess something to you. When I saw the customer satisfaction ratings for the past quarter, I didn't believe them at first. Sent them back for checking. But they were accurate, apparently. Never seen anything like it, and my day job is running an IT outfit that lives or dies by customer service. Maybe I need to pay more attention to what you're doing down here.'

'Come and have a chat about it, by all means. Any time you like. My door is always open.'

'Metaphorically?'

'Literally. I told this group when I arrived that I would listen to anything they wanted to say, and I expected them to have the same attitude towards everyone else – employees and clients. There's no magic to it. Just common courtesy, really.'

'Let's have a drink', says the chairman. 'I want to propose a toast.'

Kate narrows her eyes at him. 'To the team?'

'Of course.'

The paradox of goodness

There's a paradox at the heart of the good life: we are at our best when we are striving to give others the very things we ourselves most desire – respect, recognition, kindness and even happiness. (And we are at our worst when we criticise others for the very frailties and shortcomings we ourselves possess.) Though each of us wishes to be taken seriously, goodness involves taking *others* seriously, responding to their needs and attending to their wellbeing, while not worrying too much about whether we're getting our fair share of respect. This is the same paradox that underpinned our discussion of the pursuit of happiness in chapter 2: to pursue our own happiness is to risk misery, frustration and disappointment, but to devote ourselves to the happiness and wellbeing of others is likely to enhance our own sense of wellbeing and fulfilment. (Perhaps we should remind ourselves of the important caveat already mentioned in chapter 5: we are not promoting the wellbeing of others in order to enhance our own wellbeing. That is never the right motive for behaving well, and, in any case, a personal sense of wellbeing is never guaranteed by goodness.)

This is the paradox that explains why good sportsmanship is so attractive: it expresses humility by honouring the accomplishments of our rivals, perhaps even helping them overcome their weaknesses (as in the case of a runner who stops to help a fallen competitor to his feet or a tennis player who sacrifices a point to acknowledge that a previous point had been awarded unfairly). It's why good communicators always ask, *What will my audience do with this message?* rather than *What will this message do to my audience?* because they know the essential starting point for effective communication is to see the situation from the point of view of the other person. It's also why altruism – the finest expression of a life lived for others – is so widely regarded as our noblest impulse, as well as being the engine of a civil society. And it's why one of the essential ingredients of the good life has always been self-sacrifice (a deeply unfashionable term at present, though I'm not sure why: take a look at the motto of your local school and there's a good chance it refers to 'service', and what else is service but self-sacrifice?)

None of this requires superhuman strength, integrity or saintliness: it calls only for a little humility, the antithesis of arrogance. It is the sign that we have finally grasped an important aspect of goodness: that we cannot parade it as we might parade our wealth or our sporting prowess; goodness can be discerned only in its effects on others. In an era of wildly extravagant self-promotion and an unhealthy emphasis on self-esteem, humility has taken something of a back seat (though that's its natural position, of course). Humility doesn't involve flagellating yourself, demeaning yourself or losing your self-respect; it involves only shifting your primary focus from your own wellbeing to the wellbeing of others. It also involves a certain hesitancy in responding to praise, because humility acknowledges the role of genetics, luck and circumstance in any of our accomplishments. Modesty is the natural partner of humility.

A new way of looking at work–life balance

A lot of nonsense is talked about so-called work–life balance, as if work weren't part of life. Still, we know what's meant: we should try to strike a healthy balance between the time we spend at work and the time we devote to our private lives, including our personal relationships (time for family and friends) and our private pursuits (time for ourselves, whether browsing in cyberspace, reading, meditating, exercising or anything else we might like to do on our own). Getting that balance right is a real challenge for many people, particularly those whose working lives bring them more satisfaction than their private lives. But it's all life, which means that when it comes to the good life, there is no sensible distinction to be drawn between the way we behave at work and the way we behave in our private and social lives. *I am me, wherever I happen to be, whoever I happen to be with, and whatever I happen to be doing.* That's one meaning of 'integrity': integrating our values with every aspect of our lives. If you want to know what my values *really* are, you need to see the total picture.

If that seems like a statement of the obvious, take a look at its implications. If a good life is marked by kindness, tolerance, compassion, respect for others and a willingness to respond to their needs, then that kind of commitment can't be confined to one compartment of our lives. To say that a person is kind and loving at home or with their friends but a ruthless, exploitative operator at work is to say that this person is not committed to the good life. Being kind to the people we love is hardly a moral challenge. Our commitment to the good life is tested by our response to circumstances in which is it hardest for us to live up to the Golden Rule.

The sickening gaps sometimes exposed between a person's religious beliefs or declared moral convictions and the ruthlessness of their commercial dealings or their unequivocal surrender to the profit motive suggest that, as far as the Golden Rule is concerned, some of us have become adept at applying it selectively. Yet the rule permits no work–life distinction: the concept of work–life balance includes the idea of moral balance – moral equivalence – between our working and personal lives.

Because some occupations seem inherently good, it's tempting to assume that people who do those jobs are automatically devoted to the principles of the good life. The spiritual roots of the traditional professions, for example, lie in the concept of selflessness. Professions like medicine, law and accounting impose on their members a particular set of moral obligations that relate directly to the concept of a life lived for others. Professionals, as well as tradespeople and artisans, possess skills their clients lack, and their relationships with clients depend utterly on those clients being prepared to trust them. Such trust is based not only on the expectation of professional work of the highest possible standard, but also on the assumption that a true professional will always place the client's interests ahead of their own. (No wonder the charge of professional misconduct, whether through poor-quality work or the charging of unconscionable fees, carries such opprobrium both within a profession and in the wider community.)

Yet contradictions abound: some people who work in 'good' occupations may be quite insensitive, exploitative and self-absorbed in their private lives. (It's a cliché in psychotherapy, for example, that the private lives of therapists are often more troubled or chaotic than their clients might imagine, for people who are supposed to know so much about personal relationships.) Conversely, some people who work in occupations we might hesitate to call 'good' or 'worthwhile' may nevertheless be passionately committed to the principles of the good life in private: kind and thoughtful to their friends, helpful to strangers, generous philanthropists.

> A bloke I went to school with suddenly turned up at the golf club. Just the same. Sharp as a tack. Very funny. Very charming. We started playing together and one of my other mates took me aside after a few weeks of this and said, 'Do you know who that is?' I said of course I did, told him about being at school together, and so on. Turns out this bloke is some kind of corporate wheeler-dealer type with the reputation of a real bully-boy. All charm on the outside, ruthless as buggery underneath.

> Thinks ethics is a county in England. Anyway, my mate says it's only a matter of time before he'll crash, big time. I wouldn't know – I don't understand that world at all. Meanwhile, nice as pie around the club. I did hear his wife left him, though – apparently she couldn't reconcile his business dealings with the person she thought she'd married. She said he was like two different animals – one at work and one at home. She eventually decided that if he was a bastard at work, then that's what he was – a bastard – and the rest was an act. Bit like watching how people drive – I always think you see the real person when they're behind the wheel.

Most work done in our society is devoted to satisfying people's basic needs for food, clothing, shelter, security, transport, education, recreation and entertainment. To the extent they meet those needs, all such occupations are 'good', and the economy would grind to a halt if everyone wanted to work in society's breakdown gangs of assorted therapists, carers and advisors.

The apparent value of the work a person does is no guide to the intrinsic goodness of their life. It's perfectly possible for rogues and bullies to do good work or even for supposedly good priests to sexually abuse children. A determination to lead a good life may naturally encourage us to seek worthwhile employment in an industry whose values and practices we can respect and embrace. But whatever job we happen to be doing, the good life demands that we behave at work as we behave in our private life; that we draw no ethical distinction between the two; that goodness becomes the touchstone, the hallmark, the benchmark for everything we do.

Everyone's a therapist; everyone's a client

Religious and philosophical traditions, folklore and cultural heritage are teeming with exhortations and practical tips for living the good life. Support those in difficulty or distress. Don't dissemble or deceive. Don't make promises you can't keep.

Be kind to strangers. Suffer fools gladly. Turn the other cheek. Go the extra mile. Befriend the friendless. Live in peace. Don't let the sun go down on your anger. Don't meet hate with hate or violence with violence. It is more blessed to give than receive. The list goes on and on, and all such snippets of wisdom are grounded in the concept of the good life as a life lived for others.

Some of those well-known maxims may strike you as a bit too challenging or perhaps as being relevant only in rather dramatic or exceptional circumstances. But, in essence, they are all about the same thing: the promotion of mental and emotional health in those whose lives we touch. Love is, of course, the greatest therapy of all, which is why I have described the good life as a loving life.

So the question is, what might we do in the ebb and flow of normal daily existence to increase the quotient of goodness in our lives? Or, to put it another way, how might we best satisfy other people's need for therapeutic support? If the word 'therapy' strikes you as odd, consider this: we are all struggling with the frailty, flaws and failings that go with being human, which is why we all need emotional support and guidance to see us through the dark and difficult passages of our lives. (What's that, if not therapy?) Our sense of emotional security depends on knowing such therapeutic support is available when we need it.

> Once a month I get together with a group of my girlfriends – we've known each other since school and we've been through everything together. We often drink a bit more than we should on these occasions, and there are always tears, but I think we'd go quietly mad if we didn't have each other. Some of the husbands don't like it – I think they feel a bit threatened – but as far as I'm concerned, it's a lifesaver. I'm sure the other girls feel the same.

Sometimes, things are too rocky, too complex or too private to share with our friends, or perhaps we are passing through a stage of feeling unsupported by friends, and we may then seek the help of a psychotherapist or counsellor. But most of us, most of the time, get by with the support of a loving family (perhaps including a wise elder), the concern of friends or the strength of a caring community. In this sense, we are all, sooner or later, called upon to be each other's therapists.

> When my wife died, I couldn't believe how kind and supportive people were. Friends cooked meals and dropped them in. Neighbours called in – even neighbours I hadn't previously known very well – offering to do bits of shopping and even a spot of housekeeping. I felt almost overwhelmed by kindness. I feel so sorry for people who don't have that kind of support. I suppose they find the strength within themselves to carry on after a thing like a bereavement, or perhaps they seek help from a counsellor. I'm from the generation that believes you should muddle on the best way you can, but I must say I was very, very fortunate to be surrounded by so many caring people. Now I'm back on my feet, I think I've become more alert to the kind of support other people around here might be needing.

The reverse is also true: when we act from dark impulses like jealousy, hatred, anger, possessiveness, superciliousness, blind ambition, smouldering resentment or a desire to control someone, the effect of our behaviour on other people will be the very opposite of therapeutic. We are all perfectly capable of inflicting harm on each other – sometimes lifelong harm. Hearts can be broken by unkind remarks; spirits crushed by dismissive or demeaning words or actions; reputations destroyed by gossip and innuendo.

There are some very contemporary examples of anti-therapeutic behaviour, arising from changes in our society. Here's one:

As we tend to live longer, more people will inevitably experience various types of dementia associated with ageing, and that will challenge their families and carers to remember that the loss of memory does not imply the loss of the desire to be taken seriously. Saying wildly improbable or unintelligible things does not mean a person has lost either their own self-respect or their need for our respect. Impaired cognitive function, commonly revealed through endlessly repetitive behaviour, may sadden, disappoint or even occasionally infuriate those who have previously enjoyed a normal relationship with someone now suffering from some form of dementia, and the onset of dementia will profoundly change the nature of that relationship.

We should never assume that we know how the world looks to those who are suffering this loss of function; kindness is the only basis for adapting to the new way of being with them. To treat them like semi-persons is to demean them; it is also to overlook the possibility raised by Beverley Murphy in Betsy Peterson's *Voices of Alzheimer's* (2004):

> If you believe in the concept of a soul, then you have to believe that the soul doesn't get Alzheimer's any more than it gets cancer. Maybe the soul has an awareness of life around it that transcends the body or the ability to communicate . . . Maybe, just maybe, our people have the unique experience of being able to live in two worlds, ours and a freer one that allows them access to insights and awareness we can't even begin to fathom.

Even if you don't believe in the concept of a soul, there are still no grounds for assuming that a person with dementia doesn't respond to kindness or unkindness, or that they have no inner life. We may not have access to it, but that doesn't entitle us to assume it isn't there.

Another contemporary example of anti-therapeutic behaviour arises from the combination of increased longevity and the high rate of divorce and remarriage among people in the middle and later years of life. Human nature being what it is, some of those divorced people will have ex-partners who might react uncharitably to the news of a new romance. (*I don't want him, but I don't want anyone else to have him,* is an attitude not unknown in such cases.) Another source of pain and sadness for many couples in this situation is that at the very time when they are finding new romance and the promise of a new level of contentment in their life, their grown-up children are making the situation difficult for them by resenting (or even refusing to engage with) the new partner. While younger children are naturally a little wary of a new step-parent, at least until a satisfactory relationship with them has been established, adult offspring, who might be expected to have a more mature and tolerant attitude, can be even more difficult. Sometimes, this is because they feel fiercely loyal to the other parent, even if that parent has died, but the pain inflicted by such behaviour is often acute.

> Frank and I have never married, even though his wife died years ago, because his daughter simply won't countenance it. She scarcely makes eye contact with me and never invites us to her home together – he has to go over there by himself to see the grandchildren. We once went on a beach holiday together – the whole family. Never again. I had to come home early. She wouldn't talk to me and the grandchildren treated me like dirt. I'd love to marry him, but I don't think it's going to happen.

Such cases are not rare. They involve the same deliberate attempt to withhold the therapeutic power of kindness as when a person bears a grudge for years, refuses to accept a new person into an established work or friendship group, or behaves in a hostile way towards every person who emerges as a potential romantic partner for their precious son or daughter.

The good life, by contrast, is animated by a willingness to bestow the therapeutic effects of kindness on friends and strangers alike. Goodness is not a grand or mysterious concept. All we require are a few simple disciplines that, like compass settings, steer us in the right direction. In every case, those disciplines will be based on the idea of treating others as we ourselves would like to be treated, putting ourselves in the other person's shoes, trying to see the world from the other person's point of view.

The three great therapies of everyday life

What, then, are the signs of a good life? What does a life look like when it is being lived in accordance with the Golden Rule? In what practical ways can we demonstrate our commitment to taking other people seriously, respecting them and acknowledging their desire for proper recognition? How does humility manifest itself in practice?

There are three particular disciplines that bring out the best in us and in those around us. Think of them as the three great therapies of everyday life: to listen attentively, to apologise sincerely and to forgive generously. None of them requires exceptional skill, though each calls for some courage. If we were to integrate them into our way of living – to make them part of who we are – many other manifestations of goodness would naturally flow from them. (There is a fourth, but I'll keep that up my sleeve for now.)

Listen attentively

Why is it such a thrill when someone gives us the gift of their undivided attention? Why are we so grateful to people who actively listen to us, as opposed to simply hearing us out? The answer is obvious. When someone listens attentively to me, they are clearly demonstrating two things: they take me seriously enough to listen to whatever I'm trying to say, and they are prepared to place my interests and concerns ahead of theirs, at least for the moment.

The converse is also true. When someone is clearly not listening to me – gazing over my shoulder in the hope of catching sight of someone more interesting, perhaps, or simply glazing over and failing to react – their unspoken message is eloquent: *I don't take you seriously enough to bother attending to what you're saying*, or, *I don't regard what you're saying as being interesting or important to me.* Either way, the implication is clear: this is not someone prepared to treat me the way they themselves would like to be treated.

Michael misses his connection

Michael (he of the vomiting baby at Heathrow) is frustrated beyond words. En route to London for yet another of his lightning business trips, he finds himself pacing the concourse at Singapore's Changi Airport after a mix-up with his flight. Forced to face the fact that his plans are now in tatters, he is resigned to taking the next available flight straight back to Brisbane, mission unaccomplished. He is just off the phone from a highly unsatisfactory conversation with Jenny, his wife, who is showing serious signs of being fed up with him.

This aborted trip was meant to have involved two meetings, the first a private briefing with the CEO. He had assured Michael they could deal with the agenda by phone, but Michael, always eager for face-to-face time with his boss, had arranged a second meeting, with the marketing department at the Dagenham plant, to justify the trip.

Before he left home, Jenny had said something to him about wanting to spend a few days away with one of her girlfriends, Nina, but Michael had not paid much attention to it: he was preoccupied with plans for the trip and had never much cared for Nina anyway – he felt her effect on Jenny was not always helpful to the marriage. After her sessions with Nina, Jenny always wanted to discuss their relationship, and Michael was firmly of the view that discussing it might only make things worse. He was a great believer in just getting on with things.

Now he finds that Jenny has indeed gone away with Nina, to spend three days in the beach house Nina had prised out of her ex-husband as part of their property settlement. (Michael doesn't like Jenny being around people who speak airily of ex-husbands.) On the phone, Jenny claimed she had told him quite explicitly about this arrangement and had chosen the dates to coincide with his trip. 'I knew you weren't listening', she had said. 'I knew you had your mind on the trip and your meeting with your beloved Lord Steaming Pile' (a reference to the British CEO, Jeremy Steamford, who has recently been made a peer and now insists on being addressed as Lord Steamford). 'You're like a dog with a bone, Michael. You're so obsessed with your job,

I really don't think you hear anything I say. Did you remember to call your mother for her birthday? No, I didn't think so. I told you to do that before you left, too.'

Michael loves Jenny, has always loved her, but has found it increasingly difficult to say so. Jenny has taken to calling him the Great Communicator, after US president Ronald Reagan, whom Jenny regards as one of the worst communicators ever to strut the world stage. She was convinced the title was either meant to be ironic or was the work of a brave PR consultant. Her use of it in Michael's case is unambiguously sarcastic.

The phone conversation ended when Michael confessed he had either misheard or misunderstood the arrangements for his transfer to a different flight for the Singapore–London leg of the trip. This, he knew, would supply Jenny with more fuel for her argument that he was paying less and less attention to what he was being told by anyone not directly connected with his job.

The flight Michael was originally booked on had been cancelled because of some technical problem with the aircraft. The passengers had all been transferred to other flights, and Michael was quite sure he had been told he was being transferred to a flight leaving at eleven-twenty that night. He'd gone for a massage, a shower and a meal, and sauntered back to his departure gate with, he thought, almost an hour up his sleeve. The flight had left at ten-twenty. The next, at eleven-twenty, was fully booked. His London appointment was inflexible (his boss was leaving for the United States the next day), and the Dagenham meeting was of only marginal value anyway.

Michael secures a seat on an eleven-forty flight back to Brisbane, facing the prospect of two days at home without Jenny, a PA who will scarcely be able to believe he so comprehensively messed up a simple transfer, and a boss in London irritated, at best, by their cancelled appointment. On the flight home, Michael ponders Jenny's parting words on the phone: 'If you're not going to listen to me, why should I listen to you?'

When Michael doesn't listen to Jenny, or doesn't listen carefully enough, she is drawing the only possible conclusion: *He doesn't think I'm worth listening to.* Michael would almost certainly be shocked by that interpretation of his behaviour. *Of course you're worth listening to*, he would want to say; *it's just that I've got a lot on my mind at present.*

Sorry, Michael, but we all have a lot on our minds, most of the time. That's why listening to someone can feel like hard work. It's easier not to listen: listening is much harder than talking, because listening involves a deliberate effort of will. To compound the problem, our brain is perfectly capable of thinking of several things at once, so we have to set aside the things we might rather be thinking about and focus exclusively on what the other person is saying to us.

Most of us speak at a rate of about one hundred and twenty-five words per minute. When we think in words (which we don't always), we are capable of thinking at about five hundred words per minute. So an obvious question arises: what happens to all that spare thinking capacity of about three hundred and seventy-five words per minute? The answer is that unless we're committed to active, attentive listening, that excess capacity will be filled by all kinds of extraneous thoughts, some of which might be more compelling or seem more immediately relevant to us than the things the speaker is saying.

Active, attentive listening involves a willingness to rein in those private mental meanderings before they have a chance to blot out what is being said. The best way to resist distractions is to devote all your available thought-speed to the act of listening. Don't just hear the words; attend fully to them. Pay close attention to the tone of voice, the rate of speech, the level of energy, the pauses and hesitations, the facial expressions, the posture of the speaker, their gestures, their body language. (This is the same principle as speed reading, where we learn to scan a page so quickly that distractions can't get a look-in: it's like hanging on to a speeding train.) Another useful way to harness your excess thought-speed is to be constantly asking yourself, *How can I use this?* There's no such thing as a boring subject, only a bored listener who hasn't bothered to search for the relevance of the message to them.

In any person-to-person encounter, there's always a lot more happening than the mere exchange of words. In fact, most researchers would say the words typically account for less than half the total meaning being conveyed by non-verbal signals. Good listeners know that, which is why they are so keen to catch the subtleties, the nuances, that give them access to the rich meanings that lie behind the words. We humans usually attend more closely and respond more directly to pictures than we do to words: in a personal encounter, the visual messages (facial expressions, posture and gestures) usually convey more than the words we say. For that reason, we sometimes reveal more than we intend when we are either speaking or listening. (*My face is like an open book!*)

Anyone who is serious about listening will recognise that the hidden message in most encounters is this one: *Please try to understand me . . . don't worry too much about the words.* That plea is even more poignant if the words are contradicted by the way they are being said – as they often are. In a surprisingly large number of cases, people say the very opposite of what they mean. (*It's not the money; it's the principle of the thing. I will always love you as a friend. This is not about you; it's about me. No, I'm not angry.*)

The galloping revolution in information technology raises many questions about the new modes of communication and their effectiveness compared with face-to-face contact. The jury is still out on the effects of heavy information technology use, both on our brain and on the quality of our social lives, but it's obvious that online contact, for all its convenience and cleverness, can't approach the subtlety or complexity of face-to-face contact. For a start, the emphasis is almost all on words, and though the language of digital communication is evolving its own subtleties and nuances, most of the crucial non-verbal (especially visual) messages we exchange in a face-to-face encounter are missing from an online connection. Posture, gestures, facial expressions, tone of voice, rate of speech, the location and atmospherics: all these aspects of a face-to-face encounter give us important clues that enable us to interpret it more accurately (including our interpretation of the actual words being spoken). And all those clues are missing from the online experience. This is why misunderstandings occur more easily in emails, text messages and social media posts than in personal conversations. And it's why we are often deceived by online contact with strangers into believing they are quite different from the people they turn out to be when we meet them.

We have not yet created the online equivalent of the gift of attentive, active listening. Gazing into each other's eyes on Skype or FaceTime can't approach the subtlety of the real thing (though the online versions are excellent top-up substitutes for people who already know each other); nor can we yet match online the magic moment when one person reaches out to give another the comfort of a touch. We can exchange endless text messages, maintain almost continuous access to each other's Facebook pages and scatter Twitter messages like so much electronic confetti, and all of this can help maintain our existing relationships. It can also create a sense of immediacy and an illusion of closeness and transparency between offline strangers that might, until tested in a flesh-and-blood encounter, encourage outspokenness and recklessness leading to a more rapid assumption of intimacy than is warranted.

Like all technological aids to communication, starting with the printing press and, later, the telephone, these ever-smarter new media create the illusion of bringing us together while actually making it easier for us to stay apart. In the end, we have to come out of hiding and meet face to face if our relationships are to receive the unique boost, the unique nurturing, that only attentive listening can provide.

*

The single biggest problem we face when we are listening to another person is the bundle of preconceptions we bring to the encounter. All our previous experiences, all our beliefs, attitudes and prejudices act like lenses that distort the communication process. We are not blank slates waiting to receive whatever messages anyone chooses to send us; we are active participants in the encounter and we will inevitably try to interpret what we're hearing in the light of what we already know or think; hence, the viewer is part of the view.

It is easy to accept that we are the products of our experience, but not always so easy to accept that we are also its prisoners. Yet this is only another way of saying that we are limited in trying to make sense of what is happening to us today by what we have learnt from all our yesterdays. Our discoveries, learnings and decisions, including our attitudes and beliefs, gradually evolve into a recognisable pattern, sometimes called a 'world view', which we use as a framework – a template, a code – for making our own sense of the world. We need that framework or we would have no way of storing our experience and drawing on it to interpret what is going on around us. It is like a personal map, a guidebook or a compass.

Though this framework makes us feel comfortable and secure because we're protected by our own knowledge and beliefs (and our own prejudices, it must be said), it also frames and filters our view of the world – a bit like looking out a window through the slats of a Venetian blind where the slats impose their own pattern on whatever we're looking at. Our beliefs and preconceptions are like the slats of that blind . . . or the bars of a cage. As we grow older and acquire more experience, the bars of our 'cages' (or the components of our world view) become stronger and their patterns more complex. This makes us feel more sure of ourselves and more easily able to deflect messages that don't fit comfortably within our own personal cage. This is why two people can hear the same political speech, for example, and come away with entirely different impressions of what was said.

This personal, psychological cage does not feel like a dungeon or prison. Quite the reverse: it feels like a bright, airy, comfortable place, a place where we can be ourselves, a place where we belong. It is only uncomfortable when the bars are rattled by new or surprising information that challenges us to do a bit of demolition and rebuilding, which is why changing our minds is something we usually find hard, and sometimes painful.

In fact, our cages are not quite as stable or resistant to change as we might think. They are in a constant state of adjustment, as new experiences have to be incorporated into the existing pattern. But subtle shifts are usually not sufficient to worry us; they are simply part of the process of maturing and evolving. We may discover that we have actually changed our mind only when we read something we wrote years ago or are reminded of something we once said and realise that is no longer what we think. The real challenge comes when someone asks us to change our mind right now, particularly if it's about something we've learnt from our own experience.

If you want to see a cage in operation, look at how a typical argument evolves, with each person simply restating their existing point of view and budging not one centimetre: in fact, nothing reinforces the bars of our cage like having to defend them against an attack. You can feel the cage working whenever you find yourself making snap judgements about someone on the basis of their appearance or accent. You can feel your prejudices rise up to influence your view of the person and their message: *How can I be expected to take seriously someone who talks and looks like that?*

'Professional deformity' is the term sometimes used to describe the prejudice of a highly educated person whose specialised training has had the effect of filtering their view of the world so they see things only from the perspective of their own specialised knowledge. It is often difficult for such people to communicate openly and clearly with those who don't have the same type of training; it is also sometimes difficult for people trained in a particular specialty to hear what is being said to them in a 'language' other than their own.

> The bloke next door is some kind of computer wizard. But try having a normal conversation with him! I know I'm not the sharpest tool in the toolbox, but I can understand what most people say to me – not with him, though. His wife does all the talking for him. She's a lovely woman, but I can't imagine what they talk about at home.

Professional biases and preconceptions have led to many legal controversies surrounding the evidence of expert witnesses. In his 2008 paper 'A Defence of Rigorous Method in Clinical Science', published in *Neurourology and Urodynamics*, James Malone-Lee of University College London described one case in which 'a number of expert opinions expressed at the trials drew on strongly held beliefs unsupported by empirical evidence; these opinions were stated as fact'.

So you can see what we're up against when we approach the task of listening to someone else. Our natural disposition is to stay warm and dry inside the protective shell of our own attitudes and beliefs. But even as the shell – or the cage – protects us, it is creating a barrier between us and the person we are supposed to be listening to. We are not, by nature, open to new messages, especially those that might challenge our existing point of view, so we are very adept at filtering them out: only half-listening, thinking about what we are going to say next (instead of what the speaker is actually saying), daydreaming and, easiest of all, interpreting what we hear so we are able to remain comfortable with our existing attitudes.

Imagine someone pointing to a coat hanging on a peg and saying to you, *Try on that coat – it would look good on you.* If you were to reply, *Oh, no, I don't think so; it doesn't look my size. I don't think it would suit me at all*, that person would be entitled to say, *How can you possibly know until you try it on? Go on; walk over to the peg and try on the coat. That's the only way to be sure.* That's what attentive listening is like: only when you've abandoned the security of your own cage and tried out the cage of the other person – experimented with seeing the world from their point of view – can you be said to have truly listened to them. That doesn't mean you'll agree with them, but it does mean you'll be prepared to postpone the question of whether you agree or disagree until you've fully received and understood what they're saying. That's no mean feat: it requires courage, generosity and patience.

Our reluctance to listen is legendary, in politics, in marriage, at work or wherever we feel ourselves threatened by a challenge to our beliefs or our existing way of thinking. To listen actively and attentively to another person is to put our existing beliefs and dispositions at risk. (*What if this person is right? What if I have to change my mind? What if I have no answer for this?*) As Carl Rogers put it in *On Becoming a Person*:

> If you really understand another person . . . if you are willing to enter his private world and see the way life appears to him, without any attempt to make evaluative judgments, you run the risk of being changed yourself. You might see it his way, you might find yourself influenced in your attitudes . . . This risk of being changed is one of the most frightening prospects most of us face.

Active, committed listening – entering into the world of the other person – is fundamental to the therapeutic effect of communication. This is when the speaker feels truly valued, respected, taken seriously. This is when they realise we are prepared to put our own preoccupations and ideas on hold and to entertain their ideas. That's listening. Anything else is mere hearing. Listening like that is an act of courage: it feels risky to step away, even momentarily, from the comfort and emotional safety of our own cage.

When we listen to another person, we are offering them the gift of our undivided attention, the gift of our increased understanding of them, the gift of acceptance (even if not agreement) and, of course, the gift of taking them seriously. This is generous stuff. But there's even more to the generosity of listening. When we listen to another person we are also giving them a precious opportunity to clarify their own thoughts and feelings by sharing them with us. True listening is like undertaking a joint exploration of another person's cage.

We know what it feels like to be unsure of what we really think about something until we discuss it with another person, hear ourselves say it out loud or sense another person's response to it. Nothing is quite as reassuring and clarifying as being properly listened to. And the opposite is true: nothing is quite as frustrating and disappointing as not being listened to. Why do you think naggers keep nagging? It's usually because they haven't been attentively listened to in the past, so they've developed the unattractive habit of saying the same thing over and over, to the point where most of us are inclined to switch off. The only way to break that cycle is to truly listen and then prove you've listened by offering some feedback that makes it clear you have understood what was being said. Do that a few times, and the nagger won't feel the same compunction to keep speaking as if into a void.

Impatience is one of the great barriers to listening. The person who is jumping in before you've finished what you want to say, making a fresh point before acknowledging the point you've been trying to make or ignoring what you've been saying and using the time to prepare what they want to say . . . all these are signs not only of poor communication skills but also of a person who has not understood the therapeutic power of listening. Not to listen to someone is the equivalent of saying, *You don't matter; your opinions don't count; you're not someone I am prepared to take seriously.* To listen to someone means devoting time to the process, putting your own concerns on hold, remaining silent even when you're dying to say something. Patient listening also involves a willingness to postpone judgement about what is being said. Mostly, we want to rush in to agree, to disagree, to object, to correct; but listening demands the patience to let all that wait until the other person has finished saying to us what they want to say to us.

Committed listeners always *receive* before they *react*. If you can feel yourself wanting to jump in, you haven't been listening properly. Listening and responding are two separate acts, but we're always trying to blur them. Our patience should extend to the way we respond: instead of rushing in, we need to develop the habit of saying things like, *Let's see if I've got that straight; is this what you're saying?* One of the most reassuring things about being attentively listened to is the experience of hearing another person play back to us in their own words what we have been trying to say, just to make sure they have understood it. Careful playback usually opens up deeper layers of a conversation, because it proves that listening has occurred. Of course, playback isn't enough: we don't just want to know that we've been heard. Once we have established that our message has been received, we also need to know *how* our message is being received, what sense the listener is making of it and what interpretation they are placing on it. This is the complete feedback loop, and without it, talking is only talking – noises in the air. Active listening converts noise into communication.

We can't realistically be expected to give such patient, attentive, generous listening to everyone all the time. But when someone makes it clear to us that they need the gift of our undivided attention – they need us to be fully attentive to them – we are effectively being cast in the role of therapist to that person, in that moment. If we don't have the time or are not in a sufficiently receptive mood to be able to listen attentively, it's better to say so. Mock listening, with one mental eye on the clock or your mind on something else, is like mock therapy. To pretend to listen is far worse than simply saying, *Look, I'm sorry, but this isn't a good time for me. Can we make another time to talk?*

Michael misses another connection

Back from his aborted trip to London and feeling rather neglected because of Jenny's absence while she is at her friend's beach house, Michael catches a couple of hours' sleep. Afterwards, he scratches some lunch together and decides to spend the rest of the day at home, where he can work in peace. (He's also quite happy to postpone the moment when he has to confront the look of incredulity on his PA's face.)

By eight-thirty that night he has papers spread out all over the dining table and is deeply into some email exchanges via his iPad when he hears Jenny's car in the drive. She is home earlier than expected (possibly a whole day earlier than expected, but Michael isn't sure). He is pleased and relieved by her return, though he is in the midst of a flurry of emails with someone in the marketing department at Dagenham, and the negotiation is at a rather delicate stage.

He gets up and goes to meet Jenny, takes her overnight bag and kisses her. 'Did you have fun?' he asks.

'Fun? Since when was this ever about fun?'

'Well, I mean . . . a couple of days at Nina's beach house, and—'

'You didn't hear a word I said about Nina's daughter on the phone, did you? I suppose you were gazing at the wretched screen of your iPad the whole time I was talking. Were you?'

'Of course not, Jen. I might have been a bit distracted by that mix-up with the flight . . . ' Michael trails off unconvincingly. He now recalls that he was indeed in the thick of a message exchange with London, desperately trying to salvage his appointment with his boss. Perhaps he had missed something Jenny told him.

'I'll have a wash and put the kettle on', she says. 'Or would you like something stronger than tea?'

'Tea would be lovely.'

Michael returns to the dining table and takes up his iPad. The notoriously impatient marketing man in Dagenham is clearly waiting for an answer . . .

'. . . and so I just told Nina straight. She can't expect her daughter to be open and honest with her if she's going to go off the deep end every time Millie mentions this boy. I mean, Nina has never really given the poor kid a chance to—' Jenny glances in the direction of the dining table. 'You weren't listening to any of that, were you?'

'Any of what?'

'Make your own tea. I'm going to bed.'

Listening is not only the great sign that we are taking someone else seriously; it's also the way we discover and develop common ground between us. The more we listen, the more likely it is that we will find some point of connection with the other person; we'll learn about some sadness or difficulty in their life to which we can respond with sympathy; we'll find threads of common humanity linking us to each other.

Listening is a journey of exploration. The things we discover won't always warm us to the other person, but until we have listened we won't be equipped to know whether we have anything useful – anything good – to bring to the encounter.

Apologise sincerely

When someone has wronged, offended, hurt or upset you, intentionally or unintentionally, what do you most want from them? Without doubt, the answer is that you want them to acknowledge what they've done to you and apologise for it. And not just an airy, reflexive *Oh sorry*, but a sincere expression of regret, a statement of remorse (if the matter is serious enough to warrant that), a clear indication that they understand the hurt or harm they caused you and an undertaking not to do it again. Easier said than done, of course.

'Never explain, never apologise' is a line often, though wrongly, attributed to Henry Ford II. (What Ford actually said, after being convicted on a drink-driving charge, was 'never complain, never explain', quoting Benjamin Disraeli.) Minor variations on 'never explain, never apologise' appear through history, attributed to various royal, political and military figures, and the phrase was popularised in the 1949 John Wayne movie *She Wore a Yellow Ribbon*. The rest of the line delivered by Wayne in that movie is significant: 'It's a sign of weakness'.

A sign of weakness? How can it be weak to admit I'm wrong or to acknowledge that I have behaved in a damaging or offensive way? How can it be weak to offer someone the therapeutic gift of an apology? On the contrary, to apologise sincerely is to imply that I am secure enough in my sense of myself to admit I was wrong and to show that I am keen to rebuild the bridge between us. To withhold an apology when we know we have erred in some way is a sign not only of breathtaking arrogance but also of insecurity: it's as if the offending party is afraid of what might be exposed or lost in the encounter.

So why would so many people be drawn to the idea that apologising is a sign of weakness? And how could anyone reach the conclusion that *not* to apologise should be a matter of principle? The answer is simple. Apologising takes a double measure of goodness – one part humility, one part courage – and many people who worship the idols of power or status manage to convince themselves that to apologise is to give too much away, to erode their position of superiority, to sacrifice some authority. It's not just people in positions of power who think like that, of course.

> A fellow at my work is congenitally incapable of apologising. We all find it a huge joke – you can see him squirming when a simple apology is called for, but he just can't bring himself to say the words. I think someone must have once told him it's a sign of weakness and so he's kind of adopted that idea. My own father was the same. Couldn't do it. Drove my mother nuts. 'Go on, Geoff', she'd say to him, 'just say you're sorry. We all know you're sorry. Just say the words!' But for some

reason, he was incapable of doing it. He was a stubborn bloke, my father, so I suppose that was part of it. My mother laughed at him over it. The rest of us weren't game to laugh at him, but we did think it was pretty silly – a bit like pretending it didn't hurt if you hit your thumb with a hammer. Actually, I think his refusal to apologise, almost as if it was a matter of principle, hurt our mother pretty deeply. She certainly taught us to apologise when it was called for. Maybe it was a generational thing – with some men, at least.

The idea that apologising risks some loss of power or status is actually quite true. You can't apologise to someone in a way that will mean anything to them if you stay on your high horse. You have to dismount, stand with them, look them in the eye and apologise from that position. An apology is a gesture between equals, not something dispensed from on high. I'm apologising only because I've wronged you; the question of our relative positions in some real or imaginary pecking order mustn't be allowed to come into it. A boss apologising to an employee is precisely the same sort of encounter as an employee apologising to a boss: if status is allowed to enter the equation, the unbalanced dynamics will diminish the force of the apology.

Official apologies run the risk of losing some of their force for precisely this reason. When a government or a religious or other institution makes an apology to a person or a class of people wronged by that government or institution, it's vital that the apology is made in a spirit of equality; otherwise, it can look like yet another thing being done to the victim by the institution. Any official apology should ideally be the outcome of a careful process of consultation and collaboration. To simply apologise as a spontaneous, isolated act may offer temporary comfort to the aggrieved party, but an apology that grows out of a sustained, negotiated encounter between the two parties is likely to have a deeper and more enduring effect. Victims of sexual abuse at the hands of supposedly celibate priests, for instance, are never going to be satisfied with a formal institutional apology that offers anything less than full and frank admissions of guilt, convincing expressions of shame and remorse and, depending on the victim's wishes, symbolic acts of restitution.

As usual, we run into language problems when we deal with something as complex and emotional as a heartfelt apology. The word 'sorry' (like 'love', 'good' and many other words laden with ambiguity) can convey many different shades of meaning.

If I want to express sympathy with you at a time of bereavement or illness, I can say, with complete sincerity, *I'm really sorry to hear about that.* I'm sorry, but I'm not apologetic, because I am in no way responsible.

If I invite you to my place for dinner and it's pouring with rain at the time of your arrival, I may greet you at the door by saying, *Sorry about the weather.* Yes, it's true that I wish it had not been raining when you ran from your car to my front door, but the weather is beyond my control and we both know that. Still, apologising for it in such circumstances is a pleasant social convention.

If I'm playing tennis with you and my ball hits the net cord and bounces awkwardly, I can say, *Sorry!* purely as a sporting gesture: no one will assume I am apologising for having deliberately tried to hit the top of the net in a ruthless attempt to win the point. I'm sorry it happened, but I'm hardly responsible for it: it was a matter of chance.

If I brush lightly against you as I pass your table in a restaurant, courtesy demands that I say, *I'm sorry*, without there being any sense of a serious apology. But 'sorry' in that context does convey the idea that I did something careless and possibly mildly irritating, even if it was both unintentional and inconsequential.

Because the word so often carries no more than lightweight hand luggage, it can seem inadequate in circumstances where it is made to carry the heavier freight of a serious apology. In such cases, saying 'I want to apologise' can seem more comforting and more convincing, because it will explicitly convey the idea that

I am accepting personal responsibility for what has been done to you. As always, the test is what we ourselves would want to hear if we were being offered an apology.

> The girl next door was really horrible to me when our family moved to the city. I tried to be friends, but the worst thing was when she deliberately broke a rather special cup and saucer we were playing with in our backyard. She ran home, and I took the broken china inside to show my mother. I don't know what passed between the two mothers, but the next day the girl and her mother came over to our place to apologise. The mother had her arm around the girl the whole time, and it was the mother who did all the apologising. My mother was very gracious, very polite, 'Don't give it another thought' . . . all that stuff.
>
> Then we all waited for the girl to say something. He mother poked her and said, 'Go on'.
>
> Eventually she mumbled, almost inaudibly, 'Sorry'. Her mother praised her as if she'd done something brave and noble, but I thought it was totally pathetic. She wasn't sorry at all. I still remember that, after all these years. It was so insincere.

When we apologise to someone, there's often a moment of uncertainty when we wonder whether the apology will be accepted and, if so, whether we will be forgiven. Ideally, we'd like both things to happen together, but that is never guaranteed.

Generally speaking, apologies made in a spirit of sincerity and humility will be accepted, as long as any anger roused by the incident has subsided and the wronged party is prepared to move on. People who have been wronged are understandably sensitive to any sign of insincerity in an apology or any hint that the apology is actually a devious attempt to wriggle out of accepting any more responsibility for the incident. It's true that apologies are sometimes used as smokescreens, designed to deflect further attention from the matter without the offender fully facing up to all the consequences of their actions.

My husband had an affair a few years ago. I was devastated when I found out, of course, and he was abject. Terribly ashamed of himself, remorseful . . . He assured me he had ended it and he apologised unreservedly. The thing was, he thought apologising was all he had to do. He wouldn't really let me work through it with him. I was hurt and angry, naturally, but I wanted to understand it properly and maybe even see what we could learn from it. But every time I tried to discuss it, he'd roll his eyes and say, 'I've apologised, haven't I?' as if that was the end of it and I was in the wrong for bringing it up again. Well, it wasn't the end of it as far as I was concerned. I didn't actually feel as if I could accept his apology until I knew a bit more about what drove him to do it. It felt as if he was using his apology as a way of short-circuiting that process I needed to go through. It sounds awful, but I actually wasn't sure it was a sincere apology. He kept saying he'd turned the page. It felt more like him trying to let himself off the hook.

Most people are pretty adept at picking the difference between an authentic apology made in a spirit of genuine humility and an attempt to use an apology as a means of manipulation or control. Even an authentic apology can't always be accepted straightaway; some people may need time to let an apology sink in or to adjust their perspective on the situation in the light of the apology. Some people are reluctant to accept an apology simply because they are still seething and they enjoy seething; they are feeling resentful and feeding off their resentment, however self-destructive that may turn out to be. But most people are not like that. The sincerity of an apology will usually be enough to carry the day and to begin, at least, the process of reconciliation.

To have an apology offered and accepted can be a therapeutic experience for both parties. Relationships can be strengthened by the experience of working through the process of apology: though traces of residual damage may linger, an apology will usually accelerate the healing process, especially if it is accompanied by some compensation or reparation.

Forgive generously

The acceptance of an apology is not, of course, the same thing as forgiveness. If I have been wronged, the main thing I want is to be offered an apology. It might not always occur to me that the main thing the offender wants is to be forgiven – which is exactly what I would want if I were in their shoes.

An apology is generally made in response to a combination of guilt and shame. Those are closely related emotions, but there is an important difference between them. Guilt is a private response to the realisation that we have offended against our own moral code, leading to a sense of personal failure. Shame is a social phenomenon: the sense of embarrassment or humiliation we feel when we realise someone else has been offended, hurt or disappointed by our words or actions. Shame can only be assuaged by receiving forgiveness from the person we have wronged or offended.

Usually, an act of forgiveness will help to alleviate our feelings of guilt, but, as guilt is an essentially private matter, its complete expiation requires us to forgive ourselves as well, something many people are surprisingly reluctant to do. Yet the good life demands that we find a way of shedding our guilt; otherwise, it will increase the tendency towards self-absorption. Being self-centred is not only a product of arrogance; it can also be a sign of a person who has not found a way to relieve themselves of a burden of guilt long after they've been forgiven by anyone else involved in their misdemeanour.

There are few things more emotionally crippling or more likely to get in the way of our openness to other people than a burden of unforgiven and therefore unresolved guilt. Assuming we have apologised to the person we have hurt or offended, and assuming we have been forgiven by that person and made any necessary reparations, then the only way to lift that burden is by finding a way to forgive ourselves (with the aid of a professional counsellor, if necessary). Until that happens, we will not only be distracted by our lingering guilt but we might find that we are projecting our unresolved feelings, quite unfairly, onto other people – perhaps criticising someone for their jealousy when unresolved jealousy may be the source of unresolved guilt in ourselves; or complaining of someone's angry temperament when we are nursing unresolved guilt about our own feelings of anger; or criticising someone for being too hard on themselves when that is at the very core of our own problem. In other words, guilt needs to be dealt with if we are to rise above the pathetic self-indulgence characteristic of a person who can neither seek forgiveness from others (or quite believe they've really received it) nor find the pathway to self-forgiveness.

This is not an attack on guilt: guilt is a perfectly healthy response mechanism that rings alarm bells to warn us of moral lapses, thereby reassuring us that our conscience is in good working order. We should welcome the message guilt is sending us and then deal with it.

Forgiveness doesn't always come easily. You can demand an apology of someone, but you can't demand forgiveness: that would be yet another way of offending the person you've already offended, by applying pressure on them through an expectation that they should make you feel better by forgiving you. To have an apology accepted is a relief; to feel our guilt and shame being washed away by complete, unconditional, generous forgiveness is a relief of an entirely different order.

One of the great barriers to forgiveness arises from a crazy bit of folk wisdom that seduces us all too easily, because it sounds so wonderful: forgive and forget.

Forgive and forget? No, we can do better than that. Forgiving someone is a remarkably generous and compassionate thing to do, because we know its effects will be intensely therapeutic for the person being forgiven. Those therapeutic effects actually extend to the forgiver, as well. Moving from feelings of anger, blame or resentment to the point where we are willing to forgive is to shed the shrivelled skin of the victim and replace it with new growth that thrives on feeling once more in control of the situation. For those who forgive, there are even potential health benefits, lowered blood pressure among them, according to Ellen Waldman and Frederic Luskin's chapter in *The Negotiator's Fieldbook* (2006). So an act of forgiveness can be beneficial to both parties, though, as people in search of the good life, our concern will naturally be more for the benefit to the other person in this situation. But the suggestion that we should forgive and forget, as though forgiveness entails wiping the slate clean or pretending something didn't happen, is not only unrealistic; it's also bad advice.

Let's say someone has wronged, offended or hurt me. They've apologised and I've accepted their apology. And now I am prepared to forgive them – that is, to help relieve them of the guilt and shame they have been feeling ever since they behaved badly. End of story. Good outcome. Are we both then expected to set aside what's happened? Not learn from it? Not incorporate that process into our continuing relationship with each other? To do any of that would be to misinterpret the value of an apology and to misunderstand the healing power of forgiveness. Forgiveness is not saying, *We'll go on as if this didn't happen*; it's saying, *We know this happened, and yet we'll go on.* That's why forgiveness is such a powerful therapeutic tool. After an act of forgiveness, we don't need to pretend to each other that we have forgotten all about it; we live as if I have truly forgiven you. That is, we both know that you – like all of us – are capable of bad behaviour or the occasional moral lapse, and we go on with that knowledge.

When someone hurts or offends you, it's a stark reminder that humans are like that: the lapse could as easily have been yours as the other person's (unless you're some kind of saint). Forgiveness is not only a gift to the person who has wronged you; it's also an acknowledgement of human frailty and an acceptance of the fact that we are all vulnerable. I don't forgive you out of some lofty position of unimpeachable moral superiority; I forgive you because I see my own frailty reflected in you. I forgive you because I understand what it means to be human.

The polar opposite of forgiveness is, of course, revenge. Everything we can say about the therapeutic effect of forgiveness (for both the forgiver and the forgiven) can be reversed in the case of revenge. Revenge is the ultimate form of anti-therapeutic behaviour. It is *calculated* to inflict damage, and such malevolence is potentially as destructive for the avenger as for the original offender. It reduces the avenger to the level of the person who wronged them; it meets anger with anger, hate with hate or violence with violence; it diminishes us as surely as if we had participated in the original offence. As we noted in chapter 5, revenge is a grotesque corruption of the Golden Rule into something like: *If you treat me badly, I'll treat you badly*. What could be a worse basis than that for the life of any society?

Let's pause here to remind ourselves where we have come from and where we are going. We are approaching the end of a book called *The Good Life*, which is all about how we might increase the goodness quotient in our lives by paying more attention to the needs of other people – friends and strangers alike. The question of whether we might or might not be prepared to forgive someone who has wronged us is a stern test of whether we've engaged with the idea of the good life and, in particular, with the demands of this Golden Rule we're all so keen to endorse in theory.

There's no law that says you must forgive someone who has wronged you just because they've apologised to you. So why would you? Would it be out of mere politeness? (*It's the socially acceptable thing to do.*) Would it be because you feel the pressure of expectation from a person who badly wants your forgiveness? Would it be out of a vague sense of reciprocity? (*Maybe if I forgive this person, they'll be more likely to forgive me when I do something awful.*) There are people who manage their relationships, even their marriage, just like that, regarding a friend's or partner's lapse as runs on the board that put them in credit on the forgiveness register.

If we are serious in the quest for the good life, there is only one answer to the question of why we would unhesitatingly forgive someone who has apologised to us: we'd do it because that's the way we ourselves would like to be treated in that situation. We might still want to explore the question of why things went wrong or test whether the apology is authentic. But our underlying disposition will be this: if the apology is sincere and the matter has been cleared up, of course we'll forgive. To do otherwise would be to deny a therapeutic benefit, a healing, to the one who has apologised.

Can we forgive someone who hasn't apologised? Yes, we can. Parents do it for their children all the time. They make allowances. They teach their children to apologise, but they know it will take years before the moral force of this is really grasped. We forgive people we think are incapable of apologising because of a disorder or disability that impairs their cognitive functioning or because they lack the insight that would alert them to the implications of what they've done. At our best, we forgive people even before they've apologised, because we know how sorry they are for what they did and we know we are capable of doing the same. Sometimes, our love or care for someone means that forgiveness becomes a way of life for us, even when there's no thought of an apology.

> I finally forgave my poor mother for not being the mother I wanted her to be. She must have suffered terribly through her alcoholism – we all suffered – but after she died I realised she would never have been able to apologise to us. She wasn't capable of facing what she'd done with her life. But, yes, I forgave her. I hope she's having a peaceful death, wherever she is. Her life certainly wasn't peaceful.

But the question *Can we forgive someone who hasn't apologised?* runs deeper than that. What about someone who has wronged us, who knows they have wronged us, and who shows no remorse;

no inclination to apologise? What then? The truth about most of us is that we are likely to carry our resentment at being treated like that for a long time, sometimes for a lifetime. As we haven't been apologised to, there's been no trigger for forgiveness. And yet forgiveness may come, and it will heal us when it does.

> I was all set for a big promotion when this bloke completely white-anted me. Undermined me. It was deliberate – he spread stories that weren't true, and curried favour with the boss. Everyone knew what he was doing – he was quite brazen about it – and I thought he'd never get away with it. How naïve was I! He got the job and I didn't. I left as soon as I could organise somewhere else to go. I was completely disgusted. I knew I could never trust or respect that man, even though I gather he's made himself into a bit of a hero these days. I used to wonder if he'd ever apologise to me for what he did. Of course he wouldn't – that's not how these blokes operate. Never explain, never apologise. I doubt if he even thought he did anything wrong. *Whatever it takes* – that would be his line. He wanted the job so he did what he had to do to get it. Someone said to me I would never get over it if I didn't forgive him. How can I forgive him? He hasn't apologised. But I admit it's a thing that nags away at me. If I could forgive him, maybe I could let it go. Perhaps I will. He'd only laugh if he knew. He wouldn't know what I was talking about.

Mostly, the calls on our capacity to forgive are less complex than that. Someone has made a mistake, said something hurtful in the heat of the moment or fallen short of their usual standards of courtesy or propriety. And now they're sorry; and we need them to be sorry, because they've upset or disappointed us.

So what do *they* need? They need our forgiveness, just as we would need theirs if the roles were reversed. If we withhold it, we know the consequences: the healing of our rift won't begin; their lingering sense of guilt or shame might persist and be expressed in other, more destructive ways; our sense of having been wronged may linger, eating away at us and distracting us from our focus on the wellbeing of the other person.

Where passionate love is concerned, the situation can be more complex. It's a cliché that the line between love and hate is both fine and wobbly, and there are many examples of lovers who claim they could never forgive each other for some real or imagined slight. The loss of love feels so damaging, so desolating, so confusing, that the capacity for forgiveness is not only diminished; we may even *want* it to be diminished as a way of punishing the lover who spurned or disappointed us. Here's Wendy Cope's little gem 'Defining the Problem', from *Serious Concerns* (1992):

I can't forgive you. Even if I could,
You wouldn't pardon me for seeing through you
And yet I cannot cure myself of love
For what I thought you were before I knew you.

But time can heal even those wounds, and lovers who refused to speak to each other, let alone apologise or forgive, at the time of a tiff or a break-up sometimes manage to find a way back to civility, at least.

Make 'em laugh!

Attentive listening, sincere apology, generous forgiveness: these are the gifts we most want from others and, therefore, the gifts we should be most willing to give to others. These are indeed the three great therapies of everyday life. But there is another . . .

What type of email do we most commonly forward to our friends? This week's rib-tickler, circling the globe. Many newspaper readers go straight to the comics or the political cartoon. Pick up a copy of *The New Yorker* and what do you look at first? The cartoons, of course. Flip through *Reader's Digest* and where do you pause?

'Laughter, the Best Medicine.' Who doesn't enjoy a laugh? *Everyone wants to be a comedian* is part of theatrical folklore, because there is nothing more gratifying to an actor (or a playwright) than hearing gales of laughter sweeping through a theatre.

'Start with a funny story' is the advice often given to people feeling nervous about making a speech. The theory is that if you make them laugh, they'll warm to you and the sound of laughter helps relax a nervous speaker. It's not always good advice, though: we've all suffered through speakers' unsuccessful attempts to raise a laugh, and then we're all worse off than if the attempt had never been made. Quips that occur to you on the spur of the moment are usually best left unsaid. If you're determined to start your speech with a joke, pre-test it on at least five people to make sure (a) you've got it straight, and (b) it's funny.

When we are meeting someone for the first time, especially in a potentially romantic setting, the first shared laugh is a magic moment, because it's the moment when we discover, with relief, that the other person has a sense of humour; and a sense of humour is one of the attributes humans rate most highly, especially in a potential mate. Why? It's partly because a person with a sense of humour is generally perceived as having things in perspective, in contrast with those who seem too serious. Life is a demanding and sometimes gruelling process, and light relief is always welcome. It's also partly because we feel good about ourselves when our laughter releases endorphins, the brain's feel-good neurotransmitters that raise the pain threshold and reduce stress. Why wouldn't we be grateful to anyone who can trigger that magical response in us?

You don't have to be an accomplished joke-teller or raconteur to give people the occasional gift of a smile. It requires only a willingness to see that life is often amusing and sometimes delightfully, unimaginably absurd.

There's a man who lives in our street, a thoroughly nice fellow, who is always up for a chat, and he never finishes a conversation without striking a light note. Many of our conversations are quite dark – he's been very worried about vandalism around here and he's always banging on about the dumbing-down of the media – but he usually manages to leave you with a smile on your face. 'Let me tell you a little story that might amuse you . . .' he says. It might be about the roadworkers he saw perched on a box in the middle of the road having their morning coffee break, protected by two flagmen stopping the traffic. Or the local clergyman who was reading a wedding service from his iPad when the battery went flat. He might make them up, for all I know.

I'd better end the chapter with a joke, then. Here's one that pops up in many different versions, depending on where in the world it's told. An American rancher is visiting an Australian cattle station. He wants to impress his Australian host with the size of his ranch back home. 'My ranch is so big', he says, 'I can saddle my horse up in the morning, ride west all day, camp the night and ride all the next day, and I still wouldn't be at the western boundary'.

'Yeah', says the Aussie, 'we used to have a horse like that, but we had to shoot the bastard'.

7

A good death

I want to die in my sleep.

I want to be wide awake, fully conscious of the moment.

When I know it's time to go, I just want to be able to swallow a 'peaceful pill'.

I'd rather drop dead from a heart attack on the tennis court than have a long struggle with cancer when I'm old.

I'd like to die in my nineties, shot by a jealous husband.

I want to die at home in my own bed, surrounded by family and friends.

Most of us have tried to imagine our deaths; some of us, unable to shake off the Utopia complex, may have constructed hopeful scenarios of an ideal death. Those ideals may range from people who don't want to know anything about it – *just give me the drugs!* – to those who regard death as the next great adventure and want to be fully engaged with the transition.

Some think of death as an end: the final word of the final chapter of our lives; the closing of a door that's locked and bolted forever. Others prefer to think of it as a beginning: the opening of a new door into the Great Unknown. Most religions offer their adherents the prospect of more to come after this mortal span, but not all believers take the offer seriously: many Christians, for example, enthusiastically follow the teachings of Jesus and profess belief in a deity (ranging from an almighty creator to a loving spirit abroad in the world) without clinging to any expectation of life after death. Yet even people without any conventional religious faith may embrace one of the popular conceptions of an afterlife: a free-ranging spiritual existence in which our souls, spirits, 'shades', 'energy' or life-force persist beyond the death of our bodies (perhaps for a short time, perhaps forever); reincarnation as another person; or a post-death state in which people's performance on earth will be judged by an omniscient, omnipotent and unforgiving arbiter who will decide whether we are to be ushered in to paradise or condemned either to oblivion or some gruesome eternal punishment.

This chapter is not about any of that. When it comes to questions of what might lie beyond death, your guess is as good as mine. We can believe whatever we choose to believe. The afterlife can only ever be imagined, until we're dead, of course, when the time for speculation will have passed. Faced with such cosmic uncertainty, the seventeenth-century French philosopher Blaise Pascal proposed this wager: as we can't be certain whether God exists or not, it's better to play it safe by believing than to discover we were wrong in not believing and then be sorry. Pascal's wager has particular relevance to a reward-and-punishment conception of the afterlife: the argument can be extended to say that as we can't know what an afterlife (if any) may bring, it's a safer bet to act as if it exists than to act as if it doesn't. Such pragmatic reasoning hardly sounds like a leap of faith, but it finds an echo in the equally pragmatic contemporary view that religious faith is somehow good for us, whether or not it happens to be true – where 'good for us' might mean good for our health and wellbeing as well as providing a motivation for leading a good life.

But this chapter is not about religion. It is certainly not about rewards or punishments. It is exclusively about the idea of a good death.

The fear of death

It's not that I'm afraid of dying – I just don't want to be there when it happens.

Woody Allen

Do not go gentle into that good night,
Old age should burn and rage at close of day;
Rage, rage against the dying of the light.

Dylan Thomas

Woody Allen's flippant line and Dylan Thomas's furious poem both strike a responsive chord in many of us because we associate death with pain and loss. We think of death as the process of being separated from those we love, though separation is an idea that makes sense only in the context of our present, conscious existence: once we're dead, that existence is ended and separation is no longer an issue for us. Whatever else it might do, death frees us from the present, with all its fears, anxieties and uncertainties. As the French philosopher André Comte-Sponville puts it in *The Little Book of Philosophy* (2004), 'Death will take nothing from us (since it will take only the future – which does not exist)'.

Yet many people intuitively resist that idea. They fear death precisely because they feel it will snatch their future from them, causing them to miss out on so much. Those approaching death sometimes speak of the shock of realising that death will prevent them from seeing their grandchildren grow up, for example, or cut short some unfinished project. All such fears arise from the bizarre assumption that, after death, we will still be in a state where it is possible to miss people or to regret being unable to complete projects or participate in events or activities.

Whether you prefer to think of death as oblivion or as transportation to some plane of existence beyond this earthly realm, the idea of missing people is inconsistent with the idea that you will have left all this behind. Others might miss you, but you won't be missing them: you'll either have nothing on your mind, since your mind won't exist, or you'll be thinking in a quite different, quite unimaginable way about quite different, quite unimaginable things, getting to your grand-daughter's school concert on time unlikely to be among them. None of the promises of religion, nor any other set of beliefs about the afterlife, suggests that if you turned out to have an immortal soul it would be engaged with the preoccupations of the life you lived in your mortal body.

Some of us fear death because we anticipate a terminal confrontation with disappointment and regret: perhaps over our failure to have done all we wanted to do; perhaps over our realisation that we had our priorities wrong for too much of our lives; perhaps over a failure to have loved as faithfully as we might have wished, or to have exerted as much positive influence on the lives of others as we might have hoped to. A common death-bed experience is to wish we had loved more and desired less. Yet anecdotal evidence suggests most of us will die peacefully: if we are fortunate enough to be conscious of our approaching demise, our cares, worries, obsessions, strivings and anxieties are likely to be washed away by the sense of an ending.

Some fear death as a form of punishment, almost like an execution. Some fear the intensity of family and friends' expressions of sadness as the moment of death approaches, though, again anecdotally, it appears that a greater problem for the dying is the reluctance of their family and friends to face and discuss what's actually happening. Some fear the idea of being enclosed by terminal blackness, as though death will feel like the ultimate version of depression, though, again, those who've come close to death report that it's more like being bathed in bright light than being drowned in a black sea. Other fears are less cosmic and more pragmatic: a common fear is of being buried or cremated before we have actually expired, but modern medicine ought to reassure us on that point.

All such fears have some rational basis, since we tend to fear the unknown, and death is the most unknowable thing of all. And yet, considering that death is the only absolute certainty for all of us, it's odd that we have traditionally been so reluctant to talk openly and candidly about it, to face its inevitability and prepare for it. Not that preparing for it need be morbid: preparation for death, at the emotional level, implies nothing more than reaching a state of mind where we are no longer striving, where we have made peace with ourselves and others, and where we are able to live utterly in the moment. Sound familiar? Such mindfulness is recommended by many philosophers, psychotherapists and mystics as the best form of preparation for each and every day, wherever we happen to be in the life cycle, especially since our death may come unexpectedly.

This is certainly not an exhortation to live every day as if it's your last; that strikes me as both unhelpful and unrealistic. The psychoanalyst Carl Jung had this advice for the elderly: 'Live each day as if they'll be here for another hundred years. Then they will really live to the end'. The goal of mindfulness is to be fully present, fully engaged, fully participating in whatever the moment, the hour, the day may bring. Though it has been purloined by many other systems of thought and meditative practice, the concept of mindfulness originates in the Buddhist tradition. In *Awakening the Buddha Within* (1997), Lama Surya Das describes it like this: 'Pure mindfulness is relaxed, open, lucid, moment-to-moment present awareness. It is like a bright mirror: nonclinging, nongrasping, nonaversive, nonreactive, undistorting . . . Present awareness and mindfulness implies an understanding of what we are doing and saying'.

Ellen Langer, a professor of psychology at Harvard, describes the essence of mindfulness as 'looking for new things' in each new moment. Even for a person conscious of the imminence of death, mindfulness banishes worry in favour of moment-to-moment engagement with what is, not what might be, and certainly not what might have been. This is, after all, the only opportunity we will ever have to answer the question *What is it like to die?*

Research into Finnish young people's concerns about the future has caught the attention of social researchers around the world because of a recent escalation in young Fins' fear of death – mentioned by only 17 per cent of respondents in a 1983 survey, but jumping to 39 per cent in 2007. In that same period, adolescents' fear of war and terrorism fell dramatically, being mentioned by 81 per cent of respondents in 1983, 56 per cent in 1997 and only 11 per cent in 2007. Fears about the environment rose sharply between 1983 and 1997, but fell away in 2007 (being mentioned by only 7 per cent of adolescents). Fears about work fluctuated a little, but hovered around 40 per cent. More personal fears rose: fear of failure and making wrong choices went up from 7 to 16 per cent, and fear of loneliness from 5 to 20 per cent. But the most dramatic increase, by far, was in the number of young people fearing death.

There are good reasons to assume that Finland is not a unique case and that Western adolescents' views are probably being broadly represented in these figures. So why the sharp increase in fear of death among the young? In a paper published in the *Journal of Adolescence* in 2012, the Finnish researchers, led by Pirjo Lindfors, conclude that 'perceptions of risks have become more individualized, thus supporting late-modernist theory'. In other words, adolescents have become more self-centred, more 'internal' in their concerns, reflecting a culture shift in the direction of individualism, materialism, privatisation, fragmentation and dislocation of families and communities. This is what's sometimes referred to as a 'lifestyle' culture, characterised by self-absorption and self-indulgence, and a preoccupation with positive outcomes (hence the associated increase in fear of failure and making wrong choices). It is not, of course, a culture created by adolescents: like every generation before them, they are responding to the subtle blend of parental example and all the environmental pressures and influences – economic, cultural, technological and otherwise – of the society in which they have been raised. As the researchers note, 'adolescents' images of the future act as a mirror of the times, reflecting the values and ethos of society . . . Cultural and societal changes, including emphasis on individual choice and increased uncertainty, seem to create perceptions of uneasiness and insecurity in young people's transitions to adulthood'.

Commenting on these findings in a 2012 article in *The Futurist* entitled 'Young People's Fears for the Future: Less Global, More Personal', the Australian social analyst Richard Eckersley says that

> the existential dimension of the analysis can be taken further. In psychology, terror management theory argues that fear of our mortality is a powerful motivation for humans, and we construct personal and cultural means to manage it, to allow us to accept the inevitability of death – worldviews, values, beliefs, rituals. So the Finnish findings showing increased fear of death might be evidence of how Western culture is failing us.

The fear of death is likely to be stronger if we have allowed ourselves to be seduced by the Utopia complex or to have fallen for the belief that the goal of our lives is to be happy, since both those motivations reflect a self-centredness that may heighten our anxieties about the future and, correspondingly, our fear of death. If it's all about Me, then my demise would indeed seem like an unspeakable tragedy.

If we have embraced a materialistic ethic, death's greatest significance is likely to be that it marks the end of our ceaseless struggle for more stuff, more money, more power, more status or more security. When our goals are primarily about gaining a personal advantage rather than making a contribution to the common good, death is always going to seem premature. *Why can't*

I have more? is a question that can be asked as greedily about life as about our possessions.

If, by contrast, we have managed to develop a less self-centred, less materialistic world view coloured by the sense of being part of a continuous process of social and cultural evolution, we are more likely to regard death simply as an inevitable stage in the life cycle, to be accepted rather than feared. Death may or may not lead on to something else: that is as unknowable as any other speculation about the future and, like any estimate of future possibilities, the shakiest basis for deciding how best to live now. Once we have embraced the idea that the good life is a life lived for others, then what is death but the transition from a moment in which we exist for those others to a moment in which we don't?

Whose 'good death'?

If you've caught the spirit of this book, you'll have been waiting for me to say this: people living the good life are going to be more concerned about trying to facilitate other people's good deaths than worrying about their own. It goes without saying that we all want to have a good death, by which most of us would mean a peaceful rather than a violent or painful death, but, on reflection, wouldn't our final days be the most absurdly inappropriate time to be preoccupied with ourselves and our own wellbeing? After all, we are about to leave the stage, not enter it. Our life's work – love's work – is almost done.

In any case, so much of what will happen to us through the process of dying is a matter of luck or circumstance, it's pointless devoting too much care and worry to it, especially if we've already developed an attitude of mindfulness that allows us to live in the moment. The less we dwell on the future, the less death looms as an issue for us. We are here. This is now. That's all there ever is.

The truth is that we might end up dying in pain, though the brilliance of modern palliative care almost guarantees that won't happen. We might end up being killed in an accident, and no amount of preparation can avoid that. We might die in our sleep, and know nothing of it. If we live long enough, there's a strong chance of some form of dementia (such as Alzheimer's disease) afflicting us, even if only mildly: some geriatricians argue that dementia is simply a symptom of ageing. Our thinking may be clouded by dementia but there are no grounds for assuming a demented person has no inner life: the nature of that inner life will be one of the discoveries many of us will make as we near the end.

We might have months, weeks or days of waiting for a death we know to be imminent, and be able to arrange for the kind of death that will be easiest for us and our families and friends to deal with. Again, the message of the good life: we will want our death to be as good an experience as possible for the people around us, not just for ourselves.

One way of achieving that is to be sure we have taken all possible precautions to make our passing and its aftermath as straightforward as possible for family, friends and carers. It goes without saying that we need to have made a valid will, to minimise confusion among those who are entitled to whatever we leave behind. We should also document our wishes regarding the use of our organs for transplant operations or for medical research. We will make life easier for those caring for us – for families and friends, certainly, but also for our doctor and any medical or nursing staff who may become involved in our care – if we make some intensely practical decisions well before the time those decisions might need to be implemented about how we wish to be treated at the end.

For example, in case the situation arises, it would be helpful to have clarified our attitude to such issues as *Do I wish to be kept alive for as long as possible, regardless of my quality of life? Do I want to be relieved of pain and suffering at any cost, even if it means the loss of consciousness and possibly of life itself? Under what conditions do I think it would be time to draw the line by declining further medical intervention in favour of palliative care?* Such questions should be explored through discussion not only with loved ones, but also with medical advisors. None of these discussions is likely to be much fun, yet having all such matters settled in advance with a doctor, in consultation with close family members or friends, is one way of making your own death an easier experience for all concerned (including you) if you should find yourself in a situation where you are no longer able to think clearly or make your wishes known.

Many people do not get around to having these end-of-life discussions until they either find themselves caught up in an unexpected medical emergency or finally realise they are terminally ill. In the Australian regional city of Tamworth, analysis of hospital patients' records over a three-month period in 2011 showed that 77 per cent of patients over the age of seventy-five who died in hospital had had their first documented end-of-life discussion only three days before their death. In the case of patients admitted to the emergency department, 82 per cent had not had any documented end-of-life discussion or review by the time of their discharge. In a report on that research published in *Australian Family Physician* (2012), the researcher, Amanda Gaw, concluded that

> armed with an established relationship with the patient and knowledge of their health situation, the GP is best placed to initiate discussion concerning end-of-life care and treatment preferences, sooner rather than later. The GP can facilitate such decisions being available and honoured in acute care by . . . encouraging the patient to take a copy of their advance care plan with them if admitted to hospital.

For a growing number of people entering old age, the thorny questions of euthanasia and assisted suicide loom large in any discussion of end-of-life care. *Should I make it clear that I don't want my life to be prolonged by artificial means of support? Should I leave instructions for someone to administer a lethal drug when nothing is left for me beyond pain and suffering? Should I be allowed access to a self-administered drug to end it all?* These are intensely personal questions, and the answers will vary greatly from person to person, and even for one person at different stages of life.

Some people who hold particular religious beliefs may argue that a painful death is a sign that God has something to teach us, and it must therefore be endured. Other people – with or without religious faith – see it quite differently: many supporters of euthanasia take the view that if it's okay to take an antibiotic to 'cheat nature' when we have a life-threatening illness, why isn't it equally okay to cheat nature by opting for a dignified, peaceful death when our lives have become painful and pointless?

> I've taken all sorts of stuff to keep me alive when nature says I should die – and I would have died, too, if I'd lived at a different time in history. That's exactly what antibiotics are designed to do – cheat nature. So what's the big deal about using medication to let people go peacefully? Nature can be very cruel. Nature causes miscarriages, birth defects, and all kinds of horrible diseases. I'm not a great fan of nature, especially when someone is being forced to cling on to something they no longer want – a life that's become painful and unpleasant for all concerned.

Euthanasia has several nuances of meaning, many fine lines. It's often colloquially referred to as 'mercy killing', which is usually taken to mean administering a lethal dose of painkillers either at the patient's request (voluntary euthanasia) or at the request of close family members distressed by seeing their loved one suffering so intensely and unnecessarily (involuntary euthanasia). It sometimes means withdrawing life support when it is clear that a patient is never going to recover, though many people would regard that as simply surrendering to nature rather than actively intervening to hasten a death. Does the decision to turn a machine off amount to intervention or is it the withdrawal of intervention? Is letting someone die when you have the means to prolong their life significantly different from hastening someone's death? For some people, deciding not to proceed with any medical intervention, letting nature take its course, seems like a form of euthanasia because it represents a decision by the patient, a carer or a loved one to decline any further treatment that might prolong life.

Though the legalisation of euthanasia remains a controversial topic in many countries (mainly because of the risk of abuse of a formalised, legalised process in which convenience might sometimes be allowed to outweigh compassion), euthanasia itself, whether legal or not, is a common feature of the dying process all over the world. The motives of those involved are generally quite unambiguous: they want a terminally suffering person to be released from that suffering; they want a person to be shown the kind of compassion that would allow them to be relieved of unbearable pain or indignity.

In many countries, including Australia, access to the drugs that might facilitate a painless, dignified death is generally restricted to the medical profession, so the decision to die with dignity is not always easily implemented: it generally requires the cooperation of a compassionate doctor.

> Our GP phoned me to say our elderly mother was in great distress and conventional pain relief was no longer working. I asked what he would advise. He knew our mother had always said she didn't want her life to be prolonged artificially, but this was a bit different. No one was keeping her alive – we were just trying to keep her comfortable. Her situation got worse and although she was barely conscious, it was obvious she was desperate to be released from the anguish she was suffering. Eventually the GP rang again and said, 'I'm going to give your mother morphine. Do you understand what I am saying?' He said it very deliberately so I would get the message and of course I did. I told him to go ahead.

When the time comes to die, each of us will chart our own unique course through the process. No one else can chart it for us;

no one can predict how it will be for us or be certain of what the moment of transition will involve. No one else can prescribe how we should handle it. If we are conscious at the time, an attitude of mindfulness may mean that we are so fully engaged with the experience of dying that we lose ourselves in it and find peace in that surrender.

That's us. What about other people? How might we best facilitate *their* good death? If we are committed to the Golden Rule, the principle applies as much to dying as to living (though palliative care nurses and doctors like to say what is inarguably true: we are all living until we die). So the question is: how can we treat a person who is known to be approaching death as we ourselves would want to be treated in that situation?

The answer is simple: we will follow the same principle we would follow at any previous stage of that person's life. We will signal, as clearly as possible, that we are taking them seriously, appreciating them, responding to their needs and recognising them for who they are. We will do whatever we can to help make their dream of a peaceful death come true. We will assure them they will not be forgotten, that the value they have contributed to our life will be honoured, that their friendship has been precious. We will acknowledge the truth of what is happening to them; we will listen attentively to whatever they need to say. We will seize the opportunity to apologise for any wrongs we might have done them, or for any offence or upset we might have caused. We will reassure them that we have forgiven them for any matters that still sit – or ever sat – heavily on their conscience.

And we will, in turn, gratefully receive whatever gifts they are able to offer us: their willingness to listen to us reminiscing about shared experiences, perhaps revealing some secret we haven't previously felt able to divulge or some confession we now want to make to them. We will accept, without reservation, any apologies they might wish to make to us. We will allow them to forgive us for the ways we might have disappointed or failed them in the past.

We know how to facilitate a good death for others simply because we can imagine how we ourselves would like to be treated if the time of our own death were approaching. Perhaps we should spend more time pondering that question, not so we can set ourselves up for a perfect death (that old Utopia complex again), but so we can be better equipped to support others in their dying. In that process, we can be aided by what we might learn from history, literature and family folklore. We can learn, for instance, from Robert Dessaix's moving account of the death of the Russian novelist Ivan Turgenev, in *Twilight of Love* (2004):

> What was uppermost in his mind at the end was finding a way, as words began to fail him, of assuring those he loved of the depth and reality of his love for their goodness. What is love if not joy in another's goodness? He seemed to want not to leave them but to melt into them.

One thing we know about people's idea of a good death is that it would ideally occur in the presence of the people they love most, and probably at home. UK research (*Dying for Change*, published by the Demos think tank in 2010) has shown that 36 per cent of people rate access to friends and family as the single most important thing they would want at the end of their life, way ahead of pain relief (22 per cent) and good medical care (12 per cent). Yet the reality is different for many people. The Demos researchers say of the UK situation that many people will 'die badly in places not of our choosing, with services that are often impersonal, in systems that are unyielding, struggling to find meaning in death because we are cut off from the relationships which count most to us'.

Australian research on nursing-home patients has discovered the same emphasis on home-based personal relationships in the thinking of people contemplating the end of life, for whom 'home' might mean a nursing home where attachments to familiar and trusted carers have become strong enough for those people to feel like friends or surrogate family. A submission on advance care planning to the National Health and Hospitals Reform Commission in 2008 showed that a majority of patients in Victorian nursing homes would prefer to stay where they are and receive palliative care from familiar staff than to be moved to acute care.

Not everyone wants to die at home, but virtually everyone wants their loved ones present. In *Mortality* (2012), Christopher Hitchens's account of the year in which oesophageal cancer finally overwhelmed him, he wrote, 'My chief consolation in this year of living dyingly has been the presence of friends'. How could it be otherwise? A recurring theme of this book has been that we discover life's deepest meanings through the experience of forming and nurturing personal relationships; why should it be any different in death? What your family and friends most want at their death is the very same thing you would want at your own. Apart from being in or close to their own home, they mainly want you to be there, fully present for them, attending to them, reassuring them that they are being securely loved to the very end.

> I was booked to take an overseas trip that couldn't really be cancelled, but one of my closest friends was obviously going to die while I was away. So I went to see him, to explain all this. We had a wonderful few minutes together, said our farewells, spelt it all out, what we'd meant to each other. After he'd died, his wife told me how much that parting conversation had meant to him. Well, it meant a lot to me, too.

Your physical presence will also create the opportunity for the dying person and for you to say goodbye. People deprived of that final moment of intimacy with a deceased loved one often regret it for a very long time. Goodbyes are not always possible, but people approaching death find those moments of leave-taking precious, and they are psychologically important for the survivors as well.

> My cousin was killed in an IRA bomb blast. Everything about it was tragic – especially the fact that she was only twenty-one. I've always regretted that we didn't have a chance to say goodbye. I couldn't even get to her funeral.

Jill mourns for Jack

We last visited the Thurkettles when Jill had returned from a meeting of the LOL Club to find Jack on the floor, felled by a mild stroke. Now he has had a second stroke, of roughly the same severity as the first, but Jill was better prepared this time. She was with him when it happened and called the ambulance immediately. Jack was conscious throughout, and they both clung to the hope that this would turn out as well as the previous time.

And so it has, except that Jack's recuperative powers are much diminished, and the physiotherapy takes longer to have any noticeable effect. Still, Jack is soon home again and back to walking Horrie, though with the aid of a stick and always with Jill at his side. Jill takes extended leave from her job and, at her urging, Jack finally agrees to retirement. He is delighted by the things said to him at a farewell function and surprised by the number of people who attend.

Their three children, sensing a potentially serious situation, all come to visit. Jack spends more time with his two sons over the few days of their visit than he has for many years. Sizing up the situation, Sally moves back in, 'just for a while', she tells her mother. Sally's current romance is flourishing, so this isn't a wound-licking visit. Jack and Jill are introduced to Sally's new partner, and their initial impression is largely favourable, though Jack's private opinion is that 'he seems a bit wet', and Jill's private opinion is that no one could ever be quite good enough for Jack's daughter.

During the weeks following the second stroke, Jack often complains of a deep fatigue and spends a great deal of time lying in bed or resting in his favourite armchair. His speech has returned, though his voice is weaker and many words defeat him.

Despite mild protests from Jack, their doctor initiates a home visit to prepare what he calls an 'advance care plan', a written document that will set out Jack's wishes in the case of any need of further medical care, especially emergency care. Jack and Jill argue over the question of how much life support Jack should have in the event of a more serious stroke or other event that might disable him and put him in a coma: Jill is all for maintaining life as long as possible; Jack, despite some tears, insists that he would prefer to let nature take its course in the event of a major deterioration.

A few months after the stroke, it becomes clear to Jill that Jack is never going to regain his old strength and vitality. His tiredness seems to be becoming more of a problem to him, and walking is now an effort. Jill encourages members of the dog-walking group to visit with their dogs, and Jack is much cheered by the dogs' exuberant reaction to seeing Horrie and by receiving news of the neighbourhood. He and Jill spend a great deal of time together, often in companionable silence. They sometimes exchange endearments and assurances, revived from the years before they had allowed their intimate life to become swamped by the stresses and distractions of raising a family and making a living. Jack encourages Jill to maintain her regular contacts with the members of her book club and to keep in touch with the life of her office by phone and email. (For Jill, there's been a shift in her attitude to the LOL Club: it has become as precious a resource for her as for the other women who have needed a secure haven where sadness can be as readily and openly acknowledged as happiness, and its authenticity honoured.)

And then, one afternoon, after a visit from two of the dog-walkers, there's a third stroke. From the moment it happens, Jill realises this is far more serious than the first two. She takes the doctor's care plan with them in the ambulance. The hospital team caring for Jack seem surprised that such a document exists, but they appreciate its clarity. Within three days, Jack has passed quietly away, never having recovered consciousness except for a fleeting moment when, without his eyes opening or anything registering in his face, he is able to respond to the pressure of Jill's hand enclosing his.

The days following Jack's death are a blur to Jill: she can't recall cooking a single meal or making a single cup of tea for anyone. Who did the shopping? Who made the bed? The LOL women are constant visitors, and food keeps magically arriving. Jill catches sight of Sally's partner mowing the lawn.

Though he had agreed to the advance care plan, Jack had been adamant that the funeral arrangements would be entirely up to Jill, Sally and the boys. Various people, including the funeral director and the minister of the local church where the funeral is to be held, urge Jill to treat this as an upbeat celebration of Jack's life, but she resists that idea. 'This is a time for mourning', she tells them. 'I'm *sad*. I'm not in the mood to celebrate. Not yet. Jack's gone and I'm sad. Why should I pretend anything different? I need to stay with my sadness for a while. A wonderful man has been taken from me much, much sooner than I thought he would – can't I be allowed to mourn that? At a *funeral*?'

On the subject of burial or cremation, Jack had always been reluctant to commit himself. His own parents had both been buried; Jill's had both been cremated, and she had consistently told the children she wanted cremation for herself. But the experience of a recently widowed friend has convinced her to settle for burial in Jack's case. This woman had told Jill about the experience of going to collect her husband's ashes a couple of weeks after his cremation. As the funeral director left his office to fetch the box of ashes, he said to her, 'I'll bring your husband in now'.

All the LOLs are present at the funeral. So are the dog-walkers. Jill recognises the woman who lost her husband and son: her other son is with her. Jack's old boss is there, along with several former colleagues, including a woman Jill had once suspected of distracting Jack from their marriage. *I forgive you for hoping whatever it was you hoped, and I'm sure you discovered that Jack was never that kind of man,* Jill says, but only to herself.

The eulogy has been jointly written by Jill and the children, with some input from Jack's younger brother, who is also present with his wife and two daughters. It is read by Sally. The essential message is that Jack was an unselfish man; a good man who didn't seem to know he was good; a loving husband, father and friend who seemed bewildered by love; a wonderful neighbour who discovered his neighbourhood rather late in the day but made up for lost time. (No one feels the need to mention his foolishness, perverseness or frailty. No one ever does at funerals: we all know that about each other.)

Whether a life is short or long, we can't fully appreciate its trajectory until we are near its end, looking back. Death is the only fixed reference point we have for making sense of life. To quote Saul Bellow in *Humboldt's Gift* (1975), 'Death is the dark backing that a mirror needs if we are able to see anything'.

Not everyone has the luxury of knowing when the end is likely to come, but for those who do, a remarkable clarity becomes possible. Only then can we be sure how long we were to have on this earth; only then can we finally relax into an understanding and acceptance of the value and meaning of our lives – for us, and for those we tried to love. We receive intimations of this same clarity when we are confronted by traumatic events earlier in our lives: separation and divorce, life-threatening illness, retrenchment, bereavement, periods of upheaval or alienation. All such experiences, often described as 'setbacks', can be seen as little deaths: times when we sense that a phase of our life is over, a set of attitudes and expectations will have to be abandoned or a relationship is dead. These are the times when we are likely to reorder our priorities, rethink our goals and reset our agenda. (*La petite mort* – the 'little death' following orgasm – has a similarly cathartic effect for some people, leading to a post-coital period of melancholy reflection or, perhaps, transcendence.)

Such moments of reflection and insight are not only important pointers to the things that really matter to us; they are also a foretaste, a preparation for how it might feel when we know we are approaching the end. These little deaths might be therapeutic, too: geriatric psychiatrists say that depression is quite common among elderly people who have had a dream run – no serious health issues, no major life traumas – only to be hit with a sudden sense of mortality when they eventually become ill. Like everything else, death is easier to approach when we've had some practice.

The US poet and short-story writer Raymond Carver wrote this poem, 'Late Fragment', for his wife, after he had been diagnosed with an inoperable brain tumour:

> And did you get what
> you wanted from this life, even so?
> I did.
> And what did you want?
> To call myself beloved, to feel myself
> beloved on the earth.

Throughout this book, I have argued that we ought to pursue goodness for its own sake; that virtue is its own reward and we should expect no other; that the good life is an end in itself, not a way of gaining some personal gratification. A rich sense of fulfilment is a strong possibility, but, if it comes, it's like a collateral benefit – incidental to the purpose for which we embrace the good life.

And yet I would say this: if, like Raymond Carver, you would wish to end your life knowing you are loved, the only way to make that possible is to love, generously and selflessly. No one can promise you that a life lived for others will bring you a deep sense of satisfaction, but it's certain that nothing else will.

Postscript

Why would you willingly submit yourself to the Golden Rule?

Why would you take the tough option when there are many easier and more appealing alternatives: treating other people the way they treat you; giving as good as you get (where 'good' usually means 'bad'); staying one step ahead of the game; looking out for Number One? That all sounds reasonable enough; natural; perhaps even logical. Many people actively pursue such strategies and teach them to their children. Why, after all, should I treat a bad person well? Why should I be kind to people who annoy me? Why should I respect people with whom I profoundly disagree? Surely the Golden Rule sets an unrealistically high standard?

And then you hear that insistent message, echoing through the philosophical traditions of East and West: **treat other people the way you'd like to be treated.** Yes, we may have to qualify the rule to ensure it meets the requirements of justice and fairness, but the basic message never alters, whether your moral heritage is Socratic, Jewish, Christian, Islamic, Buddhist, humanist or anything in between.

Why such consensus across such wildly diverse cultures? Part of the answer lies in a simple sentence from chapter 3: '*Who am I?* turns out to be a less interesting and less significant question than *Who are we?*' and in a closely related sentence from chapter 4: 'It's more a case of *Who needs me?* than *Who am I?*' Neither statement is intended to imply that the quest for self-knowledge is pointless but only to suggest that the key to a good life is to acknowledge that our essential nature is social, not individual. Know yourself, by all means, but, above all, know this about yourself: you are one of us.

That's why social theorists and sociologists talk about the value of social capital: they recognise that a community's strong commitment to its common life is the most precious resource it possesses. The way we organise our governance and our social institutions (especially our public hospitals and schools), nurture our families, keep in touch with our neighbours, maintain our friendships, respond to the needs of friends and strangers alike, participate in 'herd' behaviour (book clubs, community choirs, church-going, local clubs and sporting associations), volunteer for tasks that improve the quality of life for the marginalised, frail or disadvantaged . . . any activities that promote social inclusion and community development are like glue that binds us together and creates the kind of society most of us want to live in.

The greatest monument to any of our lives will not be in stone, but in our living legacy – the influence we have had on other people at every point of connection with the human family. You don't have to be rich to leave a positive legacy; you don't have to be intelligent, famous, powerful or even particularly well organised, let alone happy. You need only to treat people with kindness, compassion and respect, knowing they will have been enriched by their encounters with you.

The ancient wisdom expressed in the Golden Rule is actually an encouragement to place a high value on social capital. It also carries an implied warning about what might happen if we don't. If we commit ourselves to an ethic of rampant individualism, for instance, we erode our social capital by fracturing and dividing society into classes – winners and losers – who would inevitably become suspicious and mistrustful of each other. Social tensions always destroy social harmony, and violence is the logical end point. Similarly, if we were to yield to self-indulgence as a way of life, history tells us that cultural degeneration would be the inevitable result, since self-indulgence erodes our sense of common purpose and mutual obligation.

As a species, we humans thrive when we live cooperatively within communities, but the stability of those communities is not guaranteed; nor is the maintenance of peace between one community and another. We are both cooperators and competitors; we are both selfless and selfish. How we reconcile those two sides of our nature determines the kind of society we become. It's not a question of survival of the fittest; ultimately, it's a question of survival of the species.

Further reading

Simon Blackburn, *Being Good*, Oxford University Press, 2001

André Comte-Sponville, *A Short Treatise on the Great Virtues*, Vintage, 2003

Alfie Kohn, *Punished by Rewards*, Houghton Mifflin, 1993

Hugh Mackay, *Why Don't People Listen?*, Pan Macmillan, 1994 (Macmillan ebook, 2013)

Hugh Mackay, *Right & Wrong: How to decide for yourself*, Hodder, 2004

Hugh Mackay, *What Makes Us Tick? The ten desires that drive us*, Hachette, 2010

Iris Murdoch, *The Sovereignty of Good*, Routledge, 1971 (Routledge Classics, 2001)

Carl Rogers, *On Becoming a Person*, Constable, 1967

Stephen Trombley, *A Short History of Western Thought*, Atlantic Books, 2011

Acknowledgements

The seed of *The Good Life* was sown by an invitation from Ann Mossop to participate in a forum on 'What Makes a Good Life?' as part of her *Ideas at the House* program at the Sydney Opera House in 2011. The impetus for writing the book came from Ingrid Ohlsson, my publisher, and I am grateful for her encouragement and guidance, and for the professional support I have received from her colleagues at Pan Macmillan.

I am fortunate in having friends with whom I enjoy continuing conversations about topics that relate to the themes of this book. In particular, Richard Eckersley, Bruce Kaye, Keith Mason and Julian Wood have, from their different perspectives, illuminated my understanding of the good life. Stephanie Wells, my assistant, proofread an early draft manuscript and offered valuable comments on the text. My wife, Sheila, has been a source of constant support, encouragement and constructive criticism throughout the writing process, and the book is dedicated to her.

Index

Acton, Lord 105
Adrian, Nathan 52
advertising 14–16, 32–3, 61
aesthetic judgement 162–4
afterlife 71–2, 90, 112, 184, 236
ageing 193, 204, 243
agnosticism 183–4, 186
alcohol 13, 61, 102, 149, 165, 230
Alexander the Great 111
Allen, Woody 237
altruism 17, 130–4, 138, 144, 189, 199
ambition 108, 129, 171, 175, 179, 204
anger 135, 170, 194, 204, 227
apologising 220–5
Aristotle 54, 66, 98
Armstrong, Neil 107–8
Arrow, Kenneth 80–1
artificial intelligence 104–5
artists 152–3
ascetism 114, 118
astrology 72, 82–5
atheism 73, 183–6
Augustine, Saint 130
authentic life 148–9
authority 105–6
awards and prizes 22, 25, 197

baby boomers 39, 195
Bacon, Francis 191
badness 135–6
Barrett Browning, Elizabeth 189
Baumeister, Roy 25–6, 99, 134
Beard, Mary 113
belief systems 70–5, 135, 149
Bellow, Saul 253
bereavement 53, 190, 223, 253
Bernstein, Peter 80–1
Blair, Tony 172
Blake, William 157
blameless life 150, 160
Bloom, Rube 117
body language 210–12
Bonhoeffer, Dietrich 187
books 34, 42, 56, 88, 149, 152–3, 160, 189
Bowles, Samuel 134, 138
Brand Me 14–26
Buddhism 64, 72, 90, 125, 169, 182, 239, 255
bullies 176, 179, 195, 201
Burger, Jerry 106
Burke, Edmund 106
Bush, George W. 172
business leaders 173, 180–1

Caligula 113
Camus, Albert 165
cancer 48, 165, 248, 254
Carey, John 153
Carver, Raymond 254
category mistake 119
Catholicism 73, 79, 135
Cavalier, Rodney 111
celebrities 17, 24, 27, 111
certainty 69–80
charity 63, 79–80, 108, 132–3, 135, 137–45, 151, 180, 185–6
charmed life 146–7
Chesterton, G. K. 129
child abuse 13, 135, 170, 202, 222
childishness *see* infantilism
children 7–14, 23, 39, 52–3, 60–1, 81, 86, 99–100, 116, 131–2, 137–8, 149, 151, 177–8, 180, 186, 189, 191, 206, 230
Christianity 43, 73–5, 88, 90, 169, 175, 186, 235, 255
church 36, 38, 61, 72–6, 112, 160–1, 185
Cohen, David 64
common good 1, 112, 117, 129, 138–46, 148, 151, 153, 158, 165–6, 181
competitiveness 135, 138, 171, 174 178
Comte-Sponville, André 237
Confucianism 169, 175, 182
contentment 43, 49, 114, 126, 128, 157
cooperation 134–5, 138–9, 159, 168, 179
Cope, Wendy 232
corruption 102, 105–7
courage 114, 131, 166, 221
courtesy 114, 149, 167, 172, 177, 194, 223

creative life 151–3
creativity 65, 98–9, 105, 126, 151–3
Creighton, Bishop Mandell 105

Dawkins, Richard 73
death 70, 82, 89–90, 122, 131, 235–54
dementia 131, 155, 180, 204–5, 243
democracy 31
Demos think tank 248
depression 8, 46–8, 102, 127, 158, 254
Dessaix, Robert 248
disappointment 32, 48–9, 52–3, 68–9, 132, 178
Disraeli, Benjamin 49, 221
distractions 82, 87, 112, 130, 180, 210
divorce 39, 58, 89, 190, 205–6, 253
doctors 24, 50, 82, 102, 150, 181, 201
Dowrick, Stephanie 97–8
drugs 13, 27, 33, 47, 51, 53, 61–2, 110
Duckworth, Angela 26
duty, acting out of 41, 66, 131
dying 239–40, 242–4, 246–53

eccentricity 152–3
Eckersley, Richard 13–14, 77, 241
education 13, 29, 103, 107, 109, 185, 187, 214–15
egalitarianism 109, 113, 159, 171
ego 42, 145
Einstein, Albert 71, 74, 76, 114
emotions 46, 49–51, 53, 55, 60–5, 158, 227
end of life 243–4, 248–9
entitlement, sense of 8, 12, 23, 29, 107–10
envy 112, 114, 150
ethics 180–1, 202
eudaimonia 54, 67
euthanasia 244–5
exciting life 149–50, 160
exercise 34, 48, 120, 126, 133

Facey, Albert 147
failure 18, 42, 49, 51–3, 144, 240
faith 71–2, 75, 85, 114, 184
false leads 69–123
fame 105–14, 122, 147–8, 179
family 18, 39, 68, 165, 204
fashion 3, 27–8, 35
fear 239–40
feeling good 42, 60, 67, 145, 164
Ferguson, Niall 89
finding yourself 91–8
food 3, 13–14, 35, 48, 60–2 , 81, 115, 118, 120, 133
Ford, Henry, II 220–1
Forgas, Joe 50
forgiveness 129–30, 150, 171, 226–32, 247–8
Forster, E. M. 149
fortunate life 147–8
Frankl, Viktor 85
friends 18, 53, 68, 204
Frost, Robert 189
fulfilment 45, 49, 127, 147, 254
full life 145–6
fully functioning person 63–7
fun 34–40, 122, 126, 149–50
fundamentalists 72–6
Furedi, Frank 31
future 80–91

gambling 87, 110
Gaw, Amanda 244
Genghis Khan 111
Gilbert, Daniel 133
Gillies, Rowan 182
Gintis, Herbert 134, 138
global warming 3, 24, 75, 89
goals 39, 43, 69, 121–2, 182
God 70, 183–7, 245
Goleman, Daniel 104
Gopnik, Adam 88
Golden Rule 1, 129, 168–79, 186, 193, 200, 229, 247, 255
good life
  lived for others 127–30, 157–91
  living 193–234
  maxims for living 202–3
  meaning of 1
good time 125–56
goodness 105, 147–8, 150, 154, 158, 166–7, 183, 188–91, 198–9, 254
Gottlieb, Lori 7–8, 12
government 17, 27–31, 70, 73–4, 182, 222–3
gratification 32, 34–5, 45, 147
greed 110–12, 129, 175
green movement 116–17
groups, exclusion from 206
growth 48, 52, 227–8
guilt 226–7

Haidt, Jonathan 163–4

happiness 41–55, 62–3, 66–8, 133
Hare, R. M. 167
hatred 136, 181, 204
Hemingway, Ernest 163–4
heroes 24, 41, 131, 134, 144
Herrick, Robert 189
Hinduism 169
Hitchens, Christopher 249
Hitler, Adolf 111, 136, 149
Hogan, Shane 173
honesty 168, 173, 181
hope 71–2, 85
Hopkins, Gerard Manley 189
Howard, John 172
humanism 72, 169, 255
human species 48, 70, 120, 257
Hume, David 162–3
humility 107–8, 110, 188, 198–9, 221
humour 114, 232–4

illness 53, 82, 159, 187, 253
impatience 82, 217–18
individualism 171, 256
inequality 109, 159
infantilism 26–9
information technology 3, 27, 32–3, 35, 211
instincts 64, 162, 164, 166–7
integrity 45, 114, 166, 200
intelligence 99–105
internet 13, 32–3, 88, 149, 211–12
IQ scores 102–3
Iraq 81, 136, 172
irrational behaviour 194
Islam 75, 90, 169, 186, 195, 255
isolation 159–60, 190–1

jealousy 204, 227
Jensen, Peter 74
Johnson, Samuel 49, 106
joy 43
Judaism 75, 88, 90, 169–70, 186, 195, 255
judgement 50–1, 161–2
Jung, Carl 239

Kant, Immanuel 68, 176
Kaye, Bruce 185–6
Keats, John 189
Keller, Helen 68
kindness 100–2, 178–9, 205–6
King, Cecil 106
King, Molly 113–14
Kingston, Huw 115
Kissinger, Henry 107
Knox, Malcolm 188
Kohn, Alfie 180
Koran, the 186
Kuhn, Thomas 77

Lahey, Jessica 12–13
Lama Surya Das 239
Langer, Ellen 239
language, use of 6–7, 97, 121, 223
Laozi 175
Larkin, Philip 91
Latour, Bruno 78–9
laughing 34, 232–4
law 159, 168, 176, 201
leadership 108, 110, 132, 136, 151
Lincoln, Abraham 135
Lindfors, Pirjo 240
listening attentively 207–20
living in the moment 64, 85–6, 91, 114
loneliness 190, 240
long-term planning 40
love 50, 68, 79–81, 128, 131, 166, 184–5, 189, 203, 254
Lowell, Amy 189
luck 146–8, 187–8, 199
Luskin, Frederic 228

McAuley, Ian 138–9
McCullough, David 11–12
Magnussen, James 51–2
Mahabharata, The 169
Malone-Lee, James 215
marriage 49, 74, 122, 132, 140, 155–6, 205–6, 225
materialism 14, 16, 112, 115, 241
meaning and purpose 35–8, 43, 57–9, 68
meaning of Life 118–23
media 13, 17, 28, 32, 234
meditation 39, 61–2, 86, 98, 126
mental disorders 13, 47, 102, 191
Milgram, Stanley 106
money 35, 63, 103, 107, 110, 112, 115, 130, 179
moral code 72, 144, 162, 175, 226
moral dilemmas 166, 177, 182
moral judgements 161–4

Index

moral justification 172
moral value 45, 158
morality 63, 68, 153, 159–66
motives 63, 92, 139, 200
movies 54, 56, 61, 105, 149, 153, 189
murder 135–6
Murdoch, Iris 93–4, 96, 166, 189–90
Murphy, Beverley 205
music 56, 61, 105, 121, 153
mysteries 69–71

Napoleonic Code 74
narcissism 8, 55–6, 92, 176
needs 67–8, 198, 200, 202
negotiation 171–2
neighbours 122, 131, 156, 191, 204
Nero 88
New Testament 87–8, 169, 186
newspapers 28, 174, 232
Nostradamus 88
nursing homes 131, 154, 248–9
Nussbaum, Martha 188

offensive behaviour 162–3, 174
Old Testament 87–8, 169
openness 64–5, 215
optimism, 43–5, 50, 56
over-parenting 12–13

Pagels, Elaine 88
pain 48–53, 68
palliative care 242, 247, 249
parenting 12–13, 126, 133
parents 9, 53, 131, 133, 177, 191, 195, 230
Pascal, Blaise 236
passion 82, 150–1
passionate life 151, 160
patriotism 30–2
perfection, idea of 18, 32, 90
Peterson, Betsy 205
philanthropy 108, 144–5, 201
Piaget, Jean 163
Pittacus 169
Plato 93, 108, 169
pleasure 45, 49, 53–4, 122, 130, 164
poetry 43–5, 56, 152–3, 189
politicians 17–21, 24, 28, 30, 50, 61, 76, 82, 102, 107, 111, 172–3
pornography 32–3, 160, 164
positive thinking 56, 62
possessions 35, 114–16, 130
possessiveness 204
poverty 112, 116
power 35, 105–14, 179
praise 7–9, 23, 183, 199
prejudice 135–6, 181, 214–15
priorities 92, 121, 156, 179
productive life 147, 158
prophecies 87–9
prosperity 157–9
proverbs 137
'psychologically free' 64–5
psychologists 86
psychotherapists 204
punishment 180

radio 28, 174, 181
realists 56, 80, 90
reciprocity 169–71, 229
recognising rights of others 159–65
reconciliation 171, 225
reflection 52, 92, 146, 168, 188
refugees 3, 75, 132, 159, 185, 195
relationships 53, 66, 68, 80, 92, 103, 116, 120, 135, 147, 156–7, 178, 200, 225
religion 13–14, 38–9, 43, 70–9, 114, 134, 183–6, 222–3
resentment 204, 225, 231
respect 159–65
response to needs/rights of others 67–8, 159–65, 198, 200
revenge 170–1, 178, 229
rewards 23, 66, 90, 112, 180–3
Rogers, Carl 63–7, 80, 92, 216
Ronson, Jon 47
Rossetti, Christina 189
Ruby, Harry 117
Russell, Bertrand 76–7, 152, 167

Sacks, Oliver 85
sadness 42, 46–50, 52–3, 66
Sandel, Michael 138–9
Santayana, George 55
satisfaction 49, 68, 87, 147, 183
Schmidt, Brian 77–8
Schurz, Carl 31
Schwartz, Barry 42–3
science 70–4, 76–9

self-absorption 8, 49, 55, 92, 158, 201, 226, 240
self-control 25–6, 32, 149
self-discipline 25–6, 166, 189
self-esteem 7–9, 11, 25, 49, 148, 199
self-examination 92–6
self-indulgence 60, 92, 130, 227, 240, 256
self-interest 17, 22, 98, 130, 143, 168, 178, 189–90
selfishness 130, 133–5, 150
self-knowledge 91–8, 255
selflessness 41, 135, 188, 201
self-promotion 16–21, 199
self-respect 162, 166, 199, 205
self-sacrifice 131, 133, 199
Seligman, Martin 26
Sempell, Andrew 74
sensitivity 68, 99, 104, 159, 179
sex 6, 32–5, 149, 161–4, 166–7
Shakespeare, William 189
shopping 16, 32, 34–5, 40, 117, 150
simple life 114–18
Smith, Ed 188
Smith, Emily Esfahani 133–4
smoking 164–5
social media 13, 16–17, 24–5, 27, 81, 212
socialisation 22, 31
Socrates 90, 92–4, 169, 255
Sophocles 53
Spengler, Oswald 88
sport 24, 32, 51–3, 87, 105, 149, 151, 174, 190, 198, 223
spouses 116, 131, 156, 165, 225
status 105–14, 146, 179, 130, 222
Stern, William 102–3
strangers, interactions with 68, 99, 160, 189, 201–3, 212
success 42, 51–2, 63, 108, 112, 114
suicide 13, 127, 165, 244
survival of the fittest 130, 168
Suzuki, Shunryu 116
Switzerland 139

Tacitus 106
taken seriously, being 193–5, 198, 204, 207
taking others seriously 198, 217
talkback radio 28, 174, 181
teachers 53, 82, 102, 113–14, 151, 177
Tennyson, Alfred 80
terrorism 75, 81, 240
theism 73, 183–5
theories 77–9
therapies of everyday life 207–32
Thomas, Dylan 237
Time magazine 115
Tingle, Laura 30
tragedy 38, 82
trauma 38, 48, 53
Trombley, Stephen 77
Turgenev, Ivan 248
TV 28
Twenge, Jean 8, 11

Utopia complex 3–40

values 25, 34, 92, 135, 149, 200
violence 13, 110, 135, 162–3, 194, 256
virtue 76, 106, 116, 166–7, 171, 254

Waldman, Ellen 228
Walsch, Neale Donald 6
war 38–9, 76, 80, 85, 131, 134–5, 147, 172, 187, 191, 194, 240
Wayne, John 221
wealth 105–14, 144–8, 158, 179
West, Mae 152
Whitman, Walt 189
wholeness 49, 54, 63–9
Wilson, Timothy 97
Winnicott, Donald 9
Winterling, Aloys 113
wisdom as happiness 53–4
Wordsworth 152
work 38, 51, 116, 120, 150, 176, 178, 187, 190–1, 199–202, 240, 253
world view 213–14
writers 24, 152

young people 13–14, 31, 240–1